BORDER BETWEEN GERMAN- AND
USSR-OCCUPIED PARTS OF POLAND
FOLLOWING THE WAR IN 1939

POLISH-USSR BORDER
BEFORE THE WAR IN 1939

THESE CHILDREN ARE MINE

a story of rescue and survival

THESE CHILDREN ARE MINE

a story of rescue and survival

by DOV B. LEDERMAN

FELDHEIM PUBLISHERS
JERUSALEM NEW YORK

The publication of this book was supported by
Stiftung Irene Bollag-Herzheimer
Basel, Switzerland

ISBN 1-58330-525-4

FELDHEIM PUBLISHERS
POB 35002 / Jerusalem, Israel

202 Airport Executive Park
Nanuet, NY 10954

www.feldheim.com

10 9 8 7 6 5 4 3 2 1

Printed in Israel

Contents

Author's Introduction

During the years that the idea of writing this book perco-
lated in my thoughts, I had the opportunity to read a number
of works describing the fate of Polish Jews like ourselves who
fled to the Russian side of the Molotov-Ribbentrop line at the
beginning of World War II.

I noticed that these chronicles were invariably written by
people then in their late teens or older, whereas I was only
eight years old when we fled Poland. Needless to say, their
more mature perspective of the events is vital for an understanding of that shattering period. But a full picture will
emerge only when some of those who were children at the
time have shared their own unique perspective of the events
that enveloped them as their lives were transformed by the
upheavals of the Holocaust. It is this perspective which this
book strives to present.

As I delved more deeply into the recorded history of the
period through which I had lived, I became convinced of the
unusual scope and power of my family's saga. It encompasses
a sequence of events that begins in Poland before the outbreak
of the war, follows our exile to the Soviet Union, and con-
cludes with Mother's heroic rescue and rehabilitation activities
on behalf of Jewish children back in post-war Poland.

As the reader will discover, in 1946 Mother was forcibly
removed from a transport carrying the Jewish orphans in her
care out of Poland—a transport which included both myself
and my sister. Undaunted, Mother continued her work in
Poland for another two years until she was finally granted
permission to leave the country, but only after being incarcerated for 14 months in a Polish jail.

It happens that none of the authors who deal with this
period have committed the story of Mother's extraordinary

rescue work to writing. This task—really more of an obligation —has fallen to me.

On the advice of various people, I researched a number of publications dealing with this period to find a record of Mother's experiences. However, I very soon discovered that almost none of the writers as much as mentioned Mother. She was given only a single sentence in the book by Dr. Zerach Warhaftig. On the other hand, Mr. Yeshayahu Druker, who was himself involved in this kind of work and, who, as a Jewish chaplain in the Polish army, was at times of assistance to Mother, invariably mentions her name whenever he speaks publicly about this period; however, there is no printed record of his words. Mother was also interviewed by a Mr. Baranovich, who interviewed a number of people that were involved in similar missions. Unfortunately, Mr. Baranovich lacked the background needed to extract a significant part of the pertinent information. In any event, no mention of her was ever made in any other publication.

In order to chronicle the activities of the two years when I was not an eyewitness to her remarkable activities, I turned to Mother's "children"—the orphans she rescued after the war. Although I gathered a large volume of data, a gap remained, because, in keeping with her generation's upbringing which dictated that the worlds of the child and the adult never meet, Mother kept her young charges blissfully unaware of the trials and dangers that made up much of her own day-to-day life during this period. In this respect, I was particularly fortunate to have met the former Miss F., now a great-grandmother, who filled me in on many of the fascinating details recorded in this book.

I cannot escape the feeling that most readers are no longer emotionally equipped to understand what it means to go hungry for several years in succession, or to live in constant terror of having done or uttered something which might be regarded as counter-revolutionary—and all this, while working, going to school, doing homework, and performing all the day-to-day functions of human life. Can those born into the world of an ever-full granary comprehend that an entire nation suffered from acute shortage of basic foodstuffs, coupled with a dire lack of clothing, medications, and other products regarded as bare essentials and whose availability is now taken for granted? Nevertheless, it is important that these readers be made aware of the fact that a large portion of the Jewish people—and the people of Europe—lived in this manner for an extended period of time. I hope that, in spite of all difficulties, the reader will be able to identify himself with the persons and events that this book records.

The reader will find it easier to follow the events described in this book in the light of a brief overview of Poland's changing borders.

Both of Poland's neighbors—Germany to the west, and Russia to the east—frequently helped themselves to sections of Polish territory. Even Sweden, which lies to the north across a vast barrier of water, the Baltic Sea, managed to occupy northern Poland at least once. Poland, in turn, was not averse to annexing parts of Lithuania, its neighbor to the north and, when the opportunity arose, also sections of Byelorussia and Ukraine, the western provinces of Russia.

This continual exchange of territory accounts for the fact that many Polish cities have two or more names: Lithuania's Vilnius and Kaunas became *Wilno* (*Vilno*) and *Kowno* (*Kovno*) when in Polish hands; *Homel* and *Huradno* were known as *Gomel* and *Grodno* under the Russians (who have no letter "h" in their alphabet); and *Bytom*, which holds a prominent place in this volume, was known as *Beuthen* while in German hands.

In 1939, when Poland's borders were as shown in the map on the inside front cover, Germany and Russia signed a secret non-aggression agreement, the Molotov-Ribbentrop Pact, according to which each country committed itself to refrain from attacking the other. In addition, Russia pledged to join Germany in attacking Poland, although with some delay; and that once subdued by the joint attack from both the west and east, Poland would be divided between Germany and Russia.

Thus, only twenty days after Germany invaded Poland on the first of September, 1939, the country ceased to exist as an independent state. A new border now divided former Polish territory more or less in half, with the western sector controlled by Germany and the eastern sector by the USSR. (See the previously-mentioned map.)

Poland came into being again as a separate political entity at the close of World War II, with the borders shown in the map on the inside back cover. As opposed to the pre-war situation when it was ruled by an extreme-right government, Poland was now a Communist state.

Acknowledgments

I wish to express my sincerest thanks to the well-known writer, Mrs. Miriam Samsonowitz, for editing the original version of this book. It was she who wisely suggested including chronicles of some of the rescued children. The interviews she conducted and the moving stories she wrote significantly enhanced this book.

Thanks are also due to my good friend and colleague Uri Cheskin, who edited the manuscript at a later stage, making it eminently more readable and enjoyable.

Another person who made a significant contribution to the final version of this book is Mrs. Miriam Rosenzweig, an author and columnist for *Yated Neeman* newspaper's English edition. Her attention to detail, her insightful and incisive queries, and her extensive knowledge greatly improved my text.

And finally, my deepest expression of gratitude to my brother-in-law, Rabbi Aharon Feldman, for "adopting" this book as his own. It was his input of time, energy, and thought that are responsible for the final version of the book, which I am proud to present to the reader.

I wish to say that I have spared no effort to insure the accuracy of the facts recorded in *These Children Are Mine*. I have re-interviewed several of the people to insure that all the names and other details are correct, to the extent that this is possible half a century later. I have also consulted geographical sources to verify the names of rivers, cities, the distances between them, and the like.

In this respect I attempted to emulate Rabbi Chaim Shapiro's book, *Go My Son*, which I very much admire for a number of reasons, his historical accuracy being just one of them. Of course, the principal merit of his book lies in its riveting presentation of the history of World War II as reflected in the life of a yeshivah student caught up in the tragic events of the times. Had I been his age, I might have had a history parallel to his own; had he been my age, the converse might have been true. I cannot help but feel that these two books complement one another.

Finally, a word of apology to the reader. The book was originally conceived as a biography of Mother, but turned out to be largely about myself. My only justification for this is that, in a wider sense, I am very much what Mother made me, so that the volume is still essentially her story. May she be blessed with much Jewish *nachas* from all her offspring and from all those she helped to preserve for the Jewish people.

PART I

THE WORLD FALLS APART

A SHELTERED WARSAW CHILDHOOD

Until the world as we knew it started disintegrating in the autumn of 1939, we led a life of relative luxury and calm in the capital of one of Europe's most anti-Semitic countries. Our home in Warsaw was a comfortable four-bedroom apartment with indoor plumbing—an amenity that was not available in many of Warsaw's dwellings. It was on the third-floor apartment in a large building located at 40 Ogrodowa Street, only three houses away from the corner of Zelazna, a vibrant business thoroughfare. Ulica Zelazna, "Iron Street," derived its name from the large number of iron-goods stores lining it. The neighborhood was mixed, with a strong Jewish presence.

Our building, like others of its kind in Warsaw, was entered through a large double gate which opened to a passage that ran underneath the second-floor apartments. The passage, about twenty feet long and spacious enough to accommodate a truck, led to a large, paved inner courtyard. The yard itself was about sixty by sixty feet, formed by the walls of the apartments making up this five-story building.

Within the entryway was the opening to the staircase, as well as a door leading to the superintendent's residence. The duties of the superintendent included admitting people into the building through a small door in the main gate after the 9 PM lock-up.

Our apartment was reached via the building's main staircase, which boasted white marble steps with decorative wrought-iron posts and polished-wood railings. At each mid-floor landing, a huge window opened onto the inner courtyard. There was even an elevator shaft, although the elevator itself somehow never got installed. The impressive double-door entrance to our apartment carried a brass nameplate inscribed J. LEDERMAN.

A typical Warsaw inner courtyard. The photograph was taken from the entrance-way. Part of its ornamental ironwork can be seen on top. Our own courtyard was similar, except that it was paved with concrete.

Upon opening the door, one entered a large foyer, which had a big coat rack and a special stand for rubbers and umbrellas. A cavernous closet built into the left wall of the foyer held our valises—destined to play an important role in our survival—and, before Passover, cases of Carmel Mizrachi wine (then considered the best kosher wine). Two of the three foyer doors led to two inner rooms, one of which Father used as his office. He was a CPA, one of the few professions accessible to Jews in Poland.

Another room was occupied for a time by some distant relatives. The third door led to our dining room, which boasted, besides the regular furniture one would expect, the latest marvels of technology—a radio and a spring-driven record player.

The master bedroom had twin beds with night tables at their sides, and a vanity table where Mother kept her great collection of jewelry. The bedroom set had ornately carved gold-plated legs; it had been purchased, in mint condition, from a Polish count, who had had it made on special order.

A black dial telephone sat on one of the night tables. Only businesses or affluent people could afford this kind of luxury.

There were two closets in the bedroom, one of them holding over a dozen men's suits, even though Father hardly

Another view of a Warsaw courtyard. This time one can see the entranceway and, above it, a typical balcony.

needed half that number. This was because of an act of benevolence by Mother to a man who had needed to sell them.

This happened some time before the war when a forlorn-looking figure carrying a valise appeared at our door. He was a German Jew of Polish origin, expelled from Germany to Poland on the pretext that Poland, rather than Germany, was his homeland.* I still remember the slightly bent figure standing in our elegant foyer. This person, who must have been well-to-do back home, was now trying to maintain his dignity while engaged in the painful act of selling his last possessions —several slightly worn, custom-tailored suits.

Father had no use for them—he had as many suits as he needed, and besides, he always had suits tailored to measure and did not want any suits that required alteration. But not

---

* These expulsions were another of the German stratagems to rob Jews not only of their jobs, but also of their possessions. People so expelled had problems selling property and were usually forced to leave Germany with only those belongings that could be regarded as luggage.

Mother. "First of all, we should buy the suits just to help the poor man stay afloat," she said. "Besides, one never knows..." Although the man would have been content to sell one or two suits, Mother bought off the entire contents of the valise. These suits paid an unexpected dividend at a later date.

* * *

Since coal was the preferred fuel for heating and cooking, each apartment house had a coal cellar, divided by brick walls into small cubicles, where each family stored its coal supply. The kitchen entrance to our apartment led from a staircase in the courtyard not far from the steps leading to the coal cellar. It was circular, with steps of rough-hewn boards well worn with time, and a wooden railing. The steps squeaked and groa ied whenever anyone—primarily household help—went up or down. This staircase also served for bringing coal up from the cellar to the kitchen, and other deliveries.

The core of our apartment was heated by a coal furnace, strategically located at the junction of the dining room, master bedroom, and children's room. But we still needed quilts in the winter, and ours were quite special. In addition to the standard reddish pink casing that held the feather insulation, each quilt was covered by a very expensive silk brocade, bright pink on one side, and an equally beautiful green on the other. Snow-white quilt covers, with a large diamond-shaped opening for displaying the colored silk underneath, went on top of this.

* * *

My earliest recollection goes back to some time before my third birthday. Without any apparent reason, Mother told me that I was going off to the country to stay with one of my aunts. When I protested, Mother promised that upon my return a special present would be waiting for me. To get the present, she told me sternly, I had to promise not to cry, and to obey my aunt.

Those were the days when the worlds of children and

adults never met and babies were delivered by stork. So I could not imagine why in the world my parents wanted to force this separation on me. But to the country I went. My main recollection of this trip is that I immediately caught a cold. The remedy then current was an aspirin and a stay in bed under a heavy quilt. This winning combination was presumed to cure the cold by making the patient perspire.

I was very hot under the goose-down quilt, and furtively poked out one foot at a time to cool off. Terrified of being caught in the act, however, I soon stopped. I didn't want to be reported as disobedient, and thereby forfeit the present. I had also reached the conclusion that poking my feet out was not helping.

Finally, I was taken home. When I awoke the next morning, I asked for my present. Mother escorted me to the master bedroom, but I could not discern any object that even remotely resembled a present. All I could see was the August sun shining through the white lace curtains, producing a beautiful pattern of light and shade, and a baby carriage standing between the twin beds and the closet. When I repeated my request for the present, my parents answered in a most unexpected way: "It is in the carriage. Have a look."

I peeked into the carriage and saw a sweet-looking baby girl—my one and only sibling, Lea. It was love at first sight, a love which has never waned since.

* * *

Our affluence came at a price. Father's success as an accountant meant that we children saw very little of him during the week. His Sabbath schedule did not leave him much free time either. As a result, Mother took over his role in child-rearing as well. Add to this the fact that I was later separated from Father for an extended period, and the result was that I did not have the benefit of his influence during my formative years.

All the same, the task of bringing us children up did not

interfere with Mother's other concerns. She had a textile-cutting workshop in a half-basement of our apartment house, which she ran on the basis of the experience acquired as a teenager in her father's shop.

With our two sources of income, we could afford more or less anything we needed or wanted. One very urgent need was a country vacation in the summer. The heat of the Polish summer—with virtually no humidity and the temperature rarely going above 77°F (25°C)—would be regarded as pleasant by the inhabitants of most of the United States and Israel, but it made Mother quite uncomfortable. Consequently, as soon as the calendar showed July was drawing near, we would pack ourselves off for the country to stay in a hotel or rented villa.

The family did not usually vacation in the winter, but the one time we decided to do so, I turned out to be the only one who went. The decision had been made and a villa rented, but something prevented my parents from going. Since the rental arrangements could not be canceled or changed, I was sent off alone, with only my governess Rachelka. I wasn't too happy the first day or two, but somewhat later, mollified by the presence of my beloved Rachelka, I became used to it and even had a good time.

Unbeknownst to me, Rachelka was a member of the outlawed Polish Communist Party, known as the PPR (Polish Workers Party). Together with many young Jewish men and women, she had been inspired by visions of equality, justice for rich and poor alike, and universal love of mankind.

Rachelka had a boyfriend, also a Communist, who was in jail for his activities. We did not know about this, but apparently many potential employers knew, and refused to hire her for any position. Hence she came to us without a recommendation; but Mother had pity on her and hired her nonetheless.

Rachelka would often tell Mother that judging from the way she treated those in her employ, she would have made a good Communist. For her part, Mother was also quite unhappy about the prevalent treatment of the working class, who toiled long hours for low pay, at times under unhealthy and even dangerous conditions. She even sympathized with the fiery proclamations about the need for change, but being deeply religious, she rejected Communism, with its materialistic-atheistic notions of Utopia.

* * *

No matter how much we spent, the money kept accumulating. The need arose to invest it in something that would bring a higher rate of return than that paid by the Polish State

Nowy Swiat (New World) Street, a main Warsaw thoroughfare. The photographer succeeded in capturing a typical situation of a trolley car coming down the street, flanked by a pickup truck and a hansom cab. An additional hansom cab can be seen at the left. The picture is completed by the rear part of a wagon that was probably delivering some kind of merchandise. Photograph courtesy of Ginzach Kiddush Hashem, Bnei Brak.

Savings Bank. My parents decided that the best investment would be a taxi fleet; so, in time, three blue Chevrolets with leather-upholstered seats were purchased and put into circulation on Warsaw's streets. These, like all other motor vehicles, were garaged in closed premises. No one would dare leave such precious property in the street overnight.

At that time, public transportation in Warsaw consisted mainly of electrically-powered trolley cars running on metal rails embedded in the street. In some places, primarily outlying areas, these were complemented by buses as well as trolley-buses. The latter were hooked up to overhead electric wires, but unlike trolley cars, they rode on regular tires over the streets. Individual travel was provided mostly by horse-drawn taxi-carriages, then much more numerous than motor taxis, although these were plying their trade on the streets in ever-increasing numbers.

After a while it was decided that a family like ours should not use public transportation; it behooved us to have our own private car. Thus, a black Chevrolet with gray-fabric upholstery

Intersection of major streets in Warsaw showing the mingling of trolley cars, hansom cabs and taxis. Photographed by M. Fuks. Courtesy Beth Hatefutsot, the Nahum Goldmann Museum of the Jewish Diaspora, Tel Aviv.

appeared in front of our house. This situation, however, did not last long. Father was disqualified from getting a driver's license—he was short-sighted and, at that time, a person could not get a driving license if he needed glasses—and this created a crisis. At first a chauffeur was hired, but eventually he was let go when it became apparent that the family had little need to travel. Shortly afterwards, the front seat of the car was moved a bit forward, two folding seats were installed in the back, and a fourth cab joined our little fleet.

* * *

A central activity of my childhood was being taken for walks, either by Mother or Rachelka, the governess. The route rarely varied. It was hardly exciting going to the same two or three places every time, but children were not consulted about their opinions. As the popular saying went: "children and fish

The Tomb of the Unknown Soldier in Warsaw. The Saski Garden is in the background. This is a postwar photograph. The original monument, which was much more elaborate, included a three-sided colonnade and a statue of the commanding officer of the Polish contingent of Napoleon's army. It was razed to the ground by the Germans. The truncated columns serve as reminder of the previous structure.

have no voice."

The tedium was sometimes alleviated by watching the changing of the guard at the Tomb of the Unknown Soldier in the Saski Gardens. Another diversion during a walk would be watching a Polish funeral, if one was "fortunate" enough to run into one. Such a funeral was usually an elaborate affair. The casket was carried in a long black hearse, pulled by at least two, and sometimes as many as six black-sheathed horses. The hearse had four brass lanterns, one at each corner, lit even in daytime, and carried wreaths for placing on the grave. A band playing funeral music followed. Curiously, no memory of the mourners remains with me.

In principle, playing with friends could have been another possible pastime. But the only place a young child like myself could make friends was down in the yard, and since this would have exposed me to undesirable friendships with children whose actions could not be supervised around the clock, it was "unthinkable." I could visit cousins, but there simply weren't many of them around.

Strictness and restrictiveness were considered the progressive way to raise children in those days. They certainly had not been the norm when Mother was growing up. Her parents allowed her to mingle with children her age without exhaustively investigating their desirability as playmates. In this way she met Fishel Finkelstein, a boy her age, with whom she became very friendly and whom she was destined to meet again as an adult under fateful circumstances.

The Sabbath brought a pleasant diversion: visiting my grandparents. My maternal grandparents in particular lived within walking distance, in an all-Jewish neighborhood. Gensia Street,* where they lived, was a long street, lined on both sides almost uniformly with drab-looking five-story buildings.

---

* Pre-War street names are preserved in Warsaw to this day. Uniquely, Gensia Street lost not only all its Jews, houses and possessions, but also its name. It is now known as Anilevich Street, after the leader of the Ghetto uprising.

Nalewki Street, lined by Jewish-owned stores. Photograph courtesy Ginzach Kiddush Hashem, Bnei Brak.

The neighborhood's exclusively Jewish character is best illustrated by the story that I heard from Mother about the gentile who once rented one of the Gensia-street stores and, naturally, kept it open on the Sabbath. His storefront window was repeatedly shattered (presumably after the Sabbath ended) in protest of his desecration of the Sabbath. This stopped only when a policeman was stationed there to announce to all that it was a non-Jewish store.

My grandparents, the Grombs, lived on the top floor of Number 12. Their apartment was reached by a creaky wooden staircase, well worn from many years of use. A tiny entrance hall had a door to the kitchen on the left and a door, straight ahead, to the dining room and the rest of the apartment.

The dining room had one or two windows which faced the yard. Bookshelves, with wooden doors, lined the wall shared with the kitchen. The furnishings were completed by a large table in the middle, and a sofa on the opposite wall, through which a door opened into my grandparents' bedroom. That room had two doors leading to the two rooms that served as Grandfather's workshop.

Mother as a teenager.

Grandfather Gromb manufactured cloth ribbons, mostly white and black. They were used mainly for funeral wreaths by gentiles, since Jews do not place wreaths on the graves of their loved ones.

Grandfather Gromb was a follower of the Grand Rabbi of Radzin, and hence wore *tzitzis* with some blue-dyed threads.*

---

* The original commandment of *tzitzis* requires that one of the four threads (folded into eight tassels) on each corner of the garment be dyed blue. The dye had to be made of the blood of a certain mollusk, the identity of which was lost with time. The Grand Rabbi of Radzin felt that he had succeeded in identifying this mollusk, and he instructed his followers to dye the *tzitzis* thread according-

Grandfather was very highly regarded by the Grand Rabbi, who would spend hours discussing matters of importance with him whenever the Rabbi visited Warsaw.

Many people looked to Grandfather Gromb, a very learned and respected man, as an arbiter in monetary disputes. The apartment drew so many people who came to resolve their disputes that Grandmother Gromb eagerly awaited the Sabbath so the family could have some privacy. According to Mother, Grandmother used to joke that there was no point in closing the apartment's door, since people were walking in and out all the time. In fact, a sign stating *Do Not Disturb* had to be posted on the front door when Grandfather took his meals.

The Grombs had eight children, four boys and four girls. Moshe Aharon was the oldest and Mother was the youngest. Before his marriage, Moshe Aharon studied under the saintly Chafetz Chaim in the Lithuanian yeshivah of Radin, despite the fact that the Grombs were a Chassidic family, who generally would not send their children to a Lithuanian yeshivah. Moshe Aharon was an unusually brilliant Torah scholar and a saintly personality in his own right. Regrettably, Mother was too young to comprehend anything about Moshe Aharon's sojourn in Radin. She does remember, however, that Moshe Aharon used to be mysteriously described as "a keeper of the Chafetz Chaim's money," although she had no idea what this meant. It is likely that the boy who wore *tzitzis* with blue fringes, mentioned in Rabbi Moshe M. Yashar's book *The Chafetz Chaim*, was my Uncle Moshe Aharon.

Mother's oldest sister was married to the son of Rabbi Klepfish, a prominent member of Warsaw's Rabbinical Council. Her two middle sisters were married to two brothers (from the Silman family), an unusual occurrence in a Chassidic household. One of her brothers, Luzer, went to Germany to avoid being drafted into the Polish army; another, Mordechai, died

---

ly. (Most Rabbinical authorities did not concur with this decision.)

at an early age; the youngest, Zalman, lived in Warsaw. He was married with two children and owned his own textile factory in some other town, as well as a textile store in Warsaw. Of all my cousins, only Zalman's children remain in my memory since they were about my age.

Mother was Grandfather's favorite child, perhaps because she was the youngest, or because she was the most inquisitive, always bombarding her father with questions. At times, it took all of Grandfather's ingenuity to give her a reply that would be comprehensible as well as educational.

Grandfather had an enormous impact on Mother. His scrupulousness in business and his concern for the poor and downtrodden shaped her attitude towards life more than anything else.

The demand for grandfather's merchandise was not too steady. There were times when there were no

Rabbi Yisochor Dov Hacohen Rosenberg, the Rabbi of Strikov, Poland, after whom I am named. He was Grandmother Lederman's father.

orders at all, and his shop, like others in the trade, remained idle. It was hence common practice to employ workers only so long as the demand lasted and then to fire them when the last order had been filled. In those times, when unemployment compensation was non-existent, this was tantamount to reducing the worker to begging for his bread, if he did not want to die of starvation.

Grandfather would have none of this. Any worker that he

hired was told that the wages in this workshop were sightly below the standard wage for the trade, but, once accepted, the employee would be assured of a salary for the entire year, irrespective of the number of days he would actually work.

Mother was extremely talented with the workshop machinery. She was so familiar with all the large and small machine parts that when something broke down and Grandfather's workers could not fix it, he would say, "Let's wait till Sarahleh comes home. She'll have the machine running in no time."

* * *

Among the highlights of my childhood were the two yearly celebrations of the Passover Seder. We always made the Seder in my grandparents' homes. It happened once when we were celebrating the second Seder with my paternal grandparents that I requested a tricycle as my reward for returning the *afikoman.** I did this even though one could ride such a toy only in the forbidden yard—against Mother's wishes. I hoped that once it was in my possession, Mother would be forced to capitulate. Alas, this was not to be. I asked and Grandfather Lederman promised—but the next day I was informed that the tricycle had been exchanged for a prestigious Omega wristwatch.

* * *

Although children entered school at the age of seven, I learned to read Polish when I was five. I eagerly devoured all the "approved" children's literature, including *The Adventures of Tom Sawyer, Gulliver's Travels,* books by the Grimm brothers, and the like.

My school was a modern religious one, which could be reached by foot in about twenty minutes, or by trolley. It could also be reached by one of our taxis. Except for certain special occasions, however, my request for taxi service was

---

* The piece of matzah that children are expected to "steal," and then return in exchange for the promise of a present.

invariably turned down by Mother, who claimed that one should not get used to luxuries that are here today and may be gone tomorrow. (Little did she know how prophetic her words would prove to be!) I received the same answer when I asked why I had to shine my shoes although we had a house-keeper and a governess working for us.

During our years in Warsaw the subject of children's education in our family began and ended with me. Lea was only five when the war broke out, too young for school. Kindergartens were then a newfangled invention, and not many parents sent their children to one. Even if Lea had been old enough, Mother would not have sent her to kindergarten. One day I over-head her speaking to someone about the horror of taking a child away from his parents and sending him to kindergarten at a tender age. If not for the war, Lea would have been enrolled in a religious girls' school conducted in a manner similar to mine.

Mother's education was much different. When she was growing up, Warsaw had no religious schools for Jewish girls, and she, like other girls in her situation, was forced to attend public school. The thought of having his daughters going to school with boys, many of whom were gentile to boot, caused her father much distress, but he apparently had no alternative. Grandfather had an equally great concern, that since she was away from home all day, Mother would not absorb enough Jewish learning from her mother, as had been the norm for Jewish daughters until then. This prompted him to take the step of hiring a woman to come to the house to teach Mother *Chumash*. The tutor began with Creation, explaining everything word for word in the most proper manner. She concluded the lesson by saying: "If you believe in it, okay. I don't." Grandfather was eager to hear what his favorite daughter had learned, and Mother repeated the lecture word for word, including the "grand finale." Shortly afterwards, Mother was informed that the tutor would not be able to continue with her any longer. Mother could not fathom why her father had put an early end to her Jewish education.

Mother did, however, continue her education in an all-girls' commercial high school, where she learned bookkeeping, secretarial skills, and Russian. (Since Poland was under Soviet occupation then, Russian was taught as an obligatory second language.)

I don't believe that Mother ever held a secretarial job, but it is certain that what she learned as a bookkeeper served her well in running her own ribbon-cutting shop housed in the half-basement of our apartment building.

Mother had other pursuits besides running her business and attending to our proper behavior. One was knitting. From her swift-moving hands came a long stream of beautiful dresses, skirts and sweaters for my sister Lea, as well as handsome sweaters for me. Another was cooking for the Sabbath. Although we had a housekeeper whose duties included cooking, Mother, as a self-respecting Jewish wife and mother, would not think of letting her do all the cooking for so important a day.

*　*　*

I don't think my parents disliked their Polish lifestyle, but with Zionism such a pervasive idea, they, too, began to think of moving to Palestine. They were apparently influenced by the precedent of a very close family friend who had moved there some years earlier.

One could not then settle in the Holy Land without a certificate from the Mandatory authorities. Palestine, as the country was then called, was under the British Mandate and His Royal Majesty's government issued these prized documents —in very limited quantities—to the Jewish Agency for Palestine, which distributed them to various political parties. With his extensive connections, Father could easily have wangled one for us. He felt, though, that he should leave this opportunity for those less fortunate, since there was another way we could gain entrance to the Promised Land.

How? By simply depositing £1000 in one of Palestine's banks. A document, known as a "capitalist visa," would then be issued by His Majesty. The sum came to 27,000 pre-war zlotys. To put this in perspective, a skilled worker earned about 200 zlotys per month; but Father had no problem finding this kind of money. The deposit was made, and the pertinent royal instructions were issued "to whom it may concern" to provide the Lederman family with the required document.

One problem remained, however: the weather. The temperature in the Tel Aviv area, our proposed destination, did not drop below the already "unbearable" point of 77°F (25°C) until September or October at the earliest. Father felt that a heat wave would make a poor welcome for Mother upon her arrival in her old-new homeland, and so they postponed the trip until late September, 1939.

HELL BREAKS LOOSE

The summer of 1939 came to a close with dark clouds gathering over Poland. There was a palpable tension in the air. Billboards urged the populace to be on the alert and watch out for spies. I don't remember the mention of Germany by name, but everyone seemed to recognize the source of the threat. The Germans laid claim to Gdansk, once a German city known as Danzig, which had been ceded to Poland as part of the post-World War I Treaty of Versailles. The Poles refused to give it up. Of course, much more was transpiring than that, but this was the one occurrence that registered in my eight-year-old mind. There was talk of gas warfare. The newspapers warned about the total lack of masks, while at the same time recalling that the Germans used mustard gas during World War I. A general call-up was announced. Father was called to the draft board only to be sent home a few minutes later. He was told that at present there were not enough uniforms or arms for people over thirty-five, and that he would be called again at some later date.

Father was, quite likely, saved from the draft by that visit to the board. There he met a good friend of his who had also been called up and who, being about the same age, was temporarily rejected for the same reason. According to this person, there were indeed rifles and uniforms for the younger draftees, but little other equipment. No one in the high command, this person averred, harbored any hopes of holding out too long against the Germans. The Polish army consisted of over thirty very-well-trained infantry divisions, but was outnumbered in tanks, ships, artillery and, above all, aircraft. Even before exposure to the German *blitzkrieg* technique it was a foregone conclusion that defeat was imminent unless England and France stepped in. On its own, the Polish army, whose *avant garde* consisted of cavalry with its horse-drawn field cannon, could put up a valiant resistance, but could not defeat the Germans. Father, like his friend, held little hope of such foreign intervention. And, since he did not believe in risking his life for a lost cause, he decided to go into hiding.

The Poles tried to compensate for their lack of weaponry through humor. Accordingly, one could purchase a piece of paper with a drawing of four identical pigs. When properly folded, this would yield the face of the German dictator. Another such "weapon" consisted of limericks which poked fun at the Lithuanians who gave up the port city of Klaipeda without a fight, and even more so at the Czechs who surrendered without firing a shot. The implication: this sort of thing could never happen in Poland.

As soon as the reality of the precarious situation set in, Mother, like many other housewives, stocked up on food. She purchased stacks of sardines (about the only kind of canned food widely available then in Poland), sacks of flour and sugar, chocolate, powdered milk, and fruit; we even prepared a large supply of candles since the Warsaw power plant would be highly vulnerable, particularly with its overhead power distribution. For a while, we had large quantities of live carp swimming in the bathtub, which had previously served this purpose only between Thursday afternoon and Friday, when the fish were cooked for the Sabbath. Mother began to fear, however, that crumbs to feed the fish might not be available too much longer, so the fish were consumed at a higher-than-planned rate. Also, she reckoned it more prudent to utilize the tub as an emergency water supply than as a fish tank. Water was drawn into the tub, used as needed for a couple of days, then the tub was drained and refilled.

With the Jewish New Year approaching, the Jewish families living in our building started thinking about an alternate place of worship should an air raid prevent us from reaching the synagogue. The eventuality of bombing was a foregone conclusion, although no one had any idea exactly what was in store. It was well known that Germany had a superior air force and that Poland was incapable of preventing bombers from dropping their loads on the civilian population. Accordingly, one day, all the china disappeared from our closet and was mysteriously replaced by a Torah scroll. As I recall, no services were held in our house in the end, although I cannot be sure.

In the days before war broke out, we followed Civil Defense instructions, which were aimed primarily at blacking out the city. Automotive headlights were to be painted blue, and windows had to be covered with dark blue or black paper. In addition, paper tape was to be pasted on the windows to prevent injury from falling glass.

I no longer remember how the War started. But I do remember that, all of a sudden, the radio, in which previously I had taken no interest, became an important tool of survival. The government used it to issue air-raid warnings on hearing which everyone was supposed to enter an air-raid shelter. There was only one problem: there were no air-raid shelters. Instead, each group of tenants chose the sturdiest section of their building to serve in this capacity.

In our building there were two alternatives. One was the coal cellar, located at the left side of the yard. Its entrance was not far from the corner between the wall to the left as one entered, and the wall parallel to the street. The other choice was the half-basement that served as Mother's cloth-tape shop. Its entrance, down a short flight of steps, was in the right-hand corner of the yard. It was spacious and spotless, its flat-bed machines were ideal for spreading bedding, and it had an excellent illumination system. It did, however, suffer from two major shortcomings: Its ceiling had large unsupported spans, raising fears that if the building suffered a direct hit, it would cave in, burying everyone underneath. In addition, it was only partially underground; its windows extended to the ceiling and faced the street.

The coal cellar was deeper, and consisted of relatively small cells, separated from one another by a brick wall. Each one held the coal supply of a different family. The ceiling of this cellar was judged better able to withstand a direct hit. Nonetheless, convenience (and cleanliness) prevailed and, on the first night of air-raid alarms, most of the tenants, including ourselves, stayed in the half-basement. The holdouts joined us the next time. On one of the first nights of the war, the power supply to the half-basement gave out. We sat in pitch black darkness until Mother managed to light the candles she had brought with her. Our area was the only one so illuminated, since no one else had her foresight.

The power supply to the entire building was on most of the time; I know because I frequently listened to our electric radio. (It should be kept in mind that except for the need to hear news, interruption of the power supply was a minor inconvenience. Since there were no refrigerators, washing machines, mixers, electric irons, and the like in those days, a typical household used electricity only for lighting. Using candles instead of electricity was not a major discomfort. Until only a few years earlier, candles had been the norm.)

During the daytime we would stay in our apartment, running down to the shelter only when the radio sounded the alarm. At night we slept in the shelter. People were afraid to be caught unawares by an alarm, without having enough time to get dressed and run down. In addition, the only sirens available at night were those of factories, situated mostly on the outskirts of the city, and no one could be sure of hearing them while asleep. This being so, the nights were spent in the "shelter."

The water supply to our building functioned most of the time, but when it did not, everyone had to run to one of the nearby wells to get water. (Everyone, that is, except for people like us, who maintained a bathtub full of water for just such a circumstance.) These wells were remnants of the old system that had supplied the city with water in previous times. Since the new centralized system had been built relatively recently, most of the old wells remained intact—a blessing under the circumstances, especially since the water was drawn by hand-operated pumps, eliminating worry over the state of the electric power supply. Still, it was dangerous to be out in the street in case of a sudden bombing raid.

In our house food did not present a problem. No food, not even bread, was delivered to the grocery stores. Bread was available only at the bakeries, and people in our building who had gone there told of long lines. But our family was not affected by all this. We had enough coal to last us a couple of months, and so, instead of bread, we ate Mother's home-baked challahs. These were delicious when eaten with sardines and washed down by tea (after the powdered milk supply ran out). Mother did not try to feed me semolina, which I hated.

A manually operated water pump. Photograph by Alter Kacinza. YIVO Archive, New York, Photograph courtesy of Beth Hatefutsot, Photo Archive, Tel Aviv.

I had never liked pears because they were extremely slippery after peeling (a household requirement) or chocolate, but in view of the new situation I actually started liking both.

Newspapers became a desired commodity. Before this, I never had any interest in them, but as the war progressed and tension mounted, I found myself reading the newspaper every day. I cannot explain how these got to our neighborhood and to our house. One news story in particular has stayed with me these many years. Indeed, I regarded it as so unbelievable that I started doubting my own memory until I read it word for word in William L. Shirer's book *The Rise and Fall of the Third Reich*:

> At one point, racing east across the Corridor, they had been counterattacked by the Pomorska Brigade of cavalry... Horses against tanks! The cavalryman's long lance against the tank's long cannon![*]

The newspaper account told of a valiant Polish cavalry regiment that had attacked a German tank unit... with drawn swords. I was dumbfounded—horses and swords against steel

Polish cavalry brigade on its way to attack German forces. The riders on white horses in the foreground are officers. Other officers within the brigade can be identified by their white horses. Photograph courtesy of the Ghetto Fighters' House Museum.

---

* Greenwich (Fawcett: 1950), p. 827, reprinted here with permission.

and cannon? I showed the story to Mother. For the first time in all my eight years, she could not provide an explanation.

We lived in fear from day to day. Surviving one air raid did not guarantee surviving the next. After a few days in which the bombs fell on the city, but not on us, a new danger appeared from an unexpected source.

We woke up one day to find a detachment of the Polish army stationed in our yard. It consisted of about a dozen soldiers who, as I recall, had no weapons other than their rifles and ammunition. They did, however, come with a field kitchen: a horse-driven wagon carrying a large vessel, fired from a metal box underneath and topped by a chimney. The soldiers were accompanied by one or two farmers to whom the horses belonged, and who refused to part with them.

With German spies presumed to be everywhere, we feared that the *Luftwaffe* would give us a more thorough "treatment" due to the presence of these soldiers. Sure enough, bombs started falling closer to the house. It is equally possible, of course, that with the bombing going into the second week, more anti-aircraft guns had been put out of service, or that the Germans were looking for new targets.

The heavy bombing went on for almost three weeks. Bombs were falling on other parts of the city every day; we had no idea how close to our house. All we knew was that the radio announcement of an air raid was followed, sooner or later, by the sickening sound of bombs rending the air. It sounded something like a long *uuh* followed by a bang, when the bomb hit its target. All this, however, happened in "some other place." I often wondered whether it was proper to feel relieved upon learning that it was someone else who got killed.

But then, on that horrible night, the war came to our building.

When the alarm sounded, we went down to the half-basement, as we did routinely, not expecting that things would be different from previous days. Then, we suddenly heard a new sound frighteningly close: *Whee-ee!* It was followed by a loud bang whereupon the building shook, the overhead beams danced to and fro, and then a deafening explosion let loose someplace above our heads. Our building had received a direct hit.

For a few moments, a frightening silence reigned in the sub-basement. Apparently people needed time to realize the magnitude of the danger. Still, there was little panic. Maybe it was because our survival until now had imbued everyone with a false sense of security, resulting in a response of numb surprise. A cry broke forth, almost in unison: "To the coal cellar!"

Everyone started running to the exit, leaving everything behind. Mother was the only one with enough presence of

Corner of Nalewki and Gensia aflame as a result of bombing. Photograph courtesy of the Ghetto Fighters' House Museum.

German bomber releasing its deadly cargo onto Warsaw's streets. Photograph courtesy of the Ghetto Fighters' House Museum.

mind to consider that it might be freezing cold in the other place. She quickly thrust a blanket under my arm, took Lea by the hand, and our trio joined the crowd that was running toward the steps leading to the yard. It was a 60-foot dash across our courtyard to the presumed safety of the coal cellar. I grabbed the blanket and blindly ran toward the exit steps. The sight that presented itself to my eyes as I entered the yard was terrifying. The sky was illuminated by red flashes interspersed with tracer bullets that hung as strings of fluorescent pearls across the sky. It was an eerie mixture of beauty and horror. My entire being was gripped with fear and, for the first time since the war started, I became acutely aware of the possibility that we might be killed.

Most likely I had no more than a fraction of a second to take all this in, when suddenly our building was hit again with the mighty force of—as we learned later—five more long-range artillery shells. Many more shells fell on the building across the street, rumored to be the headquarters of the outlawed Communist party. The concrete-paved yard rolled

Nalewki Street during a bombing raid. The photograph shows an abandoned trolleycar with top windshield blown out and a hansom cab with its unhitched horse in the far background. Photograph courtesy of the Ghetto Fighters' House Museum.

from side to side like the deck of a storm-tossed ship. The safety of the coal cellar became even more remote because of the possibility that I would lose my balance and fall, and be left unprotected under skies that were raining death. With these thoughts passing through my mind, I ran, straining mightily to spread out my hands as far as I could to prevent being toppled over without losing the precious blanket entrusted to me by Mother. It occurred to me that, given the situation, it might be wiser to run back to the half-basement, which was closer than the coal cellar. However, this required making a decision—something which at that moment was beyond the intellectual capacity of any human being, let alone an eight-year old boy for whom everything had to be decided.

I somehow managed to stay on my feet and reach the coal cellar. At first I couldn't find Mother and Lea, but within a short time they burst in. Mother had been certain that something dreadful had happened to me, and joy overwhelmed her when she saw me alive and well. She had still been in the half-basement when the second (and subsequent) shells hit. She had yelled for me to turn back, but I hadn't heard her. Now I was to learn that some of our neighbors had made it to the coal cellar before the heavy shelling and some had reached it afterwards. But I was the only one who ran through the yard when the earth shook and rolled.

The next day shots were heard in the yard, and the word went out that since Warsaw was expected to surrender any minute, the soldiers were shooting holes in their rifles so the Germans would not get them.

Daytime allowed us to survey the damage. A huge hole gaped at us from the wall diagonally opposite our apartment, where three artillery shells had hit. Two other shells had penetrated the front staircase between the first and second floors, making it dangerous to use. From then on, the service entrance acquired a new status. I no longer remember where the sixth shell hit.

Of course, at the time of the shelling we had no idea what exactly was inflicting the damage on our building. But the next day, artillery appeared to be the only explanation, because only a horizontal path could have been responsible for the holes in the walls of the building. More important, we were fortunate—had it been a bomb, we would have had no chance of coming out alive from a direct hit. Only decades later did I learn that the German dictator had ordered Warsaw shelled mercilessly despite the advice given by his generals, who deemed it unnecessary. Apparently he was incensed by the fact that the capital city was holding out even after the government had fled from it (the defenses were commanded by the city's mayor and whatever armed forces units he could muster, even after the rest of the country had surrendered).

On the day following the nightmarish shelling there were no air raids. People didn't know what to make of the strange silence. Some time later, word spread that Poland had capitulated and that whatever remained of the its army had surrendered. According to rumor, the Polish soldiers, who were being allowed to withdraw to Rumania, would be forced to march through Warsaw. This was scheduled to take place along several streets, one of which was a major thoroughfare not far from our house. I joined the crowd that went to watch.

It was a depressing sight. Column after column of soldiers, eight or maybe even ten abreast, marched down the street. Although they were in uniform, they quite obviously carried no weapons. Each column was headed by a mounted officer with his sword (or maybe only an empty scabbard) hanging from his left side.

I came home shaken up and crying. Mother tried to calm me down by telling me that the Germans had come in to rebuild what they had destroyed. Since it was inconceivable that Mother was not telling the truth, I pitied her for believing that those who had caused so much destruction would then rebuild what they had destroyed.

Long-range artillery put into position outside of Warsaw. Our house was hit by six shells from such a cannon. Photograph courtesy of Bundesarchiv, Koblenz.

Warsaw's citizens digging anti-tank trenches. Photograph courtesy of the Ghetto Fighters' House Museum.

The next day the Germans entered the city. Their route into town took them along Zelazna, the street that formed a corner with ours, a mere three buildings away from us. It was an awesome sight. Watching the procession, I saw an endless line of low, relatively small trucks traveling at a very slow pace, stretched out as far as the eye could see. Each truck carried a soldier sitting next to the driver. In his right hand the soldier had something akin to a tennis racket with a large red circle in the center. Whenever the lead truck's driver was about to brake, his companion stuck out the racket, the one behind him did likewise, and a forest of racket-holding uniformed hands instantly protruded from the column. The trucks were followed by horse-drawn covered wagons loaded to the rafters with loaves of bread.

Father returned from hiding after the Germans entered the city. One day as he was walking down the street, he was picked up by German soldiers, together with other passersby, and driven to the outskirts of Warsaw to refill the trenches

Polish soldiers in surrender march through Warsaw. Even the officer's horse looks dejected. Photograph courtesy of Bundesarchiv, Koblenz.

dug by the Polish defenders of the capital. In the evening, the entire party was returned to the street from which they had been taken and each person was even handed a loaf of bread for his work. We subsequently learned that such scenes had occurred throughout the city.

After this incident, Father did not leave the house before dark. Both my parents felt, as did many others in the city, that this was just the beginning. No one doubted that such incidents would become common as time progressed, and that the Jews would be singled out for special treatment. After all, everyone knew how the Germans had treated their polished, westernized Jewish fellow-citizens in Germany, and it didn't take much foresight to realize that Polish Jews were destined for much worse. Nevertheless, no one could have possibly imagined what was eventually to happen.

Since Lithuania was then an independent state and therefore hosted a diplomatic representative of the King of England, my parents began planning to utilize our "capitalist visa" and reach Palestine. Because of Father's particular vulnerability and the difficulty of wrapping up all of our family's affairs overnight, it was decided that he should leave for Vilno immediately and we would join him there later. (It is also possible that Father didn't feel he could provide us with proper accommodations in Vilno.) Above all, no one believed that the situation was so critical as to require a slapdash departure. Father's leaving, however, was urgent. Now that all able-bodied men avoided going out in the streets lest they be seized for work details, the Germans started going from house to house in search of manpower. Being suddenly abducted from one's home was frightening enough—even with the prospect of being returned at night. But rumors were beginning to circulate that the next step would be forced-labor camps.

The situation became even more precarious when it was learned that the Germans were stopping men in the street, taking them into the entrance halls of buildings and checking

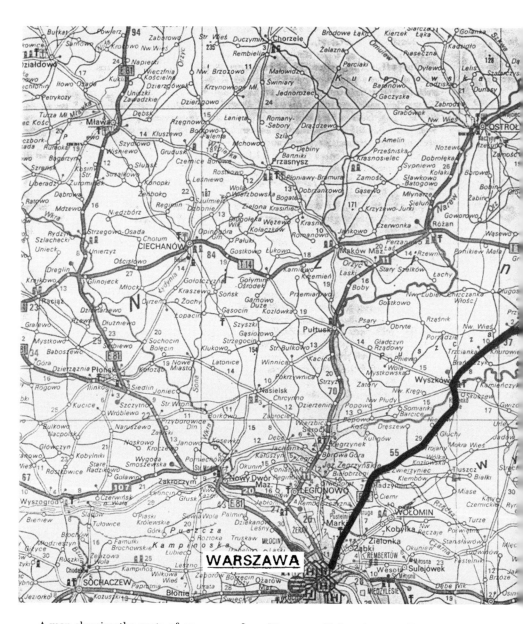

A map showing the route of our escape from Warsaw to Bialystok, via Malkinia and Czyzew.

The facade of the Czyzew
train station with a hansom
cab in front of it.

General view of the city of Bialystok.

Photograph courtesy of Beth Hatefutsot, the Nahum Goldmann Museum of the Jewish Diaspora, Tel Aviv, provided by Tomas Wisniewski, Bialystok.

The Great Synagogue of Bialystok (restored) that housed refugees during WWII, among them, the Halzband family (see Chapter 22: Two Brothers, Two Sisters).

Photograph courtesy of Beth Hatefutsot, the Nahum Goldmann Museum of the Jewish Diaspora, Tel Aviv, photo by K. Jablonski, Warsaw, provided by Marian Fuks.

A portion of the interior of the Great Synagogue of Bialystok.

Photograph courtesy of Beth Hatefutsot, the Nahum Goldmann Museum of the Jewish Diaspora, Tel Aviv, photo by K. Jablonski, Warsaw, provided by Marian Fuks.

to see whether they were circumcised. Those who were, vanished.

We found out that at least one other friend of the family had capitalist-visa privileges similar to ours, and that he also planned to go to Vilno, now called by its Lithuanian name "Vilnius." Father thus had a friend to accompany him when he illegally crossed the newly established border between the part of Poland currently under German occupation and territory previously controlled by Poland, but now annexed to Lithuania. Both families received coded messages of safe arrival, and were getting ready for the trip to the northeast that would eventually take us to the Middle East.

As soon as the bombing and shooting ended, inquiries went out concerning our taxis. We soon learned that three out of the four had been requisitioned by the Polish army for the war effort. Actually, they were used to ferry the families of officers (and, in at least some cases, also the officers themselves) to safe havens. The last taxi would have suffered the same fate, but the short, stocky army major who came with a requisition order was turned away by the owner of the garage where our cabs were stored. The first three cars were "drafted" at the beginning of the bombing, whereas for some unknown reason the major's requisition request was put in just before the city fell. The garage owner, a Polish citizen of German ethnic origin—a *Volksdeutsche*—sensed the imminent occupation by his countrymen, and refused the officer's request.

With the situation in Warsaw becoming increasingly precarious, more and more Jews started looking for ways to leave the city. The nearest and apparently simplest option was to cross illegally over the new border that had been created when the Soviet Union and Germany divided Poland between them. The Germans made no pretenses about their occupation, whereas according to the Soviets, eastern Poland had just been "liberated" from the Polish "oppressors" and was now a part of the "free, glorious" republics of Ukraine and Byelorussia.

These, together with the other similar republics, made up the Soviet Union.

There was no dearth of guides for the crossing. After all, the people living in the small villages on both sides of the border had until recently been neighbors, maybe even close family. They knew the terrain thoroughly. But borders, of course, particularly newly-established ones, are heavily patrolled. Here both Soviet and German border police kept watch at and in between the official crossings. Still, these were only patrols—by soldiers not particularly familiar with the terrain—so one's chances of getting through were quite reasonable.

In the beginning, the border guards would simply stop the fugitives, inquire as to their place of origin, and send them back. It was claimed that if one was a good talker, he could convince the guards that he had just come from the opposite side. This way he would be sent exactly where he wanted to go. The patrols frequently believed these stories since the clandestine traffic was bi-directional. There were actually many people from the Russian-occupied Poland who didn't like the attitude there toward the population, and who believed they would be better off on the German side.

Crossing the border constituted only half of the problem. It was just as hard, and maybe even harder, to leave the city and reach the village that served as the springboard for such crossings. The Germans suspected any Jew headed in the general direction of the border of intending to escape their zone of occupation by illegally crossing to the Soviet-dominated part of Poland; hence a Jew could only travel surreptitiously. The border being several hundred kilometers to the east, some means of transportation was necessary. The word got around that people who had cars could make money by ferrying fugitives at night on side roads. Although this involved some risk, at this early stage most such trips were completed without the parties being detected.

Having heard this, Mother located one of our cab drivers and asked him to take command of the remaining cab. Soon our blue Chevy joined the other vehicles in transporting people from Warsaw to the border. The car was stored in the garage during the daytime, leaving only at dusk, to pick up its passengers for their nocturnal escape, and returning to our yard in the middle of the night. I remember staying up late, waiting for the beam of light from the car's headlights to

House sheared apart by a direct bomb hit. Photograph courtesy of the Ghetto Fighters' House Museum.

illuminate the wall opposite our dining room windows. When I would awaken in the morning, the car would be gone, most likely because it had been returned to the safety of the *Volksdeutsche's* garage.

Running such an operation was probably not an easy matter, but I was not privy to everything going on. I was aware of one problem, though: obtaining gasoline. Warsaw never had the number of gas stations typically found in a modern Western city. Now, with many or even most gas stations bombed out, the situation was even worse. In addition, the gasoline supply was erratic at best, and existing gasoline supplies quite possibly consisted of "leftovers." Filling up the tank along the way was out of question. The vehicles traveled along dirt roads passing through small villages or towns. These roads were usually travelled by horse and wagon and hence had no gas stations. Driving through highways, where some gas station may or may not have gasoline for sale at a given time, was out—a German patrol could pop up any second, stop the car and ask for documents. For all these reasons, it was imperative to have a gasoline supply at hand.

Acquiring this vital commodity necessitated a scavenger hunt through the city for whatever gas station there was, then filling the tank and an additional container, since the next few days might turn out to be "dry." I was very eager to go on such a search both for the fun of it, and, much more importantly, to see what the city looked like after the bombing. Except for the two forays described above (to see the Polish army retreating and the Germans entering), I had not left the house. Of course, it was wise for everyone, even eight-year old children, to stay off the streets (although, at this point, adult men were the main target). But I pestered Mother long and intensely enough so that when the driver came up next time to get something from our house before departing on such a trip, she permitted me to go despite the danger that the driver might be picked up to join a work detail. I had to sit on the floor of the back compartment, which I shared with a huge bottle, known as a carboy. Made of plain glass, it was encased in a wicker basket to prevent it from breaking. Such containers were commonly employed in Poland for liquid food storage, and now they were pressed into service to store gasoline.

From the cab, I saw one depressing and frightening sight after another. Everywhere I looked, buildings were sheared off in front. The streets were full of rubble, which frequently lay in heaps on the roadway, producing hills and valleys on the ordinarily level streets of my hometown. Nothing escaped destruction.

We drove back with closed windows and drawn curtains to conceal our precious cargo. I got back home with an incredible headache, caused by the gasoline vapors, that took a few days to go away. For about fifteen years afterwards I would get a headache whenever I was around a gas station.

ESCAPE FROM WARSAW

One evening, as I was waiting for our cab to come in, Mother entered the room and announced that I should no longer expect its arrival: we were packing up and leaving! When I pressed her for the reason, she told me that an unpleasant person had visited us. Under the circumstances, our only choice was to leave town.

As I heard from Mother later, the visitor was none other than the Polish army major whose attempt to "requisition" our cab had been successfully resisted by the owner of the garage. Apparently he had not given up on our cab, and had followed it on its daily rounds, eventually tracing it to us. He threatened Mother that unless she paid him off, he would tell the Germans both that Father had volunteered for the Polish army (a lie), and that we were ferrying people to the border (the truth). Mother paid him off handsomely, but at the same time realized that one instance of blackmail could only lead to another. In the end, no amount of money would be enough to keep the extortionist at bay. This meant that we had to leave Warsaw immediately.

According to the original plan, we were to wait for our papers to be processed in Vilno. Father apparently had our passport with him (only one was needed per family), and he wanted to wait until the visa was stamped on it. Since not only the crossing of the border to Lithuania, but also the subsequent sojourn in Vilno until the day of actual departure were illegal, he wanted to minimize our stay there. Furthermore, he was aware that the Lithuanians guarded their border jealously, having recently regained parts of their territory wrested from them by Poland a number of years earlier. Father was afraid to have his wife and two small children cross such a border alone. Now experienced at this dangerous game, he intended to come back to Warsaw (subsequently to Bialystok) to escort us.

Since we were planning an escape from Warsaw anyway, and were simply waiting for a signal from Father in Vilno concerning the timing, all we had to do now was put the contingency plan into operation. This was a plan that had long ago been worked out to the finest detail, and so could be implemented quickly. It did, however, require a few days of organization. This gave our army major an opportunity to visit us again. Mother told him to come back in three more days, by which time she would have money. By then we expected to be (and actually were) on our way out.

Except for furniture, china, most of the cutlery and the record player, the entire contents of our house were packed into nine huge leather valises. Bed linen, quilts, and pillows found their way into the two cavernous bags formerly used for moving these items to the countryside. Most of the dishes, pots and pans, and silverware were also left behind. The china was simply too heavy and too fragile. And, in case of a search, it was considered dangerous to have dishes with a characteristically Jewish "non-smell"—from not using pork, and from using separate utensils for meat and dairy.

Last, but not least, we also left behind Mother's candlesticks. They were a magnificent pair, column-shaped with a square base and only slightly short of being two feet tall. It was difficult for Mother to part with them, but it was impossible to take them along: only Jews had such candlesticks.[*]

There was another item that we left behind: the family photo album. We did this for two reasons. Both Father and Lea had distinctly Jewish features, and we feared that if the Germans discovered the album, they would ask too many

---

[*] I saw such a set only once again. Years later, when I was invited for the Friday-night meal by Rabbi Yitzchak Schmidman, a well-known Jewish day-school principal in East New York, I entered the dining room and my heart skipped a beat. There, gracing his table, was a set of candlesticks identical to Mother's.

questions. More important, though, Mother was to have another "husband" for the trip, and the family pictures would have
given us away.

Since it was assumed that no Jew in the German part of
Poland was safe (whatever the word "safe" meant at that
time), we deposited our furniture and the other items we
decided not to take with the *Volksdeutsche* ("Mr. V." for the
sake of brevity), to be picked up again when the Germans
would be routed. We naively assumed that when the War
eventually came to an end, life in Warsaw would more or less
return to normal, and that we would be able to come back
and reclaim our furniture. No one dreamed that before the
War's end the entire city would be in ruins.

Mr. V. was also a partner in our escape plan. Either in
exchange for the goods deposited with him (about which he
may have had different expectations than we did) or for pay
(or both)—or as a form of appreciation for the kind of unparalleled customer relationship that he enjoyed with us—he
agreed to provide us the ways and means of getting out of
Warsaw with all our belongings. A private car or taxi would be
insufficient, since our belongings simply could not fit into any
standard vehicle. Instead, Mr. V. promised to arrange a truck
with a driver, and he himself agreed to ride in the cabin and
present himself as Mother's husband! After all, the only people
suspected of running away when traveling towards the border
were Jews. (There might even have been general restrictions
on inter-city travel by Jews, but I no longer remember.) Travel
by Poles was not restricted, although it is quite possible that
their documents were checked more thoroughly than those of
a *Volksdeutsche*. It was surmised that after the Germans had
checked his documents, they would not bother to check those
of his "wife and children."

All this was necessary because the dirt roads along which
our blue Chevy took other people to the border could not
safely carry a truck, and we hence had to travel on the main

highway. We knew that a German checkpoint was situated some distance beyond the city limits, and that any vehicle allowed past it had clear sailing to the border. There was always the chance that we would not be stopped but, should this happen, we expected that Mr. V's documents would grant us safe passage.

For a reason I was to learn only later, the guards used to stop vehicles they wanted to check by firing a shot in the air. Motor traffic in Poland not being too heavy, the driver of the vehicle usually had no doubt for whom the shot was intended.

The day of our departure arrived. In addition to the dishes, furniture, and other items we were leaving behind, Lea and I also had to leave all our toys—with the exception of a large "sleeping" doll which Lea tearfully clutched to her heart. My sister was placed on the front bench (trucks in those days had no proper seats), in the hope that her typical Jewish features would be somewhat hidden. The doll was placed in the storage box under the bench. Mother and I seated ourselves on the floor of the truck next to the valises and bedding. We also had with us Lea's brass crib, which was folded and tied up.

The truck rolled out of our apartment building. I do not remember going through the city or leaving the city limits, but I do recall getting onto the highway. This highway had been built (or re-paved) just before the war, and we immediately felt the difference between the bumpy city roads and the smooth highway surface. (Most of Warsaw's streets, including ours, were paved with cobblestones. Major arteries were paved with equally sized square stones, while only special streets sported asphalt.) Every minute that passed took us further away from what was home, and nearer to the checkpoint that would test the workability of our plan. Every once in a while, I peered over the cab of the truck to see whether the checkpoint had come into view. The thumping drum in my heart beat louder with each additional moment of anticipation. Although I scanned the right side of the road regularly, I also threw an occasional glance at the other side. Suddenly, a structure came into view on the left, and I instantly realized that it was the checkpoint! It was located on the other side of the road, apparently because an existing building had been taken over for the purpose. To my indescribable joy and relief, we sailed several truck lengths past the building. I stole a glance at Mother, a happy smile on my face.

Bang! I heard a shot ring out in the air as the soldiers signaled us to stop. My joy was shattered. I began to tremble with fear: Would the plan work? Would the "husband" story be accepted by the German checkpoint guards?" The following minutes would decide everything.

Then, before the guards could reach them, Mr. V. climbed down from his seat in the truck's cabin, rushed back to Mother and, shaking with fear, whispered to her: "I am not your husband! I am just the driver's helper."

All was lost! Our carefully constructed plans were demolished in seconds! Should she be asked, Mother could not provide an explanation as to what was she doing moving eastward, with two small children and all her possessions, other than that she was trying to reach the border. It crossed my mind that we would have been much better off making our way to the border under the cover of night with whatever possessions could fit into a car, rather than to bring upon ourselves a calamity of this magnitude.

Within a minute, the rear of the truck was opened and three German soldiers climbed up. One was past middle age and somewhat short, the other in his thirties, and the third a young man of about twenty. They asked Mother in German about her husband. Knowing Yiddish, Mother understood the question quite well. However, answering it immediately would have given rise to the suspicion that she was a Jew, since Poles generally didn't know German. I say suspicion, because with her fair complexion and blue eyes, and the stray strands of light chestnut hair sticking out from under her kerchief, she looked more like a Pole than a Jew—and the same was true of me. My sister, on the other hand, had a classic Jewish face. Fortunately we had thought to place her on the front seat, where the soldiers were not likely to look. Lea sat there through the entire ordeal in frozen silence, forgotten by everyone.

Mother let the soldiers work on conveying the question to her, and when she finally "understood" what was asked, she mimicked the holding and shooting of a rifle to intimate that her husband had been killed. The overwhelming tension of the situation suddenly brought upon me the urge to relieve myself. At the same time, recalling the stories about the "entrance-hall circumcision check," I was certain that if I asked to get off the truck for this purpose, one of the trio would accompany me to check whether I was circumcised. So I relieved myself in my pants. Since children were not supposed to be privy to anything that adults spoke about, and hence I wasn't supposed to know about the "circumcision check," Mother had a hard time getting over the fact that her eight-year-old son had such foresight.

The questioning over, the soldiers started to search our baggage. This was standard procedure in these cases, and, as mentioned, we had prepared for it carefully by leaving all material traces of our Jewishness in Warsaw (or so we thought). One of the valises was opened to reveal several bars of chocolate lying on top of men's suits. One of the soldiers helped himself to some of the chocolate while another proceeded to check the suit pockets. We watched mutely, our hearts pounding, as he withdrew several small items and scraps of paper. He unfolded one piece of paper and we saw to our horror that it was a receipt of a contribution to some Jewish organization, clearly marked with a Star of David. "We have been found out," I thought. "This is the end!" I felt dizzy and grew faint. My hands clenched automatically in hopeless resignation. I looked up at Mother.

I never asked Mother what went through her mind during these fateful moments. However, she did her best to show no fear, and succeeded in looking calm as the world around her collapsed.

Time stood still as we awaited the inevitable. The soldier who was searching the clothes turned to the others and said, "Aha! This Polish lady has laid her hands on Jewish goods! Good for her!"

The soldier then offered me some of our sequestered chocolate. Seething with anger at the audacity of being offered my own chocolate, I declined, even though I was aware that offending him could bring calamity upon us all. The magnitude of the injustice was just too much for me to brook. Fortunately, there were no repercussions, and the truck was soon speeding toward the village of Malkinia, on the German side of the border between the German-occupied and Russian-occupied parts of Poland.

We arrived in Malkinia toward evening and had to wait in the thatched-roof house of our guides until it grew dark. It was a typical Polish peasant abode with an earthen floor and a ceiling darkened by water that seeped through the straw roof when strong rains fell. A kerosene lamp hanging from the ceiling provided illumination. I had often seen these houses from the outside, but this was the first time I had stepped inside one. Our belongings were trucked to a second house, belonging to relatives of our "hosts" who were partners in this operation. The cargo was removed from the truck without any mishap, except for Lea's doll, which was forgotten under the driver's seat. For months afterwards Lea was desolate. She consoled herself by sewing dolls out of rags, and filling them with other rags and sawdust.

According to the original plan, we were supposed to cross the border directly from the first house. But an hour or so later we were informed that the German patrolling had been intensified in that vicinity, and that if we waited much longer, we would be accosted by a patrol as we were leaving. It was felt that the other house, located almost at the town's edge, would be safer, so we moved toward it as fast as we could.

It should be noted here that the clothing worn by peasants was much coarser than that of city dwellers, and of inferior quality. If spotted, we would be identified immediately as outsiders, and suspected of being Jewish. The Germans were aware that Malkinia served as an illegal border crossing point, and their patrols were primarily intended to prevent this activity.

Lea entered the house first and I was about to follow, but just as Mother came close to the hut, a young, rifle-carrying German soldier appeared out of nowhere. Before the soldier had a chance to utter a word, Mother pulled off her gold diamond-studded watch and handed it him. At first he refused to take it, but Mother insisted, telling him that he should give

A typical Polish thatched-roof village house. Photograph courtesy of the US Library of Congress.

it to his girlfriend as a present. Apparently this approach salved his conscience, and he slid it into his pocket. I was terrified at the sight. What was she doing? Bribing a soldier in the line of duty? In wartime to boot? Calling his attention to us instead of slipping into the house? What made her think that he wouldn't arrest her regardless? I wished I could stop her, but did not dare say anything within earshot of the soldier.

As it turned out, Mother knew best. The soldier made an about-face and left. We were saved again!

According to the original plan, we were supposed to leave close to midnight. However, since our presence placed everyone in continual danger, it was decided to advance our departure. This presented a problem because there were supposed to be ten porters to carry our baggage pieces, some of whom were scheduled to arrive only later. For this reason, another plan was put into operation. The three of us would leave immediately with half of our belongings while the other half would be brought later.

We left the house and started walking across fields, accompanied by five people carrying the valises. The night was cloudy, but at times the moon shone brightly, illuminating our group and causing us to wonder how long it would take until a German lookout spotted us. After a short walk, we reached a ditch. Our valises were deposited there, and so were we. The guides (most likely the same ones who had safely guided our taxi "customers" across the border) turned around and went back to the village for the other half of our baggage. It was imperative to move our valises out of the house from which we had departed as soon as possible because if the Germans made a search, the owners could be imprisoned for aiding in an illegal border crossing. After all, no Polish peasant could account for the possession of the kind of goods contained in our valises.

The guides soon reappeared with the rest of our baggage

and told us to wait for them. They would carry half the baggage across the border and come back for the remainder and for us. They told us they would be back soon. In frightened silence we watched the receding figures of our guides as they moved away toward a sizable clump of trees which soon swallowed them and half our possessions.

We were alone in no-man's land, totally dependent on the skills and good will of our guides. They were our only connection between what only a short time ago had been a stable and secure world, and whatever hope there existed for escaping the grip of the mightiest empire on earth.

We sat in the ditch, shivering with cold and fear, waiting for what seemed to be an eternity. Our eyes were trained on the direction where the guides had disappeared, but all we could see through the darkness were fields stretching in all directions, and the clump of trees in the far distance. We lost track of time. For some reason I had left my Omega watch in Warsaw, and Mother had parted with hers just a while ago. (Lea, only five, had not been entrusted with a watch.) We didn't know what to think. The guides were gone for a long time, or so it seemed to us. Why weren't they back? Had they been apprehended by the Germans? And if so, what should we do? Should we stay until their relatives back in Malkinia figured out what happened, and tried to find us? Would they risk their lives to try? Could they?

Our tension mounted from minute to minute. We no longer knew what to think. Suddenly the clouds parted and the moon lit up the scene in front of us. As we strained our eyes, several figures suddenly emerged from the shadow of the clump of trees and proceeded toward us. For the first and last time in her life, Mother panicked. "It is the Germans!" she said. "The guides have betrayed us! Quickly, let's run!" she whispered.

With calmness and maturity highly uncharacteristic of a child who had been protected from every kind of actual or imaginary calamity, I stood my ground and refused to budge.

After all, why would our guides bring us all the way out there only to turn us in? Couldn't they have done it in Malkinia? More important, running made no sense. "Where are we going to run to?" I thought to myself. To Malkinia? That meant to the Germans. To Warsaw? There was no way to get there— and we had escaped from there for a very good reason. I glanced at the heavy leather valises in the ditch. I could not imagine trying to even lift one of them—let alone carry it. And without their contents, how were we going to live?

Besides, I reasoned to myself, these figures might be our guides. If we stay, we allow ourselves the benefit of the doubt. They knew where they left us and they will come and fetch us. If we run, they will never find us. If it is the Germans, let them pick us up instead of our running into their hands.

As all these thoughts were flashing through my mind, the approaching figures came close enough to be counted. There were five of them. "But *Mamushiu*," I said, "these are our guides. Look—there are five of them."

"You mean there can be no German patrol with five soldiers?! Let's run fast, they will soon be here." Still, I stood my ground. "*Mamushiu*," I said, "where do you want to run?"

There was no answer. There couldn't be. I looked again. The distance between them and us diminished in the meantime and it was obvious that they did not wear uniforms and were unarmed.

"*Mamushiu*, look, they are unarmed." They were indeed our guides!

(For many, many years, I tried to find an explanation for Mother's uncharacteristic behavior. It seems quite reasonable that the two encounters—first on the truck and then with the German soldier in Malkinia—had exhausted her endurance. It is also possible that she suspected that the guides had been caught and had turned us in to save themselves.)

They lifted the remaining baggage, and we followed them. After a rather long walk, we came to a hay barn. There we met some other people who had apparently made the journey before us, and found the first part of our belongings. We spent the night trying unsuccessfully to sleep on the hay. We were only a day away from our comfortable Warsaw bedrooms, but the difference seemed like light-years.

We were already on the other side of the border, but I did not become aware of it until the next morning when a horse-drawn wagon drove up to take us on the last leg of our border-crossing journey. I was so tired by then, I must have fallen asleep as soon as I seated myself on the wagon, because I was jolted awake only upon our arrival at a railroad station. Since the total distance between the station and Malkinia is about fifteen miles, the wagon ride must have taken over an hour, although it seemed to me to have lasted not more than fifteen minutes.

If I remember correctly, this station was in the town of Czyżew. It was full of other refugees who had arrived there by means similar to ours. We were all waiting for the train to take us to Bialystok, which was the closest major city.

The day was just breaking, and it was bitterly cold. We could not enter the station building for comfort due to the presence of innumerable previous arrivals. I still remember my shock at seeing Mother pull out our quilts, encased in their snow-white covers, spread them on the dirty cement platform floor, and tell us to wrap ourselves in them.

A train pulled in, and everyone scurried to secure a seat. Most of the people were traveling light, but even those who had taken along their belongings did not have eleven valises. For a while, it looked as though we wouldn't be able to cram our luggage into the baggage car, but Mother found someone to help, and piece after piece was crammed into the jam-packed car barely minutes before the train's departure. There were no breakables among our belongings, none that is, except for our mirrored Lazy Susan. This rather exotic fixture had been taken along not as furniture, but as an item that could be sold, if necessary, for a decent price. Now, despite Mother's entreaties, a miscalculated shove jammed it against the baggage-car door, with the obvious result.

We arrived in Bialystok without problems, but were unexpectedly detained at the train station. It was our luck to arrive on November 7th, the anniversary of the Great October Socialist Revolution.* There was a Red Army parade underway, and we had to stay put until it was over.

We rented a basement room on the outskirts of town where we stayed for a while. The windows of the room looked out at a farm where pigs and other farm animals were raised. This gave me the opportunity to hear the squeals of these animals as they were being slaughtered—an aspect of life of which I had been blissfully unaware until then. With all semblance of normal life disrupted, Mother, unable to sit around doing nothing, used the time on her hands to make some heavenly-tasting jam, which lasted us throughout our stay in Bialystok.

After some time, a Russian officer came to inquire about the possibility of renting a room from our landlady. At first the lady refused, but when the officer came back for several consecutive days, she finally gave in. Mother was not happy at having such a neighbor, so we moved to another room, closer to the center of town. We spent the winter in this room. The room had a heating furnace similar to the one in my Warsaw bedroom, and this added a feeling of permanence and stability to our transient, uprooted state. As the winter progressed, our room became a drawing point for all kinds of people who had no other place to stay. Mother hadn't known most of these

---

* How was it that the "Great October Revolution" occurred in November? According to the Russian Orthodox calendar, the Revolution did indeed take place on October 25, 1917, because this calendar did not incorporate the Gregorian correction in common use everywhere else. When the Communists came to power they fell in line with the rest of the world and added the "missing" days. As a result the date of the Communist Revolution moved to November 7th.

people before, and I had no idea where they came from. We had no extra beds, so, to accommodate them, Mother "carpeted" the bathtub with old newspapers and Lea and I slept there.

A semblance of normality was provided by the Jewish school I began to attend. I no longer remember whether it was a local school, now bursting with refugee children, or whether it was one especially set up for the newcomers.

Father was informed of our new whereabouts. He had gotten the British consulate in Vilno to stamp a visa on the family passport. All that remained was for us to go to Vilno, join Father, and board the first available vessel leaving Lithuania for Palestine or some Western port not then under German occupation.

Now that all our papers were in order, Father attempted to cross the border from Lithuania to accompany us in our illegal border crossing. However, his good fortune ran out. He was caught by the Russians during the crossing and jailed in the city of Baranovich, in Russian-occupied Poland (now the Ukraine).

Somehow Mother learned of Father's fate. She also found out that his cellmate was a very distinguished Rabbi, who had previously held the rabbinical position in Sadowno, a small Polish town about fifty miles northeast of Warsaw.

Mother ascertained where the Rabbi's wife lived, and the two women made a number of trips to the jail-site in order to persuade the officials to release their husbands on humanitarian grounds. To no avail. Mother subsequently learned—too late—that young German soldiers were not the only ones willing to be accommodating in exchange for a watch or some other jewelry, which we possessed in sufficient quantities. For a long time afterward she lamented her obtuseness in failing to use the "proper procedures" with the Russian comrades.

PRISONERS WITHOUT WALLS

One day the Soviet government announced that due to overcrowding, all refugees in the city of Bialystok must leave. We were deemed too unreliable to be allowed to remain so close to the German part of Poland. Typically paranoid, the Soviets feared that our allegiance lay more with the Germans than with them, despite our having run away from the former. All refugees were asked to register the destination of their choice—and to our pleasant surprise, the choices were unlimited. One could choose to go back to German-occupied Poland, which many did, or to go deeper into Russia. Or, one could choose anywhere else as a destination, from Argentina to Zanzibar, and everything in between, including Palestine.

Those who registered for the first two destinations had their requests fulfilled. Many, including one of my maternal aunts, chose to go back to German-occupied Poland. Of course, most of the people who choose to remain in German-held territory later perished in the Holocaust. Refugees who registered to go to Russia were treated royally, given comfortable living quarters, and provided with jobs in accordance with their qualifications. Mother had no idea what to do. Father could not even be asked his opinion during the brief visits allowed in his prison because the authorities monitored all conversations.

Mother was not alone in her dilemma. A feeling of helplessness overcame anyone who had to make this decision, for everyone intuitively felt that no human being could possibly foresee what lay ahead. Not knowing when and where Father would be released, Mother could not guess what decision the twisted minds of the "comrades" might make concerning his fate. The Russians had a reputation for acting out of spite; they would not be beneath telling Father that since he had been caught illegally crossing the border with a Palestinian visa in his pocket, he could go anywhere he wished—except Palestine. The only person left to consult was Mother's brother Moshe Aharon, who had also made his way with his family to Bialystok. Moshe Aharon, the reader will recall, was a disciple of the saintly Chafetz Chaim and a great Torah scholar in his own right. Mother highly valued his opinion.

Moshe Aharon didn't even give Mother the chance to present all the sides of her argument. When he learned the purpose of her visit, he told her that he had already registered for Palestine, and that she should do likewise. Mother was shocked. She knew her brother to be violently opposed to the secular Zionist movement and she could not fathom what had happened to him. "You, Moshe—to Palestine?!" she exclaimed.

Moshe Aharon looked her straight in the eye and said, "Yes, Palestine! Now is the time to go there. This war that just started will go on for six years." Mother was beside herself. "Six years?! If the war continues that long, there will not be a single Jew left in Europe!"

Moshe Aharon answered her enigmatically, "Yes, you are so right."

Mother couldn't think of what to say. Her brother continued, "Yes, the war will last for six years, and three years later the Jews will gain their own state and...."

At this point, Mother could no longer listen. The thought of a six-year-long war was terrifying, yet sadly enough, it had a truly prophetic ring to it. But Moshe Aharon's next declaration—about a Jewish state in Palestine—especially after the calamity that her brother had predicted for European Jewry—seemed downright outlandish and absurd. But Moshe Aharon hadn't finished. "Then the Messiah will come," he said, and named a year whose last digit was five.* Now Mother was sure

---

* Their conversation was in Yiddish, in which units are mentioned before multiples. Thus she heard only the last digit of the predicted year, but not the entire number.

that he had lost his mind, and she stopped listening.

I distinctly remember that later, in 1942, when the War's outcome was far from certain, and before its fortunes started turning in favor of the Allies, Mother would try to console me by saying that "all we have to do is to hold out for three more years." When I pressed her for the source of this information she would just say, "I know." A year later, when the military situation had turned in our favor, she again announced: "Just two more years." I don't know whether at the time she herself was completely convinced that this would indeed be the case. After the War, however, when Moshe Aaron's prophecy was seen to be amazingly accurate, she told us the entire story. But, even after she went back to Poland and perceived the magnitude of the calamity, she still found the prediction of a Jewish state too incredible to believe. Only when that prediction also came true did she deeply regret not listening to the end of Moshe Aaron's declaration.

None of the refugees had too long a wait before he received traveling papers for his desired destination. With those registered for travel to German-occupied Poland and Russia out of the way, the authorities could handle the rest of the crowd at their leisure. Our marching orders came on a Friday night.

I remember that Friday quite well. Mother had run out of candles and sent me to buy some. I hated going on errands because I was always afraid of doing something wrong, but Mother insisted that I go. She cautioned me that if candles of the right size were not available in one store, I should go to another. The first store only had small candles. Since I was extremely shy, and didn't want to face the prospect of going into another store, I convinced myself that these candles would suffice, but purchased only two of them. I reasoned that next week Mother could purchase a decent supply, but that this Sabbath she would have to be content with whatever I'd bought since there wouldn't be any time left to send me to another store.

The small, slender candles were lit in honor of the Sabbath. They provided our only illumination because we slept in the same room where we ate, and would not have been able to get a good night's sleep had other lights been left on. (Jewish law forbids turning lights on and off on the Sabbath.) The meal did not last long, and soon we were all asleep. Suddenly, I woke up... just in time to see that one of the candles was no longer burning. In its place was a pool of wax and a hole in the oilcloth table covering. (Mother could not bring herself to spread a proper tablecloth on the rough kitchen table which was the only furniture in the room.) The table itself was singed. The other candle was still burning, but it was bent. Apparently, not being used to candles of this size, Mother had placed them too close to each other. The heat had bent both of them out of shape, causing one to fall onto the table. I was most likely awakened by the light and heat of the fire that engulfed the melted candle, which had eventually been extinguished in its own wax. I lay on my bed, unable to fall asleep, in dread of the verbal lashing I would get the next morning from our landlady, who was not a person to take the damage to her table lightly. It was all my fault, I realized guiltily. If only I had bought candles of the right size, this would not have happened. As it turned out, I had nothing to worry about.

After midnight, just as I was finally falling asleep again, there was a loud knock on the door. I woke Mother and she opened the door to let in three Russian soldiers or policemen.* We were told to pack our belongings and assemble alongside a waiting truck that would take us to the train station.

---

* We never knew the difference between the two, because they wore uniforms of the same color. (Blue was the color of uniforms worn by capitalist policemen, who were "a tool of the oppressors of the masses." It was therefore an inappropriate color for the authorities charged with protecting the proletariat. So the police, known as *militia,* again to distinguish them from the hated capitalist police, also wore military khaki.)

After the initial shock dissipated, we realized with dismal clarity that the entire registration process had been a farce. Our destination of choice (Palestine) and that of other people (Argentina to Zanzibar) had all been lumped together and cynically transformed into some part of the Soviet Union. In an instant we realized that anyone who had expressed a desire to go anywhere except Russia or the German part of Poland would now be given the "opportunity" of free transportation over the vast expanses of the USSR to some unknown destination.

We quickly started packing. Suddenly Mother remembered that, feeling insecure in our rented room, she had left all her jewelry with the Ackermans, a Bialystok family, whom my parents had met while on vacation in the country in the good old pre-war days. They were not refugees and hence their lives were not affected by the "new world order" the way ours were. They lived in an apartment in a new section of the city and Mother had felt it prudent to entrust them with her jewels. At Mother's request, one of the comrades who came to pick us up was detailed to accompany me on my journey by foot to the Ackermans.

We ventured into a cool and starlit night. A brisk wind blew, causing the street lamps, which hung somewhat freely from the lampposts, to sway. The streets were deserted except for a truck or two speeding by on its way to, or maybe from, a destination similar to ours. We walked briskly, our footsteps breaking the night's silence. I had the feeling of being in an unreal world—a little boy guarded by an all-powerful representative of a mighty state that had the power to get people out of bed and take them wherever it chose.

No one answered my knock. It may not have been energetic enough, or perhaps the Ackermans were out of town.[*]

---

[*] Because the Ackermans were not refugees, they most likely remained there until the Germans overran that city, and shared the fate of their Jewish brethren under German occupation.

Accompanied by my guardian, I returned, empty-handed, just as our last bundle was being loaded onto the truck. We were allowed to take everything with us except for Lea's crib, which, we were told, would have to stay behind. One of the guards informed us ominously that in any case it would not be needed where we were going. It is more likely that he planned to keep the crib for himself.

Together with countless others, we were lined up along the tracks of the Bialystok railroad station. A train of freight cars pulled up. These were cars normally used for transporting goods, with special features now added in consideration of their human cargo. Except for the space directly opposite the sliding doors, the car was divided halfway up the walls by two wooden berths. Some of the occupants were supposed to sleep on the floor, the others—on one of the two berths. A hole had been cut in the middle of the floor to be used as a toilet. Each boxcar also had four small windows, one on each side of the sliding doors on either side of the car. We were ordered to board the train with our belongings.

Boarding a railroad cargo boxcar of the kind that transported refugees into Russia. Photograph courtesy of Ginzach Kiddush Hashem, Bnei Brak.

A guard was stationed at each door. On signal, the guards locked the doors, ran to their own car, and the train started moving. People who happened to be near the small windows stuck their heads out in curiosity. This naturally obstructed our meager supply of fresh air, eliciting loud cries of protest from those unfortunate enough to be situated far from any window. This predicament was hardest on the people who had to sit (and sleep) on the floor, since their air supply was also blocked by the berths themselves. Eventually, everyone returned to his place and the situation improved. Ventilation became bearable, and several days later, it improved even more, when we had traveled a considerable distance eastward from the pre-war Polish-Russian border. Confident that by this time no one in his right mind would attempt to escape back to Poland, the guards locked the boxcar doors with only a chain lock, which left a sizable crack open for air to get in. For the same reason, we were not guarded as closely as before.

Being "low-priority cargo," we frequently stopped at stations to let other trains through. In the mornings, these stops were utilized for distributing food, primarily bread, and pails of an unidentifiable cooked food, which we didn't touch since of course it was not kosher. Mother had managed to take some food along which we ate with the bread. Refugees who needed food for small children appealed to the guards for special consideration. At the next stop some milk, eggs, and even fresh vegetables appeared and were distributed to them. A man in the car next to ours was a smoker, by now desperate for cigarettes. He asked, in Russian, for cigarettes for "the baby." This request, made in a very loud voice, was heard by most of our transport, bringing a rare moment of laughter into our bleak existence.

Food was distributed only once a day, but at any stop we could help ourselves to the piping-hot water available at all Russian train stations. Each railroad station, no matter how small, had a faucet protruding from a wall of one of its buildings, which provided an apparently endless supply of boiling hot water. At one such stop, I made another discovery: Looking beyond the station I discovered that there was only one track entering and leaving it. I was shocked. What a poor country! They didn't even have enough money to build a double track! This explained the frequent stops we had to make. We had to move over to a spur and stop not only for more important trains traveling in our direction, but also for all trains traveling in the opposite direction.

I remember waking up one morning and peering out of the car. Unlike the single-track terrain of our trip up to now, there were numerous tracks as far as my eyes could see on both sides of the car. Some of these were empty while others had long freight trains on them. Somebody ventured a guess that we were in Moscow's freight station.*

Traveling in this stop-and-start manner, it took us a full two weeks to cover the distance from Bialystok to the city of Kotlas, where we had to get off to await further transportation. The railroad continued north, in the direction of Archangel and Murmansk on the White Sea, whereas we were supposed to travel eastward. We were left overnight on a huge empty lot next to the station. There was no need to guard us; there was simply nowhere to go. We experienced our first "white" night, where the sun shone hazily throughout the night.

We didn't know it then—and the information would have been of no help to us anyway—but we were headed for a forest settlement in the Autonomous Soviet Socialist Republic of Komi. Another thing that we didn't know was that Komi was used by the Soviet regime as a dumping ground for people whose "offenses against the homeland" were not serious enough to warrant sending them to real labor camps, but who, at the same time, could not be permitted to live among ordinary, upright, patriotic Russian citizens.

The designation "Autonomous" deserves an explanation.

---

* This guess was probably correct. Many years later a Russian immigrant to Israel who had a degree in geography told me that the only way of getting from Bialystok to our destination was indeed through Moscow. This is the closest we ever got to the capital.

The Soviet Union was made up of sixteen* full-fledged republics, of which the Russian Soviet Federate Socialist Republic (RSFSR) was the largest. The other fifteen republics were populated primarily by people of similar ethnic origin; for example, the Ukrainian Soviet Socialist Republic was populated by Ukrainians. Of course, each such republic had its share of other nationalities—Russians and others (among them Jews)—but these were a minority interspersed within the general population. The situation in Russia was (and remains) different. As its name indicates, it was a federation made up, in addition to its "purely Russian" sector, of as many as thirty "minor" republics, each of which represented a population of different ethnic origin, language, mentality, and so forth, concentrated in one geographic area. Although these small republics were grandiosely called "autonomous," they, in fact, had little independence. Obviously, they could not be more independent than the "full-fledged" republics. Even these were controlled from Moscow, leaving the local government little independent authority. Still, each region had its own distinct language and literature, which were taught in schools, and a capital city with the inevitable titled officials (and bureaucracy).

Komi was (and still is) one such autonomous republic. Mammoth in size, it covers some 160,000 square miles (416,000 square kilometers). It is hence larger than reunited Germany, and only twenty percent smaller than France, the largest country in Europe. At that time, its population totaled 350,000 people** of whom 50,000 lived in the capital city of Syktyvkar. Although everyone spoke Russian, the Komis had their own language, Komi, and their own literature. The Komi people typically have a white complexion and are rather short.

---

* The "original" twelve republics were joined by Lithuania, Latvia, Estonia and the Karelo-Finnish republic, the first three "voluntarily" and the fourth through conquest.

** Presently there are close to two million.

The city of Kotlas has a port which is located to the east of the confluence between the Northern Dvina and the Vychegda rivers. The Northern Dvina originates some distance to the south of Kotlas and flows northward, discharging its waters into the North Sea. The Vychegda originates a few hundred miles to the west of the Ural Mountains and flows westward, traversing a large part of the Autonomous Soviet Socialist Republic of Komi before emptying into the Northern Dvina. The massive forests on the banks of the Vychegda were to be our final destination. The confluence of these two rivers forms

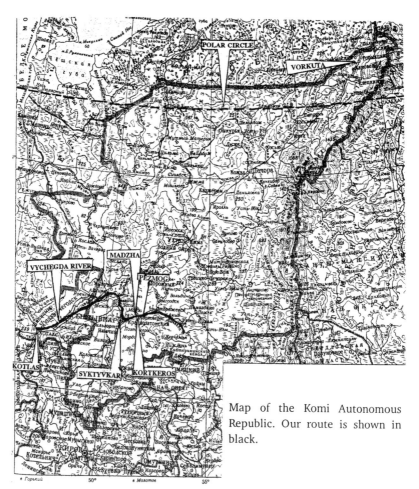

Map of the Komi Autonomous Republic. Our route is shown in black.

a huge body of water with wide, powerful streams merging to generate enormous whirlpools. This remarkable sight greeted us the next day, when we were transported to the river port.

The opposite bank of the Vychegda could not be seen. Instead, an apparently endless expanse of stormy water stared us in the face. There was a tiny island a mile or two away from the shore, with some short trees straining mightily to hold their own against the liquid onslaught. I stared at them in fascination, wondering why they hadn't been uprooted long ago. Indeed, with the opposite bank invisible, the place looked like the shore of a stormy sea rather than a riverbank. To one like myself, who had never seen a river more turbulent than the kilometer-wide Vistula flowing peacefully beneath Warsaw's bridges, this was an awe-inspiring sight.[*]

A convoy, consisting of two barges and a river-going boat that doubled as a tug, awaited us at the Kotlas river port. Mother wanted very much to get us all onto the boat, for it had proper cabins and other passenger facilities, whereas the two barges offered only a bare floor, walls, and roof. However, with our voluminous baggage limiting our mobility, we were among the last to board. We couldn't even make the leading barge, which offered slightly more comfort than the second one. It turned out that during the trip, the leading barge received a steady flow of jarred goods, including preserved fruit and similar delicacies, which somehow never reached us.

With the boarding over, our convoy started its voyage up the Vychegda, fighting the current of the fully-grown river. I

---

[*] I believe that such a merging of rivers is uncommon and deserves a more detailed description. The headwaters of the North Dvina are somewhere to the south of Kotlas, and the river flows to the north. The headwaters of the Vychegda are at least 300 miles (500 kilometers) to the northeast, and the river flows to the southwest. As a result, the Vychegda discharges its quite heavy flow broadside into the much less powerful initial leg of the Northern Dvina. It is the heavy lateral "thrust" of the waters of the mature Vychegda that give the confluence of the two rivers the appearance of a stormy sea.

remember being afraid that the available horsepower, designed to propel the boat alone, without towing the two heavily-loaded barges, would not suffice to overcome the powerful current, and that we would be swept backward into the confluence. In my mind's eye I could already picture how first our barge, then the other, and then the boat itself would be first pulled back and then swallowed up by the mighty whirlpools. Apparently the people responsible for our transportation knew better, although it did take us about two days of traveling at a snail's pace to overcome the river's powerful current and to really start moving at a decent speed.

On the barge we had our first encounter with mosquitoes. Swarms of them descended upon us and bit us mercilessly. Lea could not fall asleep and cried constantly. Mother stayed up entire nights during the week-long trip to keep these pests away from her. The mosquitoes were no less ferocious by day, but when awake even five-year-old Lea could defend herself from them.

The journey upriver continued without stopovers for another week. Finally we reached a mooring and disembarked.

Our convoy, consisting of two barges towed by a river-going ship, is moving slowly up the Vychegda River. We were housed in the cargo space of the second barge. The only source of air and daylight was an open flight of steps from the barge's stern part (not shown).

Aside from the mooring, which was so tiny that I wonder to this very day how it could handle so many people, the place was desolate. Local inhabitants driving two-wheeled horse-drawn carts were waiting to take us on the last leg of our journey. The creaky carts provided were intended solely for our belongings. We were expected to walk. The wagon drivers walked too, not only because the horses could not pull the additional weight, but also because constant vigilance was needed to prevent them from swerving off the "road."*

The "road" was simply a wide path cut through a dense forest. This soil remains frozen even in the summer, except for a thin top layer. Consequently, rainwater or melted snow takes a very long time to seep trough the frozen layer, and some of it never does. As a result, the surface is soft and swamp-like, and even moderate loads get bogged easily. When the road had to pass over a particularly bad stretch, slender trunks of birch trees were placed across the road to prevent the wagons from sinking. But this procedure was far from foolproof. The wheels of our wagons (we needed two wagons for all our baggage) would sink from time to time, and it took the combined strength of both drivers plus Mother's and mine to get the wagons moving again.

Our feeling was that of being shipwrecked on a desert island. We immediately realized that anything we did not take along with us would simply not be available where we were going. This realization was forcefully brought home to me when my orthodontic device was lost. Mother had entrusted to my special care the jaw mold that I wore at night back home, which was supposed to move my jaw back into its proper place. Due to my childish lack of care, it fell to the ground and could not be found. Mother was almost hysterical, because she knew that nothing of that sort could be obtained

---

* As we subsequently learned, except for long journeys, the native drivers would never ride a loaded wagon. The vehicle would always be loaded to capacity, and the driver walked. Our treatment was thus not discriminatory.

within a thousand miles.

Lea cried continuously that she had no strength to trudge along the boggy roads. Mother tried carrying her in her arms, but this proved too tiring. When she then attempted to deposit Lea on one of the wagons, the wagon driver would yell at her. So Mother and I alternated in picking Lea up and carrying her. By the time we reached our destination, the three of us were at the point of complete exhaustion, barely able to move or even keep our eyes open.

LIFE IN A SOVIET LABOR CAMP

Although we had traversed a distance of only several miles, it had taken us the better part of a day to reach our destination: Settlement No. 31. In a forest clearing stood one or two warehouses, a bakery, a communal kitchen, and living quarters for the settlement's inhabitants. It was a prison labor camp, albeit one without guards and without walls. Anyone wishing to escape was welcome to do so. Of course, there was no place to go.

Even if one could find his way through the woods without sinking in the boggy soil, he would be unable to survive for any length of time. Without documents, neither housing nor work could be obtained. In the camp, we had some sort of status; outside, we were non-persons. People with families were usually directed to such camps on the correct assumption that even the brave soul who would, under other circumstances, risk running away, would never so imperil his family. This was all the more true in our case, since most of the families in our camp (perhaps all of them) lacked a husband and father, as we did. Although refugees made up the bulk of the population, we were not the only people there. There was a resident colony that ran various services, such as the bakery, kitchen, and store (whose main function was doling out the daily ration of bread). Our housing accommodations consisted of a number of identical buildings. Each building was composed of four huge rooms entered from a common corridor. Forty beds (arranged with headboards against the wall) lined the walls of each room. There were also a heating stove (which could also be used for cooking, although with some difficulty), and a large table in the center. Each family was allocated enough beds for its members, and arrangements were made to keep families together while at the same time filling the room to capacity.

Mother, Lea, and I were thus thrown together with thirty-seven other people, some of whom we had met during our journey, and some whom we were seeing for the first time. All of them, however, except for a Mrs. Berlinerblau and her son Reuven, hailed from various small towns and villages, whose residents were generally regarded by city-dwellers as being less cultured. Mother, therefore, felt comfortable maintaining close relations only with Mrs. Berlinerblau and arranged for us to be assigned beds next to her.

One of the refugees who had registered to go to Russia while we were still in Bialystok was a former driver of one of our taxis, perhaps even the one who had worked the smuggling route. He had been given a well-paying job in some city in the Ukraine. Like other employees who appreciated the warm relationship which our family had extended him, he saw it as his duty to repay us. As soon as he found out where we had been sent, he started mailing us food packages of melted-down butter (which didn't spoil even without refrigeration),* preserved fruit, and other food items. He also notified other people who knew us, and within a very short time we were flooded with preserved food. The lady next to us also began receiving food packages. A large wooden crate was somehow procured to store the foodstuffs. Positioned between the beds, it was shared by Mother and Mrs. Berlinerblau.

The beds were wooden, with straw mattresses, on which we spread our quilts and placed our linen and pillows. Like every other wooden item in the entire place, these beds were constructed without nails. Like many other commodities, nails were in extremely short supply all over Komi, for without "dirty capitalist" incentives, there was absolutely no motivation

---

* The butter arrived in solid form in bottles. It stands to reason that it was melted on a fire and then poured into bottles as the sole available containers. It had to be "fished out" with a stick. I have absolutely no idea why this procedure prevented spoilage, but it did.

A log house (rather small) under construction. Photograph courtesy of the US Library of Congress.

Artist's representation of our barrack in Settlement No. 31.

to supply anything to any location—even where a demand existed. The pieces forming the bed were held together by wedges. These slipped out of position from time to time, and had to be pounded back into place. If this operation was delayed too long, the wedges would pop out and the bed would collapse. For most of our compatriots, who had barely any personal possessions, this meant, at worst, an occasional broken board. For us, a slip like this could damage the valises stored beneath our beds. So Mother was ever watchful that the wedges remain properly jammed into place.[*]

In addition to serving us for sleeping and sitting (there were no chairs and very few stools), the beds also served another group of residents: the bedbugs. The Komi species

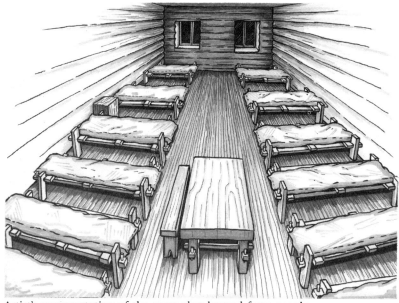

Artist's representation of the room that housed forty people.

---

[*] Because of the lack of nails and other fasteners, it took ingenuity to erect any kind of structure. The solution was to build in log-cabin fashion. This kind of work requires considerable skill. I remember that a work detail made up of refugees was once ordered to put up such a structure, but proved unequal to the task.

were large, about three-quarters of an inch long, and red, exuding a sickening smell that pervaded the entire room. There was no way to get rid of them except by killing as many as one could lay hands on. This, though, did not prevent the eggs from hatching. We fought this war with all our might, but we knew full well who had the upper hand.

Another vexing problem was the ubiquitous mosquitoes. Since our windows lacked screens, we were forced to keep them closed even in the summer. Neither glass nor wood, however, prevailed against these crafty creatures, and enough of them managed to gain entrance to make life miserable. I remember once when we tried to get rid of the insect hordes by "smoking them out." Smoldering fir branches were placed on several trays. These were carried to the wall with the windows by several people marching together, forcing the insects ahead of them. This indeed worked. But by then the room was filled with smoke, and someone opened the windows again to let the smoke out. The smoke cleared, lingering only around the rafters, while the mosquitoes were only too happy to slip back in. Instead of solving the problem, we were even worse off than before.

Obviously, the mosquito problem was worse outdoors. It was impossible to remain outside for any length of time without having a piece of protective cloth tucked under one's hat and covering one's neck.

The mosquitoes were a problem mainly in the summer, which was much shorter than what I remembered from Poland, and at the same time, much less comfortable. I was very surprised by the discomfort since I expected the Komi summer to be much cooler. Thinking back, it most probably was not heat that we felt, but the high humidity—a phenomenon virtually unknown in Poland, where the humidity levels are extremely low.

In the winter, we had other problems, foremost of which was keeping warm indoors. Our oven was too small for the room. And, believe it or not, in this seemingly endless forest firewood was scarce.

I am reluctant to reduce to myth all the popular folk tales about righteous men striding into the forest to chop down trees, saw them into logs, and stock the hearth of some poor, sick widow and her family. But the fact is that freshly cut timber barely burns. Its combustion generates a great deal of smoke and hardly any heat. Newly felled trees are damp, and logs cut from them have to be ignited again and again. (Forest fires occur because conditions there are different: moss, wind, fallen branches, and an unlimited supply of air.) To fire an oven, one needs dry wood— something we didn't have. The standard procedure is to fell trees, cut them into relatively short logs, and let them dry outdoors for several months. The people who had lived in our quarters before us had apparently exhausted any supplies of such firewood, which could have maintained us until the next season.

Those among us who were of working age were expected to work at felling trees in the endless forest. We were the first link in a chain that started with a giant tree growing in the forest and ended in a finished board, beam or sheet of plywood many hundreds of miles away. A special effort was made to fell trees in the warmer part of the season, or when the snow covered the ground lightly, so that the trees could be cut as close to the ground as possible, thus minimizing waste. The stump was then attached to ropes and uprooted, either by a team of horses, or by a large number of laborers (mostly women, who were considered by the government equals to men when it came to "gainful occupation") and later added to the supply of firewood. Sometimes, instead of being uprooted, the stumps were burned to the ground. The branches and treetops of the felled trees were trimmed and added to the pile. The felled logs were stacked according to size to await winter transportation, for no significant amount of cargo could be transported along the roads in the summer.

Refugee women forced to work as lumberjacks toiled from morning to evening felling trees.

In the winter, the situation changed dramatically. Then, sleds replaced wheeled vehicles, traveling on special sled-ways designed especially for getting the timber to the Vychegda

With barely any snow on the ground, the tractor (in the background) that is used to haul fallen trees can pull only half a dozen or so trunks; note their length. In winter sleds could be used. These were far more efficient; see the drawing on the next page.

River, which was frozen solid and could support almost any load. As soon as the layer of snow on the ground was thick enough, a fully loaded sled drawn by one or two horses traveled the path intended to serve as the sled-way. Water was then poured over the tracks left by the sled. This process was repeated several times as the snow continued to accumulate; eventually it produced a set of smooth, solidly frozen, almost frictionless reverse "rails" sunk into the snow. Once the path was securely established, a set of two sleds was tied together to accommodate the length of the logs. The trees were loaded onto the sleds and two horses had no problem pulling a load of trees that would otherwise have required a five- to seven-ton truck. The "sled train" was driven to an elevated part of the river bank where a flight of metal (or wooden) rails led down the slope to the frozen river. The horses were un-hitched, and the "train" was pushed down the incline onto the river ice. The logs were then unloaded and tied into rafts. The rest of the procedure required no human intervention. When the river thawed in the late spring, the timber would float down the Vychegda into the Northern Dvina where it would be "fished out" at one of the sawmills situated on the river's banks. Of all the tasks involved, that of the people in our group was the most difficult: felling the trees and getting them onto the sleds.

Not surprisingly, none of the refugee population had any

experience in logging. Most of them were skilled or semi-skilled artisans, merchants, clerks, and the like. However, the "right to gainful employment" was meted out equally and without exception. Since everyone had to work, and since felling trees was the only kind of work available, everyone had to fell trees. Here, too, there were a disproportionate number of females in our group: Mother was not the only woman whose husband had been incarcerated for one "crime" or another.

The Jewish refugees found logging extremely difficult work. Not only had they never performed sustained hard labor in their lives, but they also lacked the knowledge and skills that every child growing up in that vicinity imbibed with his mother's milk.

Two sleds in tandem, pulled by a team of two horses transport an enormous load of tree trunks. The sleds travel along "rails" produced by pouring water into sled tracks in the snow. The smooth ice surface that formed allowed the sleds to move with very little friction.

I no longer remember the daily work schedule, but in all probability the workday was about ten hours long. Each person was expected to deliver a specified output, known as the *norma*. The Russians had a *norma* for everything in the world, and each and every worker, man or woman, was expected to deliver it. Those who failed to do so stood the risk of being accused of sabotage, which involved various penalties and punishments.

In addition to the strain of being forced to perform difficult labor as lumberjacks, the untrained workers often suffered from work-related accidents. Felling trees calls for a special procedure. First the logger determines the direction of the wind. Then he cuts a notch in the tree on the side opposite the wind. The tree is then felled by sawing from the side facing the wind. This traditional method not only insures that the wind will push the falling tree away from the saw, thus lessening the pressure on the latter and making for an easier cut, but also that the tree will fall away from the logger, rather than on him. The saws that were used in our settlement had handles at both ends of a long blade and were operated by two people, one at each end, alternately pulling the saw toward themselves.

In the beginning, the refugees were divided into teams of two. Each team was handed a saw and an ax, and given brief instructions. Naturally, since they had never engaged in this kind of work, they had difficulty determining the direction of the wind, and some of them were injured by the falling trees. Those who had a hard time wielding axes also suffered injuries. It was therefore decided that until everyone "got the hang of it," the permanent residents of our colony would do the notching, and our crowd would stick to the sawing.

Logging injuries were not confined to our camp. Uncle Moshe Aharon's "Palestine" turned out to be a Soviet labor camp, just as it had for us. Mother somehow heard that he had injured his hand with an ax—which he probably didn't even know how to hold, let alone handle. The injury brought on gangrene in its wake, and, tragically, in the absence of medical treatment, he passed away.

Mother proved to be vulnerable as well, and broke her thumb while felling trees. Again, in the absence of medical treatment, a minor injury led to complications. The thumb healed unevenly, and aggravated her suffering from an earlier rheumatic condition.

Members of the resident colony all appeared to be "undesirables" of one sort or another. They were no better off than we were. Everyone was treated equally, and received the same food supplies, of which there was not much variety. The non-refugees, however, had the advantage of slightly more private housing and, more important, they were accustomed to life in the settlement. Getting used to the situation was the best—and only—remedy for all our ailments.

The officer who served as camp commander had a standard reply whenever anyone complained about something: "You will get used to it—because if you don't, you will die." For the word "die," he used the Russian term *zdokhnesh*, which applies to the death of an animal, not of a human being.

Another officer acted as a one-man police force in the settlement and was most likely a *politruk*, "political instructor." He took fiendish delight in entering our room, standing near the table in its center, and glaring at the crate of preserved food next to our beds. This would set him off on a tirade whose ending we knew by heart. "Hear this! You receive parcels! Hear this! You don't want to work! Hear this! Did you get me? This is all!" I always wondered what point he was trying to make, particularly since Mother and her friend, who were the main target of this tirade, worked like everyone else and just as hard.

I've already mentioned that we lacked qualified medical care. The only exception was a person known in Poland as a *felcher*, a kind of male nurse or paramedic. Actually, "paramedic" is misleading, for it conjures up the image of a person with the skills and equipment needed to treat a patient until a physician arrives. Unfortunately our man had few skills and even less equipment. But he was all that we had, and medical treatment was soon needed. Because our food lacked vitamins and other nutrients, a number of us were soon beset with itching boils between our fingers: large, watery, pus-filled boils on our feet; and scurvy, a gum disease caused by lack of vitamin C. The itching boils were treated by a salve, which was sometimes available and sometimes not. The vitamin needed for curing scurvy could not be procured. Neither could anything be done about the pus sores, except for applying a purple liquid known as *kali*. This was a water-based solution of potassium permanganate applied to boils on the verge of bursting, in order to control infection.

Our *felcher* made the widest possible use of this solution—because it was the only medicine he had. He applied it to my sister Lea's head when, to our great distress, her skull was injured accidentally by a playmate.

Compared with the grownups, we children were not expected to do much. We had no schoolwork to keep us busy because there was no school on the settlement. At one point, our parents were informed that we would be sent to a dormitory school, but this immediately gave rise to an outcry. No one would dream of having his child taken completely out from under his wings—and Mother led the opposition to the plan. I no longer remember how the controversy was resolved, but Mother stood her ground despite the demerit she earned by doing so. And so it was that we children were left to our own devices. In the summer, we entertained ourselves by sailing toy boats. The boats, little two-to-three-inch things, were carved from tree bark. I had been a whiz at carving these boats even back in Poland, and it was even easier in Komi because I was older. The pieces of bark were also larger.

The "lake" we used to sail the toy boats could be created

in a very short time. All one had to do was dig a shallow hole of the desired size, and soon enough the water that saturated every inch of the ground would start seeping into the hole. It didn't take long before we had our lake. One day, Lea, a couple of other children, and I were busy digging a particularly deep hole to create such a "lake." All of a sudden Lea stuck her head into the hole to see how the work was progressing. The boy wielding the hoe failed to notice her and struck her on the head with all his might.

Without losing a second, we ran to our *felcher*, who immediately cut Lea's hair, washed the wound, and applied the magical *kali*. He put on two layers of gauze and one turn of bandage—there was not much of it to go around, and conservation was the rule. Tetanus shots were unknown in this part of Russia, and penicillin, even if it had been discovered then, would not have been available in our location. Fortunately, however, Lea's deep, wide gash healed completely.

The *felcher* had told us to come back some time later for a change of bandage and, with Mother at work, it was I who took Lea to him. As we walked in, he opened his tall medical record book and I saw the chronologically arranged entries. All were brief, never more than three lines long, except for one item which took up a good half a page: an extensive description of the birth of his child.

Lea's mishap at the "lake" was not her only one in Komi. As you will recall, our room had a heating furnace that could also be used for cooking. In fact, we "cooked" mainly water since little else was available. During the winter, this presented no problem. In the summer, however, the heat of the stove would make the room unbearable. So, we did the cooking outdoors. We would simply place two bricks somewhat apart, start a fire between them, and cook our water on top. One day, an old lady asked Mother to boil some water for her. Mother delegated the job to Lea.

However, it was one thing to put a rather full kettle on

fire, and quite another to take it off. As Lea lifted the kettle, with all the might of a six or seven year-old, the boiling water spilled on her feet. She immediately ran to Mother. Mother knew that our *felcher's kali* solution would not solve the problem. Mysteriously, she secured several eggs, separated the whites, and applied them to Lea's burns—which healed completely. (I say "mysteriously" because we never saw any eggs at Settlement 31 either before or after the accident.)

Although Sunday was a day of rest from the tree felling which dominated the lives of every able-bodied adult, including Mother and the other women, Saturday was just another work day. No one made any attempt to avoid work on this day, the Jewish Sabbath, since this would most likely have led to deportation to a real labor camp. There, in addition to being separated from family, one would still be forced to work on the Sabbath—while standing an excellent chance of premature departure to the World-to-Come, due to overwork, malnutrition, frostbite, and other dangers.

However, the refugees could not ignore the advent of the High Holidays. Generation upon generation of faithful Jews had helped endow these holy days with an awe that inspired heroic action. And so, on Rosh Hashanah eve, when Mother declared that she would not be going to work the next day (and opined that no one else should either), her voice was heeded. The following morning, most of the labor force did not show up for work. It did not take long for our two officers to discover who was the leader of this revolt. Consequently, Mother was imprisoned for two days in the local jail, and the rest of the group, lacking a leader and seeing that our two comrades were deadly serious, went back to work. As for Mother, her wishes were fulfilled—as a result of her detention, she avoided working on Rosh Hashanah.

The jail deserves a description of its own. It was what might generously be called a room, situated near the entrance to our camp's administration building. It was less than three feet in width and depth, and had only a five-foot-high ceiling. As a result, one could not lie, sit, or stand in it. Being there for any length of time was a form of torture.

Mother was released after serving two days. But Yom Kippur was just a week later, and Mother wanted to insure that her fellow Jews would do no work on the holiest of days. Accordingly, she assembled whomever she could and gave a short speech. "Both Hitler and Stalin," she said, "are enemies of the Jewish people, but Stalin is worse than Hitler. The latter wants only to kill our bodies, whereas the former is after our souls. The least we can do for our souls," she continued, "is not to work on Yom Kippur. If all of us, or at least a large number of us, stay away, nothing will happen to us. They cannot possibly ship us off to Vorkuta" (a term that will be explained below) "for staying away from work one day a year, especially since they need us here."

After some discussion it was decided that everyone would arrive at work, and then simply refrain from doing anything. This strategy worked. Realizing that the sit-down strike would last only one day, our two supervising officers looked the other way, and the day passed without repercussions—for everyone except Mother.

When Mother made the disparaging remark about Stalin, she knew that, in spite of her (correct) assumption that the entire group would not be persecuted, she was putting her own self into extreme danger. Still, she reflected that, at one time or another, others had also made disparaging remarks about the Soviet regime. Since everyone was in the same boat, no one would inform on anyone else.

She had good reason for this assumption. Life for all the refugees in Settlement No. 31 was difficult, downright draining. Everyone complained about the hard work, the lack of food, the mosquitoes, and all the rest. Someone even composed a Yiddish song that made the rounds from building to building, in which these complaints were articulated in rhyming couplets. Of course, everyone knew the party line: that we, together with all the denizens of the Soviet Union, lived in a paradise on earth. To venture any assertion to the contrary was nothing less than high treason, an offense punishable by transfer to the dreaded "Vorkuta." However, no one ever informed on anyone else, so Mother assumed that she also was personally safe.

She was almost right. Certainly her comment about Hitler and Stalin would not have reached the authorities if not for our very noticeable crate, which was full of unobtainable goods, and the nine large valises that stored the clothing and worldly belongings of our well-to-do family.

Among the many people in our room there was a family, consisting of a mother and two grown sons. Along with everyone else, they were present during Mother's speech, and one of the sons decided to put Mother's statement "to good use." He informed on Mother to the authorities. He figured that, with Mother on her way to the Arctic Circle, he, together with the two officers who ran our camp, would help himself to the spoils. Still, for reasons known only to himself, he postponed this act for a long time.

After several months of manual labor, Mother was reassigned. She became the store's manager. This fortunate turn of events came about because the member of the resident colony who had held the job before her was transferred to another location. Mother stood out as the only candidate among the refugees who possessed all the requisite qualifications. When she had attended school as a girl, Warsaw was under Russian occupation, and hence Russian had been a required subject. By this time, her spoken Russian was not outstanding, having been in disuse for a long time, but her writing skills were perfect. Mother was not only a certified bookkeeper, but also a whiz at handling an inventory. After a few days of training with the departing storekeeper, she was handed the job.

The primary task of the storekeeper was to "sell" the daily

bread ration. Since we were wards of the state, we were not expected to pay for our food. Because of this, bread was not actually sold, but instead distributed in exchange for special metal tokens issued to each one of us regularly. The bread was doled out by weight, and here Mother's talent for assessing weight by sight held her in good stead. It was common practice in camps such as ours to cut from a loaf of bread a slice of approximately the amount needed from the loaf, weigh it, and then add increasingly smaller slices as required. As a result, a person would typically walk away with a ration consisting of one large chunk of bread and a collection of small slices. This stopped when Mother took charge. In a day or two, everyone walked out with one chunk of bread weighing exactly the right amount.

Some time later the officials decided that distributing bread was not a full-time occupation, and Mother was given the additional task of drying mushrooms. This staple was an important commodity in Komi. Mushrooms grew in abundance in the adjacent forest, and, when cooked together with potatoes (almost the only other staple available) produced a nutritious dish. During the summer, some of our crowd were assigned to pick mushrooms which were then delivered to the bakery, located in the back of the store. First they would be spread on the roof to be sun-dried, and then placed on top of the oven to remove the last drops of moisture. The person in charge of this duty had to carry baskets of mushrooms to the roof and spread them out there. Several additional climbs were needed to determine their state of dryness. When dry enough for the next stage, the mushrooms were again carried downstairs in baskets to be placed on top of the oven. I remember all this quite clearly because both Lea and I, with nothing else to do, assisted Mother in this work.

Carrying the baskets up and down was difficult enough, but handling the partially dried mushrooms revolted me because the heat of the sun had reduced them to a gooey-looking mass. My disposition towards goo being what it is, I tried my best to avoid this work. I was prepared to carry the baskets up and down as long as I didn't have to collect the mushrooms on the roof or spread them out on top of the oven.

Receiving and sending mail was another pressing problem, and one that required an immediate solution. A large percentage of the letters sent by us or to us simply failed to arrive. While brainstorming to think of a solution, we realized that postal money transfers, just like packages, never got lost. To send them, all one had to do was fill out a thin cardboard form which had a space, the size of half a postcard, left blank for writing a message. After recording the amount to be sent, one handed the form along with payment to the postal clerk. One even received a receipt. Soon enough, one-ruble money transfers were coursing between us and our correspondents. It was a relief to have at least our mail links re-established and running smoothly.

Not all the letters sent to us got lost in transit. Father's letters did reach us, although in a roundabout way. Father, like all Polish refugees, had been transferred from his jail in Baranovich to a labor camp also in the Komi Republic, about 600 or so miles (approximately 1000 kilometers) from us. The camp was in the vicinity of the town of Vorkuta.

The name Vorkuta brings fear and shivers to anyone who has ever lived in Russia. This relatively small administrative town north of the Arctic Circle is surrounded by mines (coal, iron-ore, and others) which were worked by inmates of the labor camps surrounding the town. Vorkuta is not only the name of a town, but of an entire region that was actually one huge slave labor camp. In Komi, the very mention of the name Vorkuta evoked the same reaction that mention of Siberia did elsewhere in Russia. Winter temperatures there averaged 49°F (45°C) below zero, which was 18°F (10°C) lower than those in our location. A large number of the prisoners in Vorkuta were employed in mines, where they worked under extremely dangerous and difficult conditions. Many died of exposure, undernourishment, hazardous working conditions, and untreated maladies.

All this time Father remained unaware of our fate. As soon as he was given writing privileges, he wrote to us at Bialystok. Mother had also written to our former landlady, so she was able to immediately forward Father's letters to us in Komi and our letters to him. The mail traffic between Komi and Bialystok proceeded at a snail's pace and hence it took two to three months until a letter mailed by Father reached us. We replied to the letter immediately, and expected an answer rather soon, given the relatively short distance between our camps. But this was not to be. Father, who knew Russian quite well, had immediately been assigned office work in his camp. His efficiency at the job gave rise to a competition for his services among the camp commanders and, as a result, he would be snatched up first by one and then by another camp administration. By the time our letter would reach the camp from which his last message had been sent, he was already someplace else. This happened so many times that regular correspondence was impossible as long as he was in Komi.

Water in Settlement No. 31 was provided by several wells, which were relatively deep, even though water was readily available right at ground level. Perhaps they drew on some subterranean sources that were of better quality. At any rate, these wells were a novelty to us.

Almost everyone has come across a picture of a typical village well. The top part, sometimes covered by a roof, usually consists of two vertical posts supporting a round wooden axle over the well opening. There is a metal hand crank at one end which, when turned, raises and lowers a bucket suspended from a rope. In Komi, however, not even such a contraption could be found. We had to make do with a bucket attached to a long stick, which would sit at the bottom of the well in the summer, or lie alongside the well in the winter, so that it would not freeze inside the well. In the summer, one pulled out the stick by grabbing it hand over hand. The contents of the well bucket were poured into another bucket that had to be brought along. In the winter, the bucket was first dropped down into the well to break the ice at the bottom, and only then one could fill it up.

* * *

All this time Mother continued with her daily routine. She put the Yom Kippur incident behind herself and gave it little or no thought. However, the time arrived when the informant decided to strike. He went to the camp commander and told him of Mother's counter-revolutionary statement. Soon enough, our two officers entered our living quarters and told Mother and her friend (whom they somehow implicated in the crime) that they were under arrest.

As Mother was led away by the guards, we trailed after her. At a certain point the guards ordered us to turn back. Crying, we refused and clung to Mother with all our might. Mother cried too. The guards told us several times to turn back, but we wouldn't. Finally they separated us by force. As we continued standing there, watching in shock as Mother moved on, she turned to us and tried to summon up a cheerful face. She said, "Don't cry. Look—I am also no longer crying."

Resigned to our fate, we children, still crying but now out of Mother's sight, returned to our room in the settlement. The other inhabitants of the room looked at us with pity but, of course, could be of no help. Nor was this the end of this noble execution of "Soviet justice." As a country in which the rule of law was supposed to reign supreme, the Soviet Union followed certain legal procedures when "dangerous criminals" were apprehended. In particular, there were certain procedures to be followed when a person was incarcerated and left behind only minors who could not care for themselves and for the family's belongings.

In keeping with these rules, our two officers drew up a list of our belongings, and asked us to sign it. Little did we know that they and the informant planned to divide among themselves a large portion (something like forty percent) of all that we owned. Under the law, however, all goods belonging to a criminal were in the custory of the State until the criminal was released. The guards and informant accomplished their plunder by the simple stratagem of failing to include part of our goods in their list. At the time, I was only nine or ten, and Lea was six or seven. How could we have suspected anything? I, being the older child, signed on the dotted line just as I was told. The listed property was put into storage, as required by law. The unlisted property was promptly divided, undoubtedly with much glee, among those who had brought us to "justice."

Mother suspected that the woman with her two sons were implicated in this matter. Before being taken away she had managed to approach the woman and accuse her of informing. The woman vehemently denied having had anything to do with Mother's arrest. She protested her innocence by solemnly declaring, "If I had anything to do with the matter, may one of my children drop dead!" A few days after Mother was arrested, one of the woman's sons went to work in the forest, like everyone else, but failed to return home. Apparently he was swallowed up by the boggy soil of Komi's forests.

* * *

With our mothers in custody, we children became wards of the state, and were assigned to an "orphanage" located in a large town. Although some actual orphans did live there, the place was far from being an orphanage because most of its population consisted of wards of the state—children like us of people imprisoned for all kinds of real and imaginary crimes. Upon our arrival our heads were shaven, just like those of all the other children, since this was the only procedure available to control lice. Reuven, Lea, and I soon settled into the routine of getting up, washing ourselves (without soap), eating some bread (of which there was never enough) with onions, and marching off to school. We actually marched there, usually singing some patriotic song (as far as we knew this was the only type of song there was in Russia). We, the orphanage's wards, attended school with the town's children and were not singled out in any way. In the afternoons we did homework and, from time to time, were called upon to do some work for the benefit of the Motherland. In the summer, the girls were sent to pick mushrooms, and during the winter, they had to help with the housekeeping chores. Lea suffered more than I. She was called a "dirty Jewess"—a rare expression of anti-Semitism in Komi—and was given all kinds of menial tasks.

Another task sometimes assigned to the boys at the orphanage consisted in removing felled trees that lay blocking traffic on the forest roads. The work was not overly difficult or tiring. We would be called out and marched to the place. Then forty or fifty of us boys would be assigned to a tree. No matter how big it was, it wasn't long before we managed to roll it out of the way.

Unlike me, Lea wasn't able to stomach any food other than bread. So I saved my daily bread portion—which didn't amount to much—for her. This probably kept Lea from starving to death, but it also kept me extremely hungry.

We missed Mother terribly, and were unable to communicate with her throughout her stay in prison. Mother was not permitted to write to us, and we were afraid to even ask for permission to write to her. We feared that such a request might have serious repercussions for someone jailed as a political prisoner. Despite our age, the fear of making a false step and becoming liable to an unknown harsh punishment was ever pervasive in the Soviet Union, a feeling difficult to convey to anyone who never lived there.

Mother was imprisoned for nine months. During this time she was frequently interrogated and accused of crimes against the Revolution, crimes that she couldn't even conceive of. In the end, the authorities offered to release her in exchange for a promise to inform on others. Mother agreed, thinking that if she ultimately claimed that she had nothing to inform about, no one would hold it against her. Shortly thereafter Mother was released, not only because of her deal with the authorities, but also because in honor of Stalin's birthday a general amnesty was declared for "political crimes" of a given severity, which included hers. Later, the NKVD[*] called her in a couple of times asking for "information," but Mother kept reiterating her claim that she had none to convey. The NKVD were displeased, and there is little doubt she would have been forced to spend another term in jail had her release not been part of a general amnesty.[**]

As soon as they were released, Mother and Mrs. Berlinerblau came to reclaim us from the orphanage. We had just become infected with a skin disease known as scabies, in which a kind of microscopic worm burrows under the skin. The orphanage provided no treatment despite our terrible itching, and this gave rise to large red welts all over our bodies. When Mother came to pick us up, she had a hard time recognizing us. She looked at our shaven heads and the rough, red skin and exclaimed, "This cannot be they!" Then she looked at us again, and said, "Maybe it is?" After an emotional reunion, Mother took us back to Settlement No. 31, where she somehow obtained a foul-smelling ointment that cured us of the skin infection.

---

[*] NKVD stands for *Narodny Kommisariat Vnutrennikh Del* — People's Commissariat of Internal Affairs. Although officially the Ministry of the Interior, in actuality it was synonymous with the dreaded secret police.

[**] Had she not been released, she would have been accused and sentenced under Paragraph 58 of the Soviet criminal code. This paragraph dealt with political crimes, and carried a mandatory minimum penalty of ten years in jail (actually most of it in a labor camp since there were not enough jails to hold all the "criminals"). It was only years later that I learned that people sentenced under this paragraph were known among Jews as *Bnei Noach* (Children of Noach), since the numerical equivalent (*gematria*) of the Hebrew letters of Noah's name is fifty-eight, the number of the paragraph.

Mother and her friend also went to claim their belongings, only to discover that a significant percentage had been pilfered. There was obviously nothing they could do about it. When Mother attempted to register a complaint, she noticed that one of the officers recording her charge was wearing one of Father's suits.

The loss of a part of our belongings was more painful than you might think. We had carried this bulky baggage with us all the way from Warsaw not because we expected to live in luxury, but as a substitute for currency—a means of purchasing food and other critical commodities.

RELOCATED TO KORTKEROS

Once we were reunited, our family learned that we were to benefit from the amnesty in another way, too. We, like all the refugees, were ordered to leave Settlement No. 31. Our destination: Kortkeros.

We were provided with housing and work in our new place of residence, a town no more than several dozen miles away. The town consisted of one very long street, which curved sharply in the middle, almost forming a ninety-degree angle, thus creating an enclave of several side streets which were surrounded by it. It was comprised of some three hundred houses, two office buildings, an elementary school (grades one through seven) and a secondary school (grades eight through ten), some warehouses, a shop that could, by a very long stretch of the imagination, be called a grocery store, a few workshops, and a post office. One particularly interesting site was the ruins of a church where one could sometimes find gold-embroidered pieces of cloth, remnants of vestments. Why they were there remains a mystery, since the church had probably been demolished during the Great Socialist Revolution, which had arrived in Komi at least fifteen years before we did.

The houses in Kortkeros were constructed in the same log-cabin fashion as at Settlement 31, but with several notable differences. For one, most of the homes were duplexes. Each structure had an inexplicably doorless opening centered in the front of the building, so low that one had to stoop when entering. Inside, a somewhat short and wide entry hall led to a flight of steps that terminated in a landing. Doors to the right and left of the landing opened to the two "apartments" in the duplex, each of which consisted of one fairly large room. A short flight of steps continued up from the landing to the rear section of the building with an area roughly equal to that of the two "apartments." This part of the building was intended as storage space, although during our stay in Kortkeros there was precious little to store. The rear section was more than a story high above the ground. The quite spacious area beneath was used to house two cows.

Two cows were all the private property permitted per household. Anyone holding more was considered a "capitalist" and his excess livestock was subject to confiscation by the state. Each householder was also allotted a plot of land next to his house, where he could cultivate anything he wished. Everyone grew vegetables, working the soil in a way unique to Komi. Instead of digging with a spade and turning over the soil, they dug trenches around all four sides of the row to be planted; and then deposited the soil on the row. Although there may have been a reason for this method, I was never able to fathom it.

An extremely rare photograph of a Komi dwelling, showing a grandfather with his grandchildren. Photographer: Kalju Konsin, 1967. Courtesy of the Estonian National Museum.

Our relationship with our landlord's* family was cordial, but nothing more. As wards of the state, we paid no rent. The only business we conducted with them was the purchase of milk. For some reason they had a surplus, and were willing to sell it to us. Mother would boil the milk, let it stand, and then

---

* To the best of my recollection, the houses were privately owned. At any rate, the term landlord is used figuratively, since we regarded him as such. The fact that the house was privately owned did not prevent the authorities from removing the residents at their whim.

remove the thick layer of cream that accumulated on top. This was reserved to be eaten as a special treat all by itself, or was used, in the summer, as a topping for blueberries or blackberries. Once the cream was safely put aside, Mother let us drink the milk.

It was about the time we moved to Kortkeros that Germany suddenly attacked the Soviet Union. Strange as it may seem, the War's outbreak (signaled by the bombing of Kiev on June 22, 1941) helped solve the housing problem of the former denizens of Settlement No. 31. Most of the "two-family" houses in Kortkeros had been populated by parents and married children. Now, though, virtually all the younger husbands were drafted; only the wives, children, and the elderly remained at home. In preparation for our arrival, most of the town's residents were ordered to vacate their apartments and move in with each other, i.e., the parents had to move in with the daughters or daughters-in-law, or vice versa.

Artist's representation of our dwelling in Kortkeros. Note the well, the vegetable patch and other details.

This instantly freed a large number of living units for the refugees.

In the beginning, Mother, Lea, and I were crowded into a one-room apartment along with two other families because some of the local residents had ignored the directive to move in with relatives. With time, they were discovered and forced to "move over," usually across the hall. In the end, each refugee family had an entire one-room apartment all to itself.

Each room had four parts to it. A large furnace, known as a *pechka,* dominated the far left corner, taking up a full quarter of the room. The roof of this furnace terminated about two feet below the ceiling, providing sleeping space on top. A huge wooden berth was built into the left quarter of the room at about this level. Some of the heat escaping from the furnace roof flowed into the space between the berth and the ceiling, providing for additional, comfortable sleeping quarters. The top of the furnace could be reached by built-in steps. From there, it was only a short hop over to the berth. The space beneath the berth was separated from the rest of the room by a curtain. It served as storage space, and doubled as a closet, chest of drawers, dresser, etc.

The near right corner of our single-room apartment served as the dining room. The two walls making up the corner had benches attached to them, and a table was secured to the floor. The sink located in the far right corner was quite similar to the shallow cast-iron one I remembered from our Warsaw kitchen, although with one major difference: the sink in Kortkeros had no running water. Instead, a barrel filled with water from the well in the yard served as our water supply.

The walls of every house in this distant town were, believe it or not, covered with "wallpaper." Actually, this was nothing more than old newspapers, glued to the roughly hewn log walls. Even so, we were very careful not to damage this covering because during the war even old newspapers were in short supply, and glue was virtually nonexistent. We knew quite well that if anything were to happen to the "wallpaper," no repairs would be possible.

A kerosene lamp provided our sole source of illumination. The lamp came with the apartment, and at times we could even purchase replacement glass chimneys for it. The chimneys would shatter from time to time if the wick was extended too high. Adjusting the wick to obtain maximum illumination without causing the chimney to shatter, and with a minimum of soot as well, was a special art. Actually, the major problem with these lamps was obtaining the kerosene... but more about this later.

Each yard was separated from the other by a fence made of vertical poles to which horizontal pieces of birch trees had been attached. The fence served only to establish the boundaries between the yards, and no one minded if a neighbor took a shortcut through his yard to the street. These shortcuts required special agility: one had to put his foot on the bottom piece of the fence, and then, with the other foot straddling the

Artist's representation of the inside of our dwelling in Kortkeros.

top piece, jump over with the first foot. After a while, this became a sport among the children, and we competed with one another to see who could perform the jump in one smooth motion.

The locks on the entry doors were extremely crude, and could have been picked by any amateur, but such a crime was unheard of. In fact, locks as such had come relatively recently to Kortkeros. We were told that during the reign of the Czar, when it was rare for anyone except a native Komi to venture outside the capital city, there had been no locks at all. Anyone leaving his home would simply close the front door and stick a broom into the door handle (which, even when we were there, was nothing more than a metal ring) as a sign that no one was home. As a matter of fact, many houses had storage cellars for household produce such as potatoes, cabbage and the like, which were entered by the kind of external trap door commonly used in New York City. Yet even these doors were never locked. I assume this was because stealing produce was tantamount to murdering the family, and apparently no one would stoop that low.

Of the challenges that faced us, perhaps the most immediately pressing was obtaining wood for cooking and heating. Although the wood supply was unlimited, the trees still had to be felled, allowed to dry and the logs transported into town. We could not haul them in the summer, even if we had had a cart, because the cart's wheels would sink in the boggy soil of Komi.

We had to wait for a decent layer of snow, which would allow us to use a sled. As soon as enough snow fell, the three of us went to the forest. We knew the technique by heart from Settlement 31. I notched the trees, and then Mother and I (with Lea sometimes replacing Mother) used a standard twin-handled saw to chop down one after another. We then cut them up into manageable lengths, and brought them home by sled. Pulling a fully loaded sled was hard work and required the combined muscle power of our trio. The initial batch was sawed into short lengths which were then axed into small pieces. This insured that the wood would dry quickly and become suitable for burning. The cutting up of the wood that was not immediately needed was postponed to a later date when, upon drying, it would cut more easily.

We made an arrangement with our landlord to use some of his wood until our supply was ready for use. Although he did not have much to spare, it was far better than nothing.

Although, on the whole, we had very little to do with our landlord—a widower who had moved in with his daughter (or daughter-in-law) across the hall—we did have personal contact with him on one occasion.

Food being in such scarce supply, the landlord and his family decided to sacrifice their dog. This way, they would solve two problems at once. First, they would be relieved of the obligation to feed the animal, and second, they would be provided with some otherwise unobtainable meat.

Apparently, the poor beast sensed the fate awaiting him. At any rate, one day he scratched incessantly at our door until we let him in. Once inside, he lay down near the door and refused to budge. We told our landlord, and he came in to try to move the dog. Not having much success, he left. Several hours later, the dog also left. If I remember correctly, our landlord relented and did not put his plan into action.

Like all other refugees, we lived by ourselves and hardly ever visited the local population. Once, however, I did make such a visit, and got a privileged look at how they ate at mealtime. The food was served in a single wooden bowl, and each member of the family was given a wooden spoon. The oldest person would take the first spoonful from the communal bowl. When he put his spoon down, the person seated next to him would take his spoonful, and so on around the table, repeatedly, until all the food was consumed.

There was another local custom, one I frequently encountered, that always left me furious. It found expression in our local store. This local general store sold articles that, for the most part, no one needed. This meant that although its shelves were not bare, they contained nothing usable. Since useful items would still be brought in from time to time—and one never knew when—Mother would occasionally send me to ask the saleslady about some necessity, on the off chance that it had arrived. More often than not, I was answered in the negative. This answer might not have bothered me so much if it had been given in a straightforward manner. For some reason, though, the replies were always twisted. When I inquired, for example, as to whether mittens were available, the saleslady invariably asked what size I wanted. If I asked for a small size, the answer was no. But then when I asked for the large size, I received the same answer.

When we arrived in Kortkeros, bread was in plentiful supply. There were even three kinds of bread on the market, depending on how much money you wished to spend. However, as the war continued, flour became scarce, and soon we were on bread rations of 600 grams for a worker and 400 grams for a dependent. In 1942-43, when the state of the economy deteriorated very badly, this went down to 400 and 200 grams respectively.

Except for bread, the only commodity that could be purchased in our "grocery store" was raspberry tea. Packages upon packages of this delicacy filled the shelves. It took less than a week for the newcomers to buy out the entire stock. No one dreamt of using the stuff for brewing tea—it was simply eaten as dried fruit. Since everyone worked in a workshop, he was entitled to a "cafeteria lunch," which consisted of some watery soup with potatoes and microscopic pieces of meat floating in it. This gave rise to the joke that in Komi one eats tea and drinks soup. I couldn't understand why the local residents hadn't bought out the raspberry tea supply long before we came.

There were no cigarettes in Komi. As a matter of fact, even in Poland only the affluent smoked store-bought cigarettes. Most people made do with a supply of tobacco and tissue-thin paper, rolling their own cigarettes. In Komi the only paper available was newsprint. When tobacco became unobtainable, those who could not live without it would pull out the dry moss wedged between the logs of buildings to keep the cold from seeping in, and roll their "cigarettes" from it. Despite the foul smell of the burning moss, they considered it better than nothing.

At first, Mother worked in the town's main workshop where short, white knitted men's socks were produced. The knitting needles of the hand-driven machines were arranged in a circle, with the white threads feeding into each needle from overhead rolls. The machine was operated by a continual turning of its handle. Socks came off the machine with the bottom part still open. The final stage in finishing the socks was sewing this opening up.

The workshop building also housed a bookstore and a photographer's lab. Most of the books were propaganda, in which I had no interest. The only book of use to me was a history book which was the course textbook for the current school year. I joyously purchased it and read the entire book in one or two sittings. (When the lamp went out, moonlight often provided a good enough substitute.) Some of the other textbooks could be obtained secondhand, but others were totally unavailable.

The photographer's lab was not in use because the town photographer had been drafted. It happened that we had among us a Polish gentile who specialized in topography. He had listed this occupation when filling out one of the official forms, and soon enough was told to start taking pictures and otherwise run the lab. His protests that he knew nothing about photography were to no avail, for no one in Kortkeros had ever heard of topography. Once the officials had classified him as a photographer, they could not be convinced otherwise. Fortunately for him, he was a rather intelligent lad, and it was not long before he started producing pictures just about as good as the equipment allowed.

From her first job at the sock machine, Mother moved on to becoming kitchen manager. There she came face to face with a commonplace Soviet mode of behavior: stealing. Her potato supplier would bring her a smaller quantity than specified, yet would, at the same time, make her sign a paper saying that she had received the full amount. Mother, with the trauma of her imprisonment fresh in her bones, dutifully complied. Then that same person demanded that she hand over some other commodity available in the kitchen. This Mother refused. The next step was all too predictable. The supplier informed on Mother, accused her of stealing potatoes, and led a search party to examine the evidence.

Mother had anticipated that this might happen and had made sure to subdivide the week's potato supply into daily portions. This way, the shortage in each pile would be relatively minor and harder to discern. Her hope was that, at the worst, she would be let off with a reprimand. When the investigation was made, though, the inspector who accompanied her supplier insisted that short weight is just that, and that it doesn't matter whether it is short by a lot or a little.

Mother was arrested and tried. Since stealing was considered an ordinary crime (rather than a political one), the trial was public and took place within a day or two of her arrest without prior interrogation or further investigation. Here Mother was in for a surprise.

The trial took place in the evening in the community hall that doubled as courtroom, and it was packed with all the workers from the shops (mostly women, the bulk of the men being in the army). They came because Mother, from the time she began working as kitchen manager, had enriched the daily soup with all the foodstuffs she received, unlike the previous kitchen manager, who would "tithe" the supply for his own personal benefit. As soon as the accusations were read, the women began shouting in unison: "She is innocent! Release her right now!"

The judge, who was actually just a town official appointed for this job (and who lacked any legal training, a common condition in townships of this size), did the only thing that seemed sensible to him under the circumstances: he acquitted Mother on the spot.

CLANDESTINE BUSINESS

After this latest unfortunate incident, Mother was unwilling to go back to her job in the workshop. But on the other hand, to be out of work was to be a "parasite" and a "counter-revolutionary" and carried all kinds of penalties, even imprisonment. Besides, bread rations were issued only to workers and their dependents. Without work, not only Mother, but we, too, would have found ourselves without our bread coupons, a sure ticket to starvation.

Fortunately, the position of accountant in one of the offices became vacant, and Mother took it. On the first day on the job she was in for a surprise. The bookkeeper was none other than Fishel Finkelstein, the son of Mother's neighbors, whom she had known as a child. Ironically, Mother's job outranked his, despite the fact that he was a full-fledged CPA and attorney while Mother only had a bookkeeping diploma. This was because Mother's command of Russian was superior to his. Also, he was alone and depressed, and his apathetic demeanor did nothing to impress his superiors.

One day, as Mother was walking home after work, she saw the outline of what looked like a human body lying alongside the road. A quick glance sufficed to tell her that it was Fishel Finkelstein who, for lack of warm clothing, had collapsed and was rapidly freezing to death.

There were two bachelor brothers among the Kortkeros refugees: Shai and Julek Neikron. Mother ran to their house as fast as she could, told the brothers what was happening, and guided them to the motionless body. There she handed over to them her most prized possession—her husband's thick woolen winter coat. (Mother's two fur coats were by then warming the wives of our two officers from Settlement No. 31.) The Neikrons wrapped Fishel in the coat and carried him to our place.

Once there, they rubbed him down with snow (the accepted cure for frostbite) and poured huge amounts of warm liquid down his throat until he regained consciousness. When he became aware that Mother and the brothers had saved him, he quoted the well-known Polish saying that "one mountain never meets another, but people do." This meant that he promised them that the act would be repaid in kind, some day, somehow.

Mother graciously gave him one of Father's suits and a few other articles of clothing to help him survive the freezing cold of winter. Later, when we were allotted powdered milk supplied to children by a Western charitable organization, Mother gave some of it to Fishel. She explained to Lea and me that while we could rely on her to supplement our daily ration, Fishel had nobody.

Suits of the kind Mother had given Fishel were not to be found in Kortkeros, and most likely not anywhere else in Komi, either. After Fishel appeared at work wearing his new suit, Mother was besieged with requests from her bosses to sell them similar outfits, of the ones that had been returned to her after her release from jail. Mother was reluctant to part with them, since all she was being offered for them was money, and money had almost no value. The only things that could be purchased with money were the daily bread rations, whatever happened to be available in the bookstore, and maybe another item or two. A worker's salary covered these needs very nicely. Foodstuffs such as potatoes, turnips, cabbage, and onions, on the other hand, were in short supply. The fortunate individuals who possessed these items kept them to feed their families, and would not dream of parting with them for something as worthless as money. Although high-ranking officials could purchase things such as butter, sugar, and other goods unavailable to the general public, they would not dare offer them in barter for fear of being caught speculating in restricted-purchase goods.

Mother was in a dilemma. On the one hand, the money seemed almost valueless, yet on the other, she had no use for the suits. After deliberating, she decided that cash in the pocket is still better than goods packed in valises, and sold them.

It turned out to be a wise decision, because a short time later we discovered a man who was willing to take money for goods—and who indeed had goods to deliver. This man was the warehouse manager of a hospital located in Pezmog, a town several miles away from ours. He firmly believed, unlike the vast majority of the population who could not think ahead to the end of the war, that money would regain its previous value. He was therefore willing to sell salted fish and wheat and sometimes oats for 100 rubles per kilo. Naturally, these staples were pilfered from the warehouse. There was simply no other way of procuring items that could not be grown in the home garden except for theft.

Our warehouse manager, however, was not always in a position to steal the goods. Furthermore, he was willing to conduct the transaction only if his "customer" would come up to the warehouse to pick up his "order." To find out whether the time was opportune, one had to phone him. That is how I came to be sent by Mother to the post office one day. Our local post office had three phone booths. A caller was assigned a booth where he lifted the receiver, gave the desired number to an operator who sat behind the counter, and waited to be connected. At times, the connection was poor, and the would-be caller had to repeat this procedure several times. This time, after several attempts, I succeeded in speaking with the warehouse manager, and arranged to see him the next day.

It was winter, with standard temperatures ranging from thirteen to thirty-one below zero, Fahrenheit (minus twenty-five to minus thirty-five Celsius). The town of Pezmog was situated up-river, on the opposite bank, but this presented no problem. The river was so solidly frozen that you could drive a five-ton truck over the ice without difficulty. I got up in the morning, dressed appropriately, packed some food (one third of my daily bread ration), and was admonished by Mother to eat it only at lunchtime. I took our sled and the money, and off I went.

The admonition, in spite of coming from Mother herself, was not effective. On this and subsequent trips, a powerful struggle ensued between the gnawing feeling of hunger that accompanied all of us throughout our stay in Komi and the fear of disobeying Mother. But the temptation presented by the slice of bread I carried was just too much to overcome. Accordingly, this time—and all the other times—I consumed my ration within an hour of leaving the house.

To protect ourselves from the bitter cold, which, fortunately, was not accompanied by strong winds, we had to dress properly. We wore quilted trousers, a quilted jacket, and a fur hat with ear flaps. A scarf covered the nose and mouth, leaving only the eyes exposed. On our feet we wore felt boots, known as *valenki*. Our mittens were also quilted. The fact that only the thumb was free to move separately made handling things a bit difficult, but we managed. Indeed, dressed in the entire ensemble, we were comfortably warm. I remember that once the temperature dropped to forty-nine below zero, Fahrenheit. School and all other activities, including work, were canceled. I went out for a stroll and didn't feel cold at all.

How did we purchase these special winter outfits when none of the clothing was available in local stores? Mother acquired it by bartering other items of clothing that we had brought with us and which were not available to the populace. In all likelihood, these winter clothes had been produced clandestinely by someone who had access to cloth and cotton stolen from some government supply, or left over from pre-war times when goods were more easily obtainable.

So I set out in my winter gear on what proved to be an

uneventful journey to the warehouse. First, I crossed the frozen river and followed the winter "road." This road was not too frequently traveled, and was outlined rather weakly by tracks left by several horse-drawn sleds that had preceded me. I had been given a description of the warehouse on the phone, and thus had no trouble identifying it.

I waited briefly for my supplier to appear. Before he took me into the warehouse, he looked around to make sure that we were not being observed. Inside, six hundred rubles changed hands. I then deposited my precious cargo of three kilograms of salted fish and a similar amount of wheat on my sled, and started the trek back home.

As evening approached, it began to snow. Little by little, the tracks I was following towards home became less visible. I plodded along the path, feeling the snow under my feet becoming increasingly soft, and the sled more difficult to pull. Soon, there were no tracks to be seen at all.

I continued walking in the direction of what I believed was the path when all of a sudden, with no advance warning, I found myself sunk in snow up to my knees. I took a few more steps, and, when this did not bring me to firmer-packed snow, tried to retrace my steps in order to return to the point where I first started sinking in the snow. To no avail. I could not find the trail! I was lost!

There were no markers of any kind to guide me. The "road," really nothing more than a path, passed through a sparsely wooded area which, for all I knew, might have extended for miles in any direction. This meant that the real road might have passed through an infinite number of paths, each one being a different treeless passage. My situation was precarious. I didn't dare leave my expensive purchases behind, which meant that I must pull my sled, although it was not suitable for riding on soft snow. Its relatively narrow runners were good for riding on snow that was packed to some degree or other, but now they sank into the virgin snow and the sled rode on its "belly" making it extremely difficult to pull. All this, while I had to extricate each foot, every step of the way, from knee-deep snow.

I knew quite well that, barring a miracle, my survival hinged upon my finding my way out on my own. In Komi everybody was on his own, and even the term "search party" was unheard of. I decided to try not to panic, and in this I succeeded. Still, I kept thinking about what would happen if I couldn't manage to find my way out.

I felt that as long as I was walking, even without a definite direction, I was making an effort at survival, since walking was the only thing I could do to save myself from freezing to death. So I plodded along in the direction I thought was right, trying all the while to decide what to do.

All this time I had my eyes focused on my immediate surroundings with the hope that I would at least not find myself following my previous footsteps. Then, without much

Lost in the woods and knee-deep in snow, I am pulling a sled with a precious load of 6 kg of salted fish. Note how the sled's runners also sink into the snow.

thought, I lifted my eyes to the sky and noticed that there was much more light coming from the direction in which I was headed.

"The river! The moon is full," I thought, "and its light must be reflecting strongly from the river." I still had about a mile to traverse, but now there was hope. I renewed my efforts, and within half an hour I reached the leg of the road that, after a ninety-degree turn, ran parallel to the river up to the crossing point. (The river could not be crossed at just any point because snow was piled up very high on its surface.)

I finally walked into the house several hours later than I should have. Mother was beside herself with worry, and had already imagined the worst. But all was forgotten at the sight of the six-kilo treasure I brought with me.

This exchange, however, was only one part of Mother's plan. The second part called for securing some potatoes. Mother could not find anyone in Kortkeros who would willingly part with any of his supply, but in a way I will never know, she found some people in the town of Madzha, down-river from Kortkeros, who were willing to barter their potatoes and turnips for salted fish. Accordingly, a few days later I was sent to Madzha. Mother also discovered that Madzha had a shop which sold earthenware pots and plates, items that we needed. As a government-owned shop, its prices were extremely low and, thankfully, the purchase could be paid for with cash.

I set out for Madzha by crossing the frozen river and following a path, again produced by horse-driven sleds, along its opposite bank. This time most of the travel was along the riverbank. When the town came into view, the path turned right and it took less than fifteen minutes to reach my destination.

I purchased the pots and plates, and went to the people who were willing to exchange their potatoes and turnips for salted fish. By that time darkness had fallen. Extremely apprehensive that I might get lost again, I hinted broadly to my bartering partners that I would like to sleep over at their place. They did not like the idea, however, and told me that there was still "enough time to get to Moscow." I had no choice but to head for home in the dark.

I tied the produce, topped by the earthenware, to the sled and started on my journey. By now it was night, with only a very pale light shed by a waning moon. I walked toward the river, intending to follow the path by which I had come. To do this, I needed to get within a few yards of the river and then turn left to follow the snow road until the crossing opposite our town. Somehow, in the almost total darkness of the night, I overshot the turn and continued on straight ahead. Suddenly, I found myself flying down a couple of feet onto the frozen river with the sled following me at breakneck speed. The sled arched over me, gave me a solid bang on the head, and landed close by.

I picked myself up, righted the sled, and looked around. The thing to do was to climb back up onto the bank and try to find the road. But there was no way I could do it—the drop from the bank down to the river was too steep. The other bank, the one on which our town was located, looked much lower. More importantly, from afar, there seemed to be a line of saplings at regular intervals, possibly indicating a road. I decided to cross the river over there.

However, things were not that simple. When I got there, I did find the line of young trees, but the path, if it was a path, was covered with ankle-deep snow. Still, it appeared passable, and, since I did not have much choice, I kept on going. The snow grew deeper and deeper as I continued plodding in the upriver direction. After a while it became very difficult to walk while pulling the sled. Not only that, but the path went through a forest, which although not too dense, obscured whatever view I had of the surrounding terrain. And I desperately needed that view if I wanted to find my way.

This was because someplace midway between the two

towns there was a relatively small settlement where we had friends, the Lifshitzes. That settlement had some kind of facility that was operated by electricity and therefore it possessed a generator, which also provided power to the facility's many employees, including the Lifshitz family. The light bulbs, which shone much more brightly than kerosene lamps, made the settlement quite visible at night. In addition, the generator powered a floodlight which hung from a pole in the middle of the settlement. All this caused the settlement to be visible from afar. The floodlight was even strong enough to be seen from Kortkeros. I very badly needed to see these lights, particularly the floodlight, so that I would have some idea of the distance and direction to the settlement.

Right now I had no choice but to descend onto the frozen river in order to get a view of the settlement. To my dismay, when I finally reached a spot from where I was able to take a good look, the settlement appeared far away. Its lights were faint, and even the strong light of the floodlight could not be seen. I decided that I must still be very far away from reaching the refuge of the Lifshitz home. One fact bothered me: I knew that the distance between the floodlight and me was less than the distance between it and Kortkeros, yet from Kortkeros it had always been quite visible. The fact that I couldn't see it now demanded an explanation. The only plausible one I could think of was that the floodlight must be facing away from me.

I took stock of my situation. I was exhausted. I was standing there all alone late at night on the frozen river, knee deep in the freshly fallen snow. I felt too tired to pull the sled, but I knew that if I did nothing and just stood there passively until the morning, I would freeze to death.

Making my decision, I abandoned the sled with its hard-won goods and started walking along the riverbank in the general direction of the settlement. To my surprise I reached it in only half an hour. It turned out that the generator had broken down that very night and that the faint lights I had seen were those of kerosene lamps, and not electric bulbs. The floodlight, naturally, was not working at all, and that is what caused me to misjudge the distance.

I was welcomed by the Lifshitzes, who put me up for the night. Early the next morning I went down to the river. To my surprise, I found the sled with its precious load still intact, although only a dozen yards away from where I had left it, lumberjacks were busy preparing logs for transport after the spring thaw. They could easily have spotted it, but inexplicably, did not. I was also surprised to discover that had I gone in a somewhat different direction the night before, I would soon have encountered this very spot, an area on the ice that was cleared of snow. Not only that, but there was a beaten path from this clearing straight back to Kortkeros.

I followed the path and arrived home at about 10 AM. Mother, who had by then assumed that I was irretrievably lost, was overwhelmed with joy. She told me that when I had failed to arrive the previous night, she and Lea had run to the outskirts of town hoping to catch sight of me trudging home. With no sight of my return, they went home and prayed to the Master of the Universe for my well-being. Then they went out again to scan the horizon in search of me. On and on through the night they continued this pattern. By the time I came home, Mother was exhausted and shaking, so distraught she was hardly aware of her surroundings.

Lea was not home to greet me upon my arrival. She had no choice but to go to school as usual, since the authorities considered missing a day of school a very serious offense. Indeed, the same consideration had prompted me to set out on my shopping expedition to Madzha in the afternoon rather than in the morning, which would have given me more daylight hours for the trip. We assumed that one truancy (to make the initial trip to Pezmog) would be tolerated, but a second would not.

I unpacked my load and found that some, but not all, of

the earthenware had cracked. Another unexpected effect of the overnight storage conditions was that the potatoes I brought became so sweet after cooking that they could be eaten only with difficulty—this despite our being chronically hungry. We asked about the phenomenon, and were told that the sweetness resulted from freezing. The damage could be remedied, the local lore had it, by keeping them outside, frozen, until cooking time, and then dropping them directly into boiling water. Sure enough, the next time we found ourselves with frozen potatoes, we followed this procedure. It worked beautifully.

I made the trip to the warehouse in Pezmog twelve or thirteen times, until our "supplier" could no longer deliver the goods. Not all the trips, however, resulted in the anticipated exchange. I was supposed to call the man before coming, but sometimes, after not getting a connection on the first try, my bashfulness prevented me from asking the operator to try again. I would then go home and tell Mother that "everything was arranged." Not surprisingly, though, I would as often as not come home empty-handed after the more than ten-mile round trip. Sometimes I would return before noon having already consumed my bread portion for the day—despite Mother's admonition. Of course, the scolding I received was only for my benefit, but I was too young to appreciate that fact.

In the summer, one of the ways we crossed the river to the warehouse was by ferry. This ferry was nothing more than an ordinary boat "propelled" by the hand-over-hand pulling of a rope which straddled the river in the water itself. The rope had to be left quite slack because the river was traveled by full-size vessels that would have cut right through a tightly stretched rope. The two men who ran the ferry in shifts charged a full ruble for passage. This was a large amount compared with other official services, but still affordable. Thinking back, this must have been a private, rather than official, service. If so, it was the only "free enterprise" in our region that I knew about and the only place where money had some worth.

The other way to cross the river was by passenger boat. This boat presumably operated on some kind of schedule, although like any other esoteric information of this kind, it was known only to a select few in the town's administration. At any rate, the boat would call first at our town and then continue on to Pezmog where the hospital was located. Since these towns were not particularly important, the boat would usually arrive at inconvenient hours: close to midnight at our place and very early in the morning in Pezmog.

The trip wasn't much of a pleasure. Because the boat came infrequently, its decks were packed with standing-room-only passengers. I remember falling asleep while standing, and waking up as my knees buckled. Even worse, the temperatures on the exposed decks were frigid—even in the summer. Obviously, I could not wait for the boat to finish its route all the way upriver and back before I headed home. So, my journey to Pezmog in the summer would begin with a walk to the river crossing, and end with a ferry ride back to Kortkeros.

I made at least two more trips to Madzha after that frightening one, each time to exchange the salted fish and some wheat for potatoes and the like. Happily, those other trips were uneventful. We did not exchange all the fish and wheat; some of it we ate ourselves. Mother, of course, made the decision as to what should be done with each delivery.

One time, Mother found out that one member of our community had managed to acquire a substantial quantity of potatoes and was willing to barter it for another food, and sent Lea to conclude the deal. She admonished Lea to look carefully at the scales to insure that we were not being cheated, but Lea proved too bashful to supervise. When she came back with the potatoes, Mother lifted the package, which weighed three or four kilograms, and said with conviction, "Half a kilo is missing." Poor Lea had to return to the man and ask for the missing potatoes. He, on his part, was amazed that Mother had been able to detect the shortchanging without a scale and meekly made up the shortage.

Mother had other enterprising ways to bolster our pantry. Soon, all the exquisite wool dresses she had knitted for Lea were reduced to skeins of wool from which she knitted sweaters both for us and for "her ladies" (as she called the women who ran the town's shops). In addition to selling whatever item or two happened to be delivered for distribution, they were also in charge of supplying high-ranking officials with commodities such as butter, sugar, kerosene, and other items unavailable to rank-and-file comrades.

The silk brocade outer linings of all our quilts were carefully removed and transformed into beautiful dresses. Little by little these pieces of clothing found their way to the wardrobes of Mother's "ladies." In exchange, we received butter, sugar, kerosene, and other needed goods. Frequently, I had the privilege of effecting this transfer of goods. I would go to the store, wait patiently in line with everyone else, and buy some item that was currently in stock. I would then be handed, under the counter, a slab of butter, a bottle or two of kerosene, or some other item agreed upon between Mother and the lady.

Obviously, the butter couldn't be eaten by itself. Since Mother claimed that bread is delicious enough to be eaten without a spread, she put the butter to a unique use. She discovered that the wild nettle which grew in profusion around our settlement was extremely nutritious. Turning this knowledge into action, we collected the nettle, and Mother chopped it up fine, rolled it in oat flour (which we produced ourselves by pounding oats—another acquisition from the store ladies) and then fried the batter in butter. It would be a slight exaggeration to call these patties "tasty," but they were definitely edible. Yet, although they were nutritionally beneficial, they could hardly fill our hungry stomachs. The feeling of unending hunger accompanied us as long as we were in Komi.

*   *   *

Mother's accounting job did not last long, and soon she was back in her old place of employment, the sock factory. By now, another item had been added to the shop's output: fishing nets. The workshop did not produce complete nets, but only netting, a mesh of strong string with hexagonal holes. Mother was assigned to the net production in the shop, and after a while discovered a way to improve her work conditions while at the same time increasing our bread rations.

Her suggestion to the shop's boss was simple: She would work at home, and both Lea and I would also be registered as workers. The idea was accepted, and in the winter of 1942, about two and a half years after our arrival in Komi, our family began its "cottage industry." There being three of us, we were expected to produce three *normas*. Mother decided on a system by which we would reached this goal: She would produce two *normas* and Lea and I would produce half a *norma* each. I still remember the wide netting fastened to the wall in our "dining room." We worked together, weaving the wooden shuttles on which coils of string were wound back and forth. The extra pay we received from fulfilling three *normas* was insignificant, but having our family's daily bread ration raised from a total of 800 grams to that of 1200 was of paramount importance. Mother was the only one in town to strike such a deal, and to this very day I cannot understand how she managed to register us as workers when, according to the law, we had to be in school (as indeed we were).

Taking work home solved another acute problem. Mother always did everything she could not to work on the Sabbath. I no longer remember what excuses she came up with every week, but she somehow managed to get away with it, at least most of the time. It was, however, a highly nerve-wracking endeavor. We lived with the ever-present threat (real or imagined) of being sent farther up north, to the Vorkuta labor camps, if her true motives became known. So when the authorities permitted her to produce the netting in our house, Mother could finally breathe free, and allow the Sabbath to reign supreme. True, we had our shuttles ready and waiting in case someone poked his nose into our house on Saturday, but fortunately this never happened. Slowly, as we sensed that we were not being observed, our fear of being discovered diminished and eventually disappeared entirely.

Mother's struggle to observe the Sabbath was probably made easier by the fact that she was alone in her persistence, whereas most people in our group had given up and resigned themselves to working on the holy day. If others had joined her, the authorities would soon have realized that she was acting out of religious considerations, something routinely classified as a counter-revolutionary activity, punishable under Section 58 of the Criminal Code—the "political crimes" section. As for communal observance of Jewish religion, there simply was none. Most of the Jewish refugees were women and children, which precluded any attempt at organized communal prayers. Religious observances such as blowing the *shofar* or holding the four species on Succoth were very far from everyone's mind. Every household maintained its own standards and, in those that regarded themselves as observant —not too many—every family head, usually a woman, did what she regarded as proper under the circumstances.

At some point between her several jobs in Kortkeros, Mother was given the task of supervising the local basic-commodities warehouse. (This job may even have been in addition to the net-making.) To the best of my recollection, most of the commodities consisted of grain. Mother had no idea why the previous supervisor had quit, or why she was offered the job— but she soon found out. The procedure upon taking charge was to weigh all the contents, and check the weight against storage documents. In Mother's case, the "weighing ceremony" took place in the summer, when the actual and recorded amounts were found to be in agreement. Some time later, in the winter, Mother quit the job or was asked to leave. But this time, to Mother's chagrin, the weight was short, i.e., she had less grain than the documents indicated.

Mother panicked. She was certain that there would be no repeat performance of her release when she had been accused of stealing potatoes. Stealing the equivalent of sacks of grain from the entire town's commodities supply was far more serious than a few kilograms of potatoes! And this would be her second "offense." In addition, there were no women workers to defend her. To add to her fears, she learned that a special commission was to come from the capital to draw up a protocol. To Mother, the capital represented, first and foremost, the location of the jail in which she had been imprisoned.

Even more perplexing, Mother could not figure out how the grain had disappeared. The possibility of theft was precluded since the number of sacks on hand was exactly the same number that she had received. Equally puzzling was the fact that each sack was short of its supposed weight. This gave rise to only one reasonable supposition: the previous warehouse administrator must have pilfered some grain from each of the sacks. If so, he must have been able to duplicate a key (no mean task in the tool-less town) and slip in and out of the warehouse without being seen. This combination of events was, although not impossible, highly unlikely. In addition, the warehouse was located just several meters from our dwelling, and could be seen through the window. Mother felt that either she or some neighbor would have noticed the comings and goings, particularly since the person had to carry the grain on him.

To solve her dilemma, Mother discussed it with someone she felt she could trust. This acquaintance smiled broadly and asked her when she had begun the job. When Mother replied that she had taken charge in the summer and left in the winter, the acquaintance burst out laughing. "Don't you know," she said, "that grain absorbs humidity in the summer and dries out in the cold of the winter?" This accounted for the weight difference. The previous administrator, anticipating his relinquishing the position some time in the summer, did indeed pilfer some grain from each sack, but was careful to take just as much as would be compensated by the rise in humidity. (Most likely he had the job for a couple of years, so he knew what to expect.)

At this point Mother had an explanation, but, unfortunately, no solution to offer the investigative commission about to arrive any day. She feared she would be sent to the dreaded Vorkuta coal mines or, at the very least, be separated from her two children.

The commission arrived and a protocol was duly drawn up. Mother lived in fear for a month or two, but when nothing happened, she decided that the protocol's sole effect would be to prevent her from holding any administrative position in Komi. Since she wasn't expecting to ever again hold such a position, she had nothing to worry about. As it turned out, she was right.

*　*　*

School was obligatory. We first attended the elementary school, a single-story, rather plain-looking building, which was not far from our house. Since it was wartime, all the teachers were women except for two men. One was past the age of service, while the other had lost a hand in the fighting. The latter was our UMT (universal military training) instructor. We were taught how to take apart a rifle, how to march, how to use skis, how to throw a hand grenade, how to dig trenches and other similar useful wartime skills. To us, most of this was fun, in particular the marching, skiing, and even reciting the eleven parts of the rifle by heart. As I recall, though, we never actually took a rifle apart and put it back together again until we entered secondary school.

The sudden call-up of the male custodial staff had left the school without a supply of firewood for the winter. Consequently, during the first year of the war the classrooms were not heated. However, the insulation provided by the log walls was so good that most of the time the temperature did not drop below forty-eight Fahrenheit (nine degrees Celsius). On the few occasions that it did, the cold made it impossible for us to write.

Classes were, as is customary in many places in the world, fifty minutes long, with a ten-minute recess between them. These breaks presented a problem, since there was virtually nothing to do during them. I no longer remember what the girls did, but we boys played a game I had never seen before: Any boy who took a step or two in any direction outside of the classroom instantly became a candidate for getting himself thrown to the floor or against the wall by another boy. The local boys were very adept at falling "softly", and no one was ever injured.

When we first arrived in Kortkeros, I entered school in midyear, and was thus blissfully unaware of this athletic pastime. During the first recess, I left the classroom and suddenly found myself thrown to the floor. I got up and made my way back to the classroom. As the rest of the class returned to their seats when recess was over, I remained standing and said, "Listen, boys—I am out of this game." The word spread to the other classes, and my position was accepted by all. I was exempt from the game until I graduated.

Nonetheless, I found it best to stay in the classroom during recess and do homework. This way, by the time I got home after school I was free to help Mother.

Although I got out of participating in the game, I was not spared entirely from unpleasant encounters with some of the local boys. There were two teenage rowdies in town of whom everyone was frightened. They thought it great fun to beat up a passerby for no reason at all. At the very beginning of our stay one of them jumped me, but for some reason, he let me go without giving me a beating. Still, I was frightened to death to walk in the street for several days afterwards. It took me a while to learn how to spot them from afar, and run away to escape another encounter.

Lea was not as fortunate. She was once pounced upon by the rowdies and given a beating. Needless to say, she tried even harder than I to avoid these two boys.

However, typical of the Komi mentality, there was a special kind of insurance against being beaten up by these two, actually by the one who was extremely violent. (A story circulated that he had, in one of his violent moods, spilled boiling water on someone!) Many people carried the workshop cafeteria's allocation of watery soup home to eat. Anyone carrying this was automatically spared by the rowdy, since an attack would cause the soup to spill—and food was considered sacred.

I have no idea what provoked the rowdy's behavior, but I am sure it had nothing to do with anti-Semitism. Firstly, because anyone living in the town was equally victimized, irrespective of race or nationality. And secondly, the people of Kortkeros had never before seen Jews, did not even know we were Jewish, and had never been told that Jews are different from anyone else. To them we were simply Polish refugees.

We never knew where our teachers had received their education. It stands to reason that since they were native Komis, there must have been a teacher's seminary or even a college in Syktyvkar, the capital city. Otherwise, they would have had to travel over a thousand miles to attend school, which is difficult to imagine. To my surprise, our teachers were of extremely high caliber, very intelligent, as well as being understanding and considerate. This stood in stark contrast to the otherwise backward state of affairs in Komi.

I have to confess that I was a Communist in good standing for a brief period in my life. Some time during our stay in

Kortkeros, one of our teachers walked into the classroom and announced that we were being given an opportunity to join the Pioneers, a para-political organization for school children. From the Pioneers, one graduated to the Komsomol (Communist Youth Union), and finally to full-fledged Party membership. All the children had been expecting this. Their parents told them whether or not to join, so that when my classmates were asked in class, they had their responses ready. Most joined, but I myself had no idea what to do, and naively told the teacher that I would speak to my mother.

Mother was furious, and for good reason. Here she was, a former political prisoner, put on the spot by her son! Of course she did not want me to join the Pioneers, but now she was unable to refuse the offer, lest this be interpreted as counter-revolutionary. I was told in no uncertain terms that from now on, when it was dangerous or impossible to ask Mother, I was to rely on my own resources. But since I had already drawn Mother into the picture, there was no choice now. My answer had to be in the affirmative.

The following day we were officially initiated into the Pioneers. We were subdivided into three groups, each of which was expected to conduct some activity. Each group was assigned a leader. When it came to the third group, mine, the teacher hesitated about whom to choose. Silence ensued, and then one of the pupils sitting in the front row whispered to the teacher, "Lederman." That settled it. The planned activities came to nothing. We either met once or not at all, and no mention was ever made of our "glorious" membership in the Pioneers during the rest of our stay in Kortkeros.

We were also divided into groups—teams is a better word —in the Universal Military Training (UMT) class. Now, too, there were three teams, but this time the entire class was included. Again, the instructor appointed two leaders without much difficulty, but appeared unsure of the third. But this time, before he even had a chance to look around, the entire class roared "Lederman!"—a response I never fail to be surprised by till this very day! As can be surmised from my rejection of the recess game, I was very far from being an active participant in the school's social life. In fact, I barely spoke to most of the pupils, and went home right after school. My only possible claim to fame was that I was the top student in the class, and the others had respect for scholarship—respect rarely found in public schools nowadays.

I appreciated school because it kept me occupied. Far worse was the long summer vacation during which there was almost nothing to do. I read the few books I could get my hands on, and performed all the tasks that had to be done in the house. Still, boredom was my companion most of the time. One of the ways I grappled with the daily boredom was by visiting my friend Reuven, whose mother had spent time in jail together with Mother. They lived on the far end of the town, which meant that visiting him had an additional advantage beyond socializing: I could kill an hour just coming and going, and even consider it time well spent. For some reason I never discovered, Reuven was usually not at home. Yet I always considered the trip worthwhile.

I soon discovered that occupying my time physically wasn't satisfying enough. I still needed to occupy my mind with something. The utter boredom drove me to start mentally compiling a mathematical table of numbers squared (up to a hundred). The results of these calculations stayed with me for many, many years—and even now I can recall almost instantly most of these figures.

GETTING USED TO EXILE

Not all the summers were a specter of unrelieved boredom. In the summer of 1943, when the general food supply became precarious, the authorities directed us to grow our own vegetables. There was no unused land in the town. Each householder had some land next to his house, which he cultivated for his own needs. On the other hand, there was more than enough land at the town's outskirts. So one Sunday we found ourselves walking to the outskirts of town to be assigned our own plots of land.

No work could be done on that Sunday because we were not told to bring tools along. Tools, like most other items, could not be purchased anyway, but had we known, we would have borrowed them from our landlord, which we indeed did the week after.

We came back the following Sunday and started working. Having seen Polish peasants tilling the soil by turning it over, the three of us could not bring ourselves to follow the previously explained Komi custom of digging trenches around the row to be seeded.

We worked until sundown, at which time the official in charge of this project came over to see what we had accomplished. He severely criticized our tilling technique, but even worse, he claimed that we had cultivated the wrong plot. According to him, our plot actually lay in another clearing farther away, past a row of trees. He warned us not to return to this plot again! Having no choice, we did exactly that. And in due time we had our own turnips and several other vegetables capable of growing during the relatively short, surprisingly warm, and very humid Komi summers. Unfortunately, we could not grow potatoes, our staple. The order to plant had come too late in the growing season, and, besides, we had no potatoes for planting. Our other vegetables grew from seeds, which were either distributed free or could be purchased in our store for next to nothing.

The manner of seeding was also typical of Komi conditions. Since seeds were practically free, they could be spread liberally all over the prepared plot. When they sprouted, a thick green lawn blanketed the entire area. We then removed the excess density to facilitate optimal growth. I don't know what other families did with the green matter they had thinned away, but Mother took it home to make her unique patties.

Incidentally, someone else subsequently cultivated the plot we first tilled, much to Mother's chagrin. The vegetables there grew as lushly as they did everywhere else, despite our having cultivated the soil the "wrong" way.

To my best recollection, this was the only time our superiors expressed any real concern over our sources of nourishment. Perhaps some higher-up had sent out instructions to have the Polish refugees cultivate their own vegetables. I infer this from the fact that for the preceding two years or so, no one had taken the slightest interest in how we managed to avoid starvation on the miserably insufficient official rations.

By that time Sunday was the entire Soviet Union's official day of rest.* Workshop employees had been told shortly after the outbreak of war that production would continue on Sundays as part of the war effort. At that time we had no idea whether this was a directive from above or something dreamt up by Comrade Mikhaylov, the workshop boss. Since tending our gardens cut into the shop's output, we concluded that the decision must have been dictated from above.

* * *

Picking mushrooms was another summer diversion that

---

* In an earlier period the Soviets had experimented with a six-day week, the sixth day being the day off. Although this was supposed to have been instituted for the benefit of the proletariat, it may well have been intended as still another way of weaning people, Jews in particular, away from religion.

busied us on occasion. The common wisdom was that these would be most easily found deep in the forest, since the forest's edge was presumed to have been picked clean already. Mother, however, reasoned that with everyone following this dictum and doing their mushroom hunting deep in the forest, no one actually picked the areas closer at hand. And she was right. We did our picking very close to the edge of the forest, and would daily bring back basketfuls of medium-sized, perfectly shaped, brownish, nourishing mushrooms.

Other staples ripe for picking in the summer were blackberries and blueberries. At times, we ate them with the cream skimmed off the milk, but usually all by themselves. Mother didn't make jam out of them even though we had some sugar. Apparently, she thought the berries were tasty enough by themselves. The little sugar in our possession found use as a spread for bread.

The problem of getting sufficient food was foremost in our minds throughout the year, but never more so than before Passover, when Jews do not eat bread or other leavened products. During our years in Russia, our most important concern was where to get enough potatoes to survive the eight days of the Holiday. Our bread ration proved to be the key: Mother would give her bread coupons to one of the non-Jewish ladies who would pick up our rations, and compensate us with some other commodity, most often potatoes.

One year, Mother decided that we must have matzah. For this purpose we saved some of our wheat supply, crushed the grains in our mortar, and baked matzah from the coarse flour. I do not know whether these conformed to all the *kashruth* specifications—after all, Mother was inexperienced in matzah production—but we tried our best. We kashered the stove by heating it up until the top metal plate grew red hot, and then we laid the rolled out dough on it. In this manner, we produced nine more or less edible matzos.

We did not use our *pechka,* the large heating furnace, to

bake the matzos. Actually the *pechka* did not operate properly, and thus was rarely used. Instead, we had a square stove made of bricks with a metal top, which was used both for heating the room and for cooking. It required much less wood than the *pechka*, and provided heat more efficiently.

Once, during the winter, this stove started smoking. We endured the smoke for at least a month before resigning ourselves to the necessity of climbing to the roof to check the chimney. It turned out that the brick chimney had fallen apart, with the bricks scattered all over the roof. No wonder our stove was malfunctioning! Now, in the middle of the bitter cold winter, we had to fix that chimney urgently.

But how? Repairmen were nonexistent in Komi—everyone was supposed to be proficient in fixing whatever equipment he used. Chimneys were no exception.

We had noticed long before that nights in Komi were a bit warmer than days. During the day there might be some wind, adding to the wind-chill factor, but nights were always calm. We thus decided to attempt the repair job at night. Fortunately, we were blessed that no clouds obscured the full moon which shone that night.

Working together, Mother, Lea, and I fashioned a primitive ladder to facilitate our climb to the roof. We got hold of clay, boiled a large pot of water to prevent it from freezing, lifted the water and clay to the roof, mixed the clay, and rebuilt the chimney by putting the bricks back in place.

The night was clear and calm, and the view from the roof enchanting. The satisfaction of having completed the job raised our spirits, and left us one of our most enjoyable memories. When we descended and fired up the stove, not a trace of smoke appeared.

Not every job elicited such satisfaction. One of the things I disliked most was washing the floor. I was quite happy to haul water from the well to fill the water barrel—both summer and winter—but for some inexplicable reason I absolutely hated being at home when the floors were washed, even by someone other than myself. I used every excuse possible to be away during these occasions. Mother, on the other hand, disliked going to the well, even when absolutely necessary, but didn't mind washing the floor. In light of these proclivities, division of labor came about by mutual agreement.

Although I cannot claim to be an expert on Komi, the years I spent there did allow me to observe at close range this vast, barely populated, little known area of the world. The Autonomous Republic of Komi stretches from the Ural Mountains in the east to (very roughly) the 48th meridian in the west. Its northern border starts some distance from the Arctic Ocean and extends south for about 400-500 miles. The southern part of the republic is covered by thick forests beginning at the Arctic Circle that slowly yield to low-growing brush.

The native language is Komi. I have been told that it sounds somewhat like Lithuanian, but I have no way of gauging the accuracy of this comparison. In any event, the language is entirely different from Russian, being entirely non-Slavic.

The language itself is a paradox. On the one hand, the grammar is extremely complex. Nouns in Komi have sixteen (!) declensions. This, as compared with six in Russian, seven in Polish, something between four and six in German and French, and none in English. On the other hand, some very basic words simply do not exist, and had to be imported from Russian. Words such as "school", "country" and, less surprisingly, "airplane", are imports. Komi has its own native literature, part of which revolves around the tales of a national fool who would, for instance, discharge his duty as watchman of a town's doors by taking them off the hinges and guarding them in bulk.

The language of instruction in our school was Russian, while Komi was taught as a second language. Komi language and literature were obligatory—like all subjects, in fact. Although I spoke and read Komi rather well, I had no interest in acquiring an in-depth knowledge of the language, but as long as I attended elementary school, I had no way of wriggling out of it. An opportunity for release presented itself toward the middle of the first year of secondary school. By that time, a small group of Russian refugees who had fled from areas close to the battlefront had come and settled in Kortkeros. Some of them took over as teachers in the secondary school, and some of their children attended as well. These children were even less happy than I about learning Komi, since the language was entirely foreign to them. I, at least, could speak and read it fluently. Someone in the Russian group came up with the rationale that since Komi was not their native language, they should be exempted from studying it. For some inexplicable reason, the administration accepted their position. When I saw their success, I came forward and made the same claim, but for a different reason: I wanted to get out of these classes because they were extremely boring. I, too, was excused, but this left me with nothing to do during class time but pace the corridor. This proved to be equally boring, if not more so, but at least I had my way.

Secondary-school curriculum in Komi included all the subjects considered standard everywhere in Russia, such as language, literature, math, geography, history, life science and physical science. Of all the subjects that I studied there, literature made the deepest impression on me. Emphasis was placed on the Russian classics, the works of Pushkin, Lermontov, Turgenev, Nekrasov, and others whom I no longer remember. We also studied some modern writers, including, first and foremost, Mayakovsky, the poet of the Revolution, and Gorki and others. The poetry of the classical poets was the kind I liked, with rhyme and rhythm, and everything in place. Mayakovsky was different. He wrote blank verse, but created a rhythm so powerful and unique that I was willing to forgive him—and only him—for his lack of rhyme. I liked Pushkin's short poems, but felt bored by his longer works such as *Ruslan and Ludmila* (except for the lovely opening paragraph) and others. It would only be decades later, in the Russian department of the Fifth Avenue branch of the New York Public Library, that I would discover that the works we were taught in Komi had been tampered with to conform to the Socialist line.

The UMT instruction which had begun in elementary school continued on into secondary school. Now we were actually given full-size army rifles (rendered inoperable) to disassemble, clean, grease, and reassemble. Once, we were also taken for target practice and given special target rifles for this purpose. I was an extremely poor marksman, but my instructor generously gave me the top mark for UMT so as not to spoil my overall record. We were brought up to date about chemical warfare, and shown mockups of gas masks and the like.

Our teachers spared us some of the more extreme praises of Comrade Stalin, the common fare of school children for many years. I never heard of his being endowed with the power to cause the sun to shine, the tides to rise and fall, etc., as did others. We *were* told, of course, that he was the smartest and most talented person who ever lived; that he was concerned with every event, big or small, that happened in the country; that he was Justice and Concern personified, as well as the possessor of many other superhuman qualities which I no longer remember. We knew all about our Great Father in the Kremlin from history books and numerous song lyrics. With this heavy reinforcement all around us, our teachers did not need to exert themselves in describing this great personality to us.

Strange as it may sound, no one saw—or perhaps no one permitted himself to see—that the benevolent, shining personality of our great leader stood in stark contrast to the heavy atmosphere of fear and paranoia that pervaded the entire

Soviet Union. For those who have not experienced life in an oppressive regime, it is hard to imagine how lack of freedom affects everyday life.

One small, yet telling, vignette stands out vividly in my mind. I stood in line once with a group of people waiting for a store to open (a favorite Soviet national pastime). This group included two women who apparently knew each other well. One of them was a sled driver who had just come back from a long out-of-town trip. As usual, the entire group on line waited in complete silence. All of a sudden, the sled driver turned to her friend and said, "Believe it or not, I haven't seen you since last year."

I was shocked. What? Someone speaking to another person in public? It was unheard of!

I wasn't the only person to be shocked. The other woman didn't even answer her erstwhile friend. As for the rest of the crowd, they all continued to stare in stony silence at the woman who had dared to speak in public.

An even rarer instance of speaking one's mind occurred in our secondary school, where some of the teachers hailed from parts of Russia more intellectually advanced than Komi. Apparently Stalin had committed some act of extraordinary cruelty. How this information reached the public, I have no idea. It might have been conveyed by the papers as something done "by our Great Father [sic] for the glory of the Homeland," or perhaps made its way through the grapevine. Normally, such an event elicited absolutely no public reaction, for fear of even worse repercussions.

But this incident was apparently too much for our Russians, and one of the teachers voiced her opinion about it in the teachers' room. She was apparently joined by other like-minded individuals, and vociferously opposed by yet others. The discussion heated up, and the volume of voices rose to a feverish pitch—at which point some of the students put their ears to the door of the teachers' room. Once I realized the

gravity of what had happened, I was positive that the "criminals" would be caught any moment and hauled straight away
to a labor camp. Much to my surprise, no one informed on
them, and there were no visible consequences—something
normally unheard of.

As I mentioned, although most of the secondary school
staff were women, we did have some male teachers, one of
whom was a Russian refugee. This poor fellow was extremely
undernourished—and looked it. He must have come without
family or, even more likely, was not resourceful enough to
find enough to eat in his new environment. One day in class
I was shocked to hear him deviate from the lecture topic and
instead discuss fishing with some of the boys in the class. He
was obviously intent on picking up good fishing tips in order
to secure himself some food. To me, diligent pupil that I was,
devoting classroom time to anything other than studies was
blasphemous.

But not only my teacher was preoccupied with warding off
hunger pangs. A frightening rumor began to make the rounds
in our town that someone in another town had killed a person
for food. No one wanted to believe it—until the hard facts
came in. A Russian refugee engineer had killed a bookkeeper
in his place of work, and eaten him. A trial was held, and the
court handed down a death sentence. The trauma of this event
stayed with us for a long time, lingering in the back of our
minds when we were hungry, which was nearly always.

Hunger was an ever-present companion during our entire
stay in Komi. Despite all of Mother's efforts to get us as much
food as possible, we were constantly famished. I was older and
able to take the suffering philosophically. Not so Lea. One
night, when she couldn't fall asleep because of hunger pangs,
she started crying bitterly and woke Mother. Mother tried to
calm her by reminding her that in the morning, the bread
ration would be picked up and then she could eat. But Lea just
went on crying, and was soon joined by Mother, who could no

longer stand her daughter's suffering. In an act of maturity beyond her years, Lea finally realized that she was causing Mother unbearable pain, and stopped crying, saying, "Mother, I was just joking. I am all right and not at all hungry." Mother hugged her and cried some more, until they fell asleep in each other's arms.

Even bread took on the proportions of a fantasy. On her eighth birthday Lea was asked to make a wish. Her wish was that her next birthday be celebrated with a large loaf of bread, which could be sliced an infinite number of times! "There will also be herring," she said, "and we will eat as much as we want and will still have some leftovers."

In fact, from the time we moved to Kortkeros, Mother fasted every Monday and Thursday in the time-honored tradition of pious Jews. She had, of course, another motivation for this: whatever she didn't eat, she could give to us. She left herself one half of her daily ration—200 grams, slightly less than half a pound—to consume in the evening after her fast, and gave the rest to us.

ENTERTAINMENT, KOMI STYLE

One nice winter day we were treated to the sight of a truck—a vehicle most Komis knew only from pictures—making its way down the only street in town. This particular winter the snow had fallen in a bizarre pattern, turning the main street into a series of alternating peaks and valleys flanked at both sides by piles of soft snow. The poor truck driver, probably an out-of-towner with no feel for the width of the frozen street, had only advanced a couple of feet before one of the truck's wheels slipped off the beaten path into a snow drift. Most likely, the chassis was only as wide as the sled-hardened passage, which made it difficult or perhaps impossible to stay on course.

The truck, moreover, ran on self-generated gas. It was during the most difficult years of the war when fuel could not be spared for civilian use. Instead, fuel came from a reactor, a large vertical, cylindrical vessel filled with finely chopped birch wood. Once the wood was ignited, it burned slowly, producing a gas that was fed to the engine. This arrangement compounded the truck driver's problems. When the truck tilted at a certain angle, the relative position of the fire and the wood shifted, and the gas generation process stopped. Restarting the whole thing was a project of its own.

It took the poor driver a full day to negotiate a small stretch of the street. What fate eventually befell the truck, we never found out—because by late afternoon we had gone home.

The road situation being what it was, it was not surprising that cars were nowhere to be seen. The highest official in town had a horse—and he was the only one. I still remember this beautiful huge stallion as it was put through its paces (at a gallop) up and down our main street. Since the rider was a boy of school age, I often wondered how he managed to get out of school to exercise the horse at all hours of the day.

There was other Komi-style entertainment available besides watching a truck sink in the snow. The town had a communal hall where, from time to time, movies were shown. Since there was no electricity in Kortkeros, the movie projecting team would arrive with its own generator. The films were long enough to warrant an intermission, during which the hall was illuminated by a single electric bulb hanging from the ceiling.

We were shown Westerns, with dubbed-in subtitles, or Russian patriotic films. One that stands out in my mind was about the war between Russia and Finland. According to Soviet propaganda the Finns attacked the peaceful and friendly Soviet Union one fine day—without any reason or warning. The brave Red Army took up the challenge and, although the fighting was quite fierce, achieved victory. As a result, part of Finland was annexed to the Soviet Union, by popular demand of none other than the Finns themselves. And thus a new autonomous region—the Karelo-Finnish Republic—was created.

I knew the story from school, and didn't need the movie to fill me in on the details. But after seeing the film, I couldn't help but wonder how a country as small as Finland had the nerve to take on a giant like the Soviet Union.

I also wondered about some of the songs we had been taught. They called upon the citizenry to be on the lookout for foreigners, specifically Japanese, who might get the notion that attacking the Soviet Union was a good idea. It seemed very strange to me that a peaceful and benevolent country like the Soviet Union, concerned only with its citizens' welfare, should have so many potential enemies.

As for the songs, no matter what one's opinion of the lyrics, the melodies were beautiful. The music was written by the country's foremost composers. The lyrics were also resplendent, although at times it was hard to believe that the bountiful life they described had anything to do with reality. I kept in mind, though, that we were in the middle of a war and that, quite likely, before the war things must have been different. There was no way for me to confirm whether or not the descriptions portrayed by the lyrics were true, since any questions in that direction would have been met, at best, with stony silence.

The Soviet national anthem—at the time, the *Internationale* —turned out to be problematic for even the Soviet Union. The elevation of this song to the status of national anthem was tantamount to asserting that the Soviet Union was the spiritual father of all movements, all over the world, which sought to forcefully overthrow regimes that "oppress their workers." Then one day it was announced that "in order to dispel any misunderstandings, the Supreme Soviet had decided to relegate the *Internationale* to being the anthem of its Communist Party, as is the custom everywhere in the world; it will henceforth cease to be the national anthem of the Soviet Union." It was rumored that this was one of the concessions made by the Soviets to the Allies in exchange for their aid in the Russian war effort. The Soviets were desperate to implement the lend-lease plan, under which thousands of tons of equipment were to be supplied to the Soviet army. They also wanted the Allies to conduct the war in Europe in a manner that would lift as much of the load as possible from the extremely hard-pressed Soviet armed forces.

This left the Soviet Union without a national anthem. The problem was remedied by taking the music from the Communist party anthem and supplying it with new lyrics.

Somewhat later, the reputations of Czarist generals were "rehabilitated." Prior to the war, they had been depicted as lackeys of the Czar, who aided him in maintaining his cruel dictatorship over the Russian people. Suddenly, they were elevated to the status of national heroes valiantly protecting Mother Russia from foreign invasion. One could detect an undercurrent of "they-should-have-known-better, they-should-have-overthrown-the-Czar," but the main emphasis was very positive. Names like Suvorov, Kutuzov and others—previously unmentionable—started appearing here and there. Soon, even battlefield medals were named after them.

A related change could be observed during this period, this one in the insignia of Soviet officers. When we first met Soviet military personnel in 1939, they had no epaulets, these being deemed a strictly capitalist invention. Instead, the officers wore on their uniform lapels ruby-colored insignia in various shapes (triangular, square, and a five-pointed-star), to indicate their rank. Now, it was announced that "in order to improve visibility on the battlefield," these insignia were to be replaced by epaulets "as is customary in most of the world's armed forces." Again, this was attributed to a demand by the Allies to downplay the proletarian image of the Soviet armed forces.

As a further step in seeking Western assistance, the Soviet Union established diplomatic relations, some time in 1941 or 1942, with the highly rightist Polish government-in-exile located in London.

Soon after this breakthrough, the Polish government-in-exile set up committees all over the Soviet Union to offer assistance to the Polish refugees. A committee was also established in our area, and one of its functions was the distribution of clothing. Indeed, the committee received a sizable shipment of British army uniforms and blankets for this purpose. The people in charge, however, had no intention of dividing the clothing fairly, and instead distributed most of it to their cronies. I remember going with Mother one day to apply for an allocation. We were given one or two items, and told that there was no more. Just that second a man came out of an adjacent room, all fitted out from top to bottom, starting with a beret and ending with a pair of sturdy army shoes. The head of the committee turned to Mother and tried to gloss over the obvious by saying, "Do you see how nicely we have outfitted

Captain (his rank in the pre-war Polish army) So-and-So?" There was nothing that could be said, so we picked up whatever we had been given and walked out.

Two other items distributed by the committee were powdered milk and a "specially prepared nourishing formula." Powdered milk was distributed only to families with children (at least officially). For this reason, Fishel Finkelstein, mentioned above, had not been eligible—so he received some from Mother.

The "nourishing formula" is a story in itself. It was produced in the United States by a concern that represented it as a complete food containing all the nourishment needed by the average person. It consisted, as far as I can remember, mainly of ground peas with some spices and flavorings, and was supposed to be cooked in water. The taste, to put it mildly, was nothing special. Years later I read that the entire project was a scam.

RELOCATED AGAIN

The committees set up by the Polish government-in-exile had at least one task far more important than distributing commodities: they were in charge of issuing identity papers and travel permits to Polish citizens who had a valid reason for moving from their current place of residence.

This arrangement was part of a much wider agreement negotiated by the above-mentioned Polish government, according to which the Soviets agreed to release Polish citizens imprisoned on political grounds, or on charges with political overtones. This applied primarily to people incarcerated in places like the notorious Vorkuta labor camp. Upon their release, they were automatically issued personal documents and travel papers which enabled them to travel to another location within the Soviet Union.

A travel permit was needed because the civilian railroad facilities provided by the Soviet government, inefficient even in peacetime, was severely restricted now that it was harnessed to the war effort. Since rail travel was (and still is) the primary means of transportation, not only in Russia, but throughout Europe, this meant that one could not travel a significant distance without official documents. (Even in the wealthy United States, travel was curtailed during the war, as evidenced by the famous slogan "Is this trip necessary?")

This created something of a paradox for us. Unlike the labor camp inmates, we were not prisoners, and therefore neither travel passes nor personal identity papers were automatically issued to us. The issuance of these documents was left to the questionable discretion of the local Polish committees, and no mechanism existed for appealing their decisions.

Father, like the other Polish citizens, was released from his labor camp, and took the first available train to the south of the Soviet Union. He set his sights on Tashkent, one of the major cities of the Uzbek Republic. The climate in Tashkent (and elsewhere in the Uzbek Republic) was considerably milder, living conditions were much better, and a large native Jewish community resided there. Not surprisingly, everyone allowed to leave Komi was heading for Tashkent. Although Father did not have our address, he knew we lived somewhere in Komi. When the new changes in status for Polish citizens came into effect, Father logically assumed that we were among those permitted to leave Komi. He was certain we would make our way to one of the southern "cities of refuge," and hoped to locate us there.

Alas, the fate he imagined for us was not to be. Mother's application for the necessary papers was turned down by the committee. The man in charge told her frankly that if she were to leave, he would be left with only provincials, a term applied to anyone who did not hail from a big city and who were regarded as inferior by big-city dwellers.

I argued with Mother that his decision was grossly unjust,

Postcard written by Mother to Father when he was still in Russia.

and that we should not allow ourselves to be made into pawns of this committee head, the very same person who had so heartlessly refused to issue us even one extra article of clothing. I also claimed that his statement had no basis in fact because we were not a part of his (as a matter of fact, of any) social circle and our presence or lack of it had no meaning to him. Mother, however, having experienced the terrors of being a political prisoner, was too frightened to oppose any official openly, or even to ask the committee head to reconsider. She felt she had no choice but to give up the idea of leaving Komi under the privileged status conferred by the Polish government-in-exile in London.

Father remained unaware of our plight. While our hopes of leaving Kortkeros were dashed, he was traveling farther and farther south, buoyed by the hope of being reunited with his family. As Providence had it, just before arriving at his final destination he met someone who gave him a full report of our

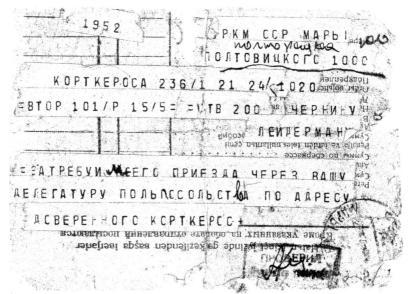

Telegram sent by us to Father asking that he demand that we be allowed to join him in southern USSR.

frustrating situation. Father was faced with a dilemma. Although the logical thing to do would have been to travel to Komi to meet us, this could not be done: his traveling papers were "one way" only. He therefore continued on to Tashkent to try to see what could be done for us from there.

The travel pass, issued to Father by the NKVD office at the time he held an official Soviet Government position. The pass specifies the locations from which and to which he was allowed to travel. A careful examination of the document reveals that the Russian words i obratno, meaning "and back," have been crossed out.

When he finally arrived in Tashkent, he discovered to his chagrin that there was very little he could accomplish for us. With no other real options, he reluctantly decided to stay there, and hope for the best. Within a short time he was appointed as regional food distribution administrator, a post he held until, later on, he joined the Polish Army.

All along, the Soviet government had treated us as foreign citizens. As a result, the few men still left among us had not been drafted. The same applied to the droves of men who were now released from labor camps. The Soviets, however, needed fighting men and were hence happy to allow the Polish government to establish its own fighting force, which would bolster the Soviet army on the European front. A large number of Polish citizens joined their new national army, which immediately started training for war.

Father was one of those who enlisted. He did this on the assumption that as a serviceman, he would have a better opportunity to reunite the family. For a Jew, joining the Anders Army (so named after its commander-in-chief) was not a simple matter. This army, from the top command down to the bulk of the privates, was composed of rightist Poles, many of whom were violently anti-Semitic. They used every possible pretext to avoid accepting Jews into their ranks. Yet Father was not one to be pushed around easily and he also knew how

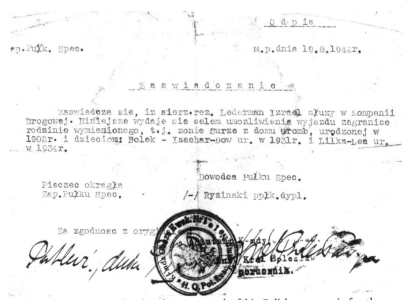

Document issued to Father by the command of his Polish army unit for the purpose of getting us out of Russia.

Father's traveling orders, issued by the Polish Army Command in Iran, that allowed him to travel to Palestine.

to make himself useful. Soon enough, he joined the army with the rank of staff sergeant.

This idyll of cooperation between the leftist Soviet government and the extremely rightist Polish government in London was short-lived. Disagreements arose, and for reasons better known to historians, it was not long before the Soviets allowed the entire Anders Army to leave the USSR for Iran. This departure also signaled a break with the previous, reactionary, capitalist government-in-exile. The Soviets didn't lose time. They immediately proceeded to set up a Polish puppet government, comprised of leftist Polish refugees, which they henceforth regarded as our sole representatives.[*]

---

[*] The original Polish government-in-exile, based in London, consisted of government officials and army officers who had somehow managed to get out of Poland at the start of the war in 1939. Poland thus now had two govern-

Father left with his unit for Iran. He felt that he would be able to do more for us in the free world than from within the Soviet Union where, should he decide to stay after the Polish army left, he would revert to being a plain, ordinary Polish citizen. In particular, he hoped that he would be able to make his way to Palestine and re-activate the "capitalist visa" which he had obtained before the war and enable us to immigrate. Immediately upon arrival in Iran, he set about finding ways of getting to Palestine. Within a short time he managed to get traveling papers to Palestine from his army unit stating that he was traveling on army business.

Upon reaching Tel Aviv, Father immediately set about trying to bring us over. But because Mother was afraid to write that we were prevented by a Polish bureaucrat from leaving Komi (all letters were censored), Father assumed that we were being held back by the Russian authorities. Reasoning

Postcard written by Lea to Father when he was already in Palestine. It was considered safer for a child write to a parent living in a capitalist country than for a wife to write to her husband.

ments-in-exile.

that his standing as a serviceman would help get us out, he dispatched several letters to the Polish authorities in Tel Aviv, asking for their assistance in the matter.

I have no idea whether and when he learned that all his efforts were in vain. Since the Russians had installed their own people as the government-in-exile around that time, they were no longer responsive to requests coming from the Tel Aviv representatives of the capitalist Polish government. To add to his inability to help us, at a subsequent date Father was induced to desert the Polish Army and join the Jewish underground in Israel. This immediately rendered him a "non-person" in the eyes of the Polish and British Mandatory authorities.

Although World War II continued to rage as our personal saga unfolded, Mother, Lea and I never knew what was actually going on. Amazingly, newspapers were delivered, weather permitting, by a light plane that dropped them once a week on an island in the Vychegda River right near our town. They arrived a week or two late and carried standard stories about the brave forces that performed the necessary maneuvers, moved to pre-planned positions, and so forth. Even if more concrete facts had been reported, we would not have believed them, as we had good reason not to believe any official information.

The papers were full of complaints against the Allies, who had supposedly promised to open a second front in Europe, but had failed to do so. After a while, we were informed that they had indeed opened a second front, although what specific military act by the Allies constituted this second front remained a mystery. At any rate, the government-employed journalists appeared to be satisfied.

We knew next to nothing about the war with Japan. We were never told about Pearl Harbor. The only information brought to our attention was that the Japanese had attacked the Americans, and that the latter were fighting back. It was

Sierżant
Lederman Israel-Izchok
M.E. 15.

M. P. 8.9.-43 r.

Do
Ekspozytury Delegatury
Min. Rob. i Op. Społ.
Tel-Aviv
poprzez Komendę Placu

Prośba

Rodzina moja, składająca się z nast. osób:
żony, Lederman Sura lat 40, imię i nazw. ojca Wigdor Gromb
dzieci: syn Lederman Berys-Izachardów lat 12, Israel-Izchok Lederm.
. córki Lederman Lea lat 9 . . . . . .
— urodzona i zamieszkała w Warszawie, wywieziona została pod władze
sowieckie z Białegostoku, gdzie czasowo zamieszkiwała, do
Komi A.S.S.R. Syktywkarska Oblast, sjeło Korzkieros
gdzie zamieszkała przy ulicy Pierwomajskaja 252.
Żona moja na tym „posiołku" została w swoim czasie
zaaresztowana i skazana za działalność patrjotyczną, skazana
na długoletnie więzienie, a dzięki amnestji w myśl umowy
polsko-sowieckiej zwolniona. Otrzymałem telegram przed
paroma dniami, że znajduje się jeszcze w Korzkierosie.
Bardzo proszę o łaskawe umożliwienie mojej rodzinie
przyjazdu w razie ewakuacji najbliższym transportem,
roztoczenie opieki i udzielenie zapomogi.

KOMENDA PLACU
TEL-AVIV

Sierżant

Letter written by Father to the Polish Army Command in Tel Aviv asking
for assistance in getting us out of the Soviet Union.

all presented as quite secondary and minor, with a significance conferred upon it to the proportion of the Falkland Islands affair as compared with WW II.

The fortunes of war turned sometime in 1943, and toward the end of the winter of 1944 there were persistent rumors that the leftist Polish government-in-exile had succeeded in arranging for our relocation to some place in the southern part of the Soviet Union. Such rumors had also circulated in the previous year. We did not lend the new rumors any more credence than we had lent the old. In the end, though, they turned out to be true. As ice broke on the Vychegda and navigation became possible, we were informed that, by agreement with the Polish government-in-exile, we were to be moved to a new location where conditions would be better than in Komi.

The big day finally arrived. A huge, paddle-wheel river boat arrived for us at the Kortkeros mooring. This time it was much easier to transport our baggage. First, the town of Kortkeros was located at the river bank. Second, our baggage was a far cry from what it had been when we entered Komi. We still had our down quilts and some other items, but by now all of the men's suits, including those acquired from the German refugee as an act of charity, as well as most other items of value, had been sold. This, in addition to the forty percent of our goods that were "lawfully" stolen.

This time each family was assigned its own cabin and there were enough cabins for everyone. The comfort of the cabins was nothing out of the ordinary, but we were on our way to a better place, a destination that could only be to the south of Komi. At the very least, the climate would be more bearable.

We again traveled on the Vychegda, but this time we went downstream. I fully expected us to disembark at Kotlas, just as we had on the way up four years earlier. I did not know that in the meantime, as a part of the war effort, railroad tracks had been laid to Vorkuta (with a spur to Syktyvkar). This meant that we were now much closer to the rails than when we came. Accordingly, we disembarked at a different spot, where railroad transportation awaited us.

The trains looked almost the same as the ones that had brought us to Komi. They were average-size freight cars, now with the middle berth missing, and more significantly, the doors left open at all times, and no guards in sight. I no longer remember how we were supplied with food, but apparently we were no worse off than we had been in Komi. Rumor had it that we were heading for a part of Russia previously occupied by the Germans and now liberated. We traveled, in time-honored fashion, as low-priority cargo, stopping frequently at minor stations along the way to allow more important trains to pass. As usual, piping-hot water was available at these stops, but nothing else.

During these still frequent stops we would usually leave the cars to stretch our legs. Here I noticed a new sight: a new breed of steam locomotives. Because of the urgent need to supply goods to a fighting army numbering in the millions, Soviet industry had been spurred into efforts unheard of during peacetime. The traditional huge, hundred-boxcar-long trains needed to travel fast, much faster than the pre-war locomotives could pull them. To solve this problem, the existing machines were scaled up.

It was a young boy's delight to stand next to *his* train, put his ears to the tracks and listen to the music of an approaching train. Soon it was time to move aside as a strange, huge silhouette appeared on the horizon. It did not take long for even the longest train to come into full view because it was pulled by a two-story steam locomotive. Its huge wheels, taller than a full-grown adult, seemed to float along the rails, pulling a snake of cars at breathtaking speed, and disappearing from view before one could take in the sight. There were three types of such locomotives, differing mainly in size; the most powerful one being named *IS*, for Iosif Stalin.

An IS locomotive.

It took us approximately two weeks to reach our destination. As we moved southward, the late-spring weather became increasingly more bearable—not much different from what I remembered of Poland. The trip proved relatively uneventful, except for the day that we were switched around through sidings at a huge freight yard. The train was moving slowly when all of a sudden we found ourselves traveling past a virtual mountain of sunflower seeds. A cry went out: "Pails, pails, whoever has a pail come to the car doors!" But by the time these materialized, the seeds were out of reach. Fortunately, though, on the next switching pass the train traveled along a different face of the same mountain, and pails upon pails of these seeds found their way into our car (and I presume into others as well). Since this was Soviet government property, appropriating such was not regarded as stealing but as repayment for years of forced labor.

Part of our group, including my family, was instructed to detrain at the fairly large station of Rossosh. This was a central railroad terminal, through which all trains traveling to or from Voronezh, a major Russian city located about one hundred and thirty miles northwest of Stalingrad, not far from the Ukraine, had to pass. (Prior to its being named after Stalin, Stalingrad was know as Tsaritsin, "the Czar's city." After Stalin fell into disgrace, the city was renamed Volgograd.)

We got off our train at a distant siding, next to a set of narrow-gauge railroad tracks. Soon a small locomotive, pulling a short train of equally small boxcars and a lone passenger car, pulled into view. As usual, those who traveled light had a head start on us and took seats in the passenger car. The rest of us had to settle for the standard comfort of the boxcars. The locomotive, which looked more like an oversized spring-driven toy, didn't appear as if it could pull us to anywhere. We did not in fact travel at a decent speed; yet, after an hour or two we arrived at our new residence, a town called Olkhovatka, about fifteen miles (twenty-five kilometers) from Rossosh.

The locomotive stopped in front of a closed gate, and we were told to get off and move into our living quarters. These were located a short walk from the train station in a four-story red-brick edifice—the only multi-story residential building in town. Like all the other dwellings, it had no electricity and no running water. Toilet facilities were nothing more than several outhouses in what was euphemistically called the "backyard." For a while, we shared a room with another family. When they moved out, we had the room to ourselves. It had a single window, and a stove similar to the one we used in Komi. In Komi, however, we could fell enough trees to build up a supply of firewood, but there were no forests around Olkhovatka.

We encountered a more significant difference with regard to the refugee population. First, we had some families who had not been with us before; second, we were now put together with Catholic Poles, known for their enmity to Jews. Throughout our stay in Olkhovatka we maintained correct relations with them, but we kept our distance from them, except in school.

In Olkhovatka a more comfortable existence began for us. The weather was much milder than in Komi, there were no swamps and mosquitoes, and (except for the lack of firewood) survival proved somewhat easier.

OLKHOVATKA

Olkhovatka was a small town, roughly the size of Kort-keros, but its buildings were arranged in a square pattern rather than being strung out along a single main street. The whitewashed houses resembled one another, but I was never able to determine of which material they were constructed. Most of the residents not employed in agriculture or in one of the few service industries, worked at the sugar refinery, or "factory" as it was called. As a matter of fact, there were two such refineries—an old one and a new one. The old one was housed in a large and ornate multi-storied building of gray and white bricks. Its huge chimney, built of the same bricks, dominated the view. The new refinery was a complex of one- and two-story buildings, built of drab red bricks (as are all factories and jails in Europe and most buildings in New York City) with a much shorter and less impressive chimney. The new refinery, however, lay empty. Apparently, the machinery was just about to be started up when Axis (actually, Italian) occupation became imminent. The equipment was hurriedly loaded onto a train and shipped to Siberia, which was thought to be out of reach of the Axis forces.

The old refinery produced sugar from beets. These were hauled in by the narrow-gauge railroad by which we had arrived, as was the coal needed to fuel the furnaces. The refinery's output, granulated sugar, was shipped out in boxcars by the same railroad. As matter of fact, this railroad was built expressly (probably before the Revolution) to serve the refinery. This train also carried paying passengers. At the time we arrived in Olkhovatka, they still enjoyed the luxury of sitting on wooden benches lining the walls of the lone passenger car. Later, the car traveled with locked doors, and still later, it vanished entirely. After this, those who traveled did so either in the empty beet or coal flatcars that returned from the factory, or on top of the beets (depending on the direction of travel); or, when the train carried only coal, either in a graciously provided empty flatcar or on top of the coal.

The train would typically stop in front of the closed gate, actually part of the fence enclosing the entire refinery grounds, for passengers to disembark. Then the stationmaster would open the gate to admit the train. Together with an official in charge of weighing, he would walk down to the weighing shack, where the locomotive would pull the first car onto the scales. The weight would be recorded, together with the tare weight of the car. Then the stationmaster would signal with a flag by day or with a lantern by night, for the locomotive to move forward by a pre-measured distance. The operation was then repeated with the next car. The same procedure was applied to the departing trains carrying sugar. As always in the Soviet Union, "another destination" was the place where the finished product was shipped; nothing was left for local consumption.

In addition to sugar, the refinery produced two byproducts: molasses and beet residue. The molasses was stored in two huge cylindrical tanks over two stories high, located on the grounds; the beet residue, which consisted of chopped up, spent beets, was dumped from small dump carts into a cavernous pit also located not too far from the refinery building. Periodically, the beet residue was also shipped out—again, to another destination—as animal fodder. To load the residue, workers with pitchforks would form a human chain from inside the pit all the way out to the open-roofed boxcars. (It always seemed to me that there ought to be a better way of doing this than by unloading and re-loading.) The molasses was an exception—although most of it was also delivered, again elsewhere, in tanker cars, some did remain for local consumption.

I became quite familiar with all these details because, soon after we settled down, all refugees were assigned jobs in the sugar factory, primarily as unskilled workers. Mother, too, was put to work, but she landed a relatively plush job as a weighing official—one of three at the railroad station. Since the trains that passed by were not especially long—no more than three twenty-car trains a day, and sometimes only that many in a week—Mother had plenty of time to herself. She did have to stay in the station while on duty, but made good use of the time by knitting. As in Komi, the wool came from taking apart the remainder of Lea's woolen dresses, most of which had already met the same fate back in Komi. Like most other commodities, wool could not be purchased anywhere.

Considering our circumstances, the work-hours suited us perfectly. Mother's tour of duty was twenty-four hours at a stretch followed by forty-eight hours off. Sunday was not a day off at the railroad, but Mother couldn't have cared less. First and foremost, she had no Sabbath problems because the other two weighing officials were more than happy to switch their tours of duty with her in order to have Sunday off. Also important, the job gave her unlimited access to the factory grounds, which meant that in a short time she became friendly with all the guards on the premises.

The guards were women. They were armed with rifles left behind by the fleeing Italians. (Most probably these rifles had no ammunition in them.) They guarded all the strategic locations on the refinery grounds. Among these were the gates, which with the exception of the gate entered by the train were usually left open to let the workers in and out, and the pile of large-lump anthracite coal that was sifted specially for the small locomotive. (The refinery's pit-type furnace could burn coal of any size and shape, and actually thrived on coal dust, whereas the locomotive would run only on lump coal.) Periodically, a carload of coal would be delivered to a sifting site. There workers would toss the coal onto sieves, letting the smaller pieces and dust sift through to leave the lumps. The residue was transported to the refinery.

The station-house had two doors, one leading to the out-side, and the other to the refinery grounds. It also had a heating furnace, and, from time to time, Mother or the station-master would fill a pail with "locomotive coal" and bring it into the station. It didn't take long before an additional pail would make the same trip into the station. Then I would come, leave by the outside door, and carry the much-needed fuel home. This went on for several months before I was caught.

In order to avoid the guards at the gates, as well as the entire plant site, which was patrolled, there was only one route that I could take to our house with the precious pail of

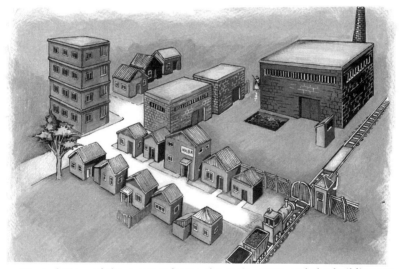

General view of the sugar refinery, the main street and the building we lived in while in Olkhovatka (the four-story building). The narrow-gage railroad, carrying coal and sugar beets is about to enter the refinery grounds after the stationmaster or the weightmaster unlocks the gate. The weighing platform and the booth where the scale is read are seen at right, in front of the old refinery building. An extra pail of coal made its way (with Mother's assistance) from the heap of locomotive coal (not visible) by way of a back door to the station house (at the right of the gate, also not seen). Then I would come in the evening, carry it out the front en-trance, along the main street (right past the NKVD building), to our one-room apartment.

fuel: through the main street. The walk was short, less than five minutes, but it took one directly past the NKVD (Secret Police) building. That's how it happened that late one evening, as I was strolling down the town's promenade with my life-saving loot, none other than the NKVD chief himself walked out into the street, apprehended me, coal and all, and ordered me inside.

Coal was available by only one means: stealing from the refinery grounds. There was no question but that I had been caught red-handed. The chief himself conducted the interrogation. I told him that a train had just rolled into town and that all I had done was collect a few lumps of coal that had fallen from it. I didn't for a minute expect him to believe my story, but I had to say something. He, of course, offered to take me for a stroll along the tracks to see if any more fallen coal could be found to corroborate my alibi. I innocently claimed that I had already picked up everything that had fallen. This was the end of the interrogation. He left me sitting in the NKVD headquarters and walked out.

Lea, who expected me home, became alarmed. She went to Mother, who had more or less guessed what had happened, but could do nothing about it. It turned out, though, that our NKVD chief also had a problem: I was only a minor; this was my first offense, and there was nothing political involved. Even more important (as I knew from the experiences of others), the authorities had orders not to arrest, imprison, or try foreign citizens unless the offense was sufficiently serious. So, at about two AM, I was released.

Mother was still on duty at the railroad station, and I went to her. I expected that after soothing me she would tell me to go home and get a good night's sleep. But she took a much more creative approach. Just as her intuition had told her that most people would pick mushrooms deep in the forest, leaving the ones closer by untouched, now, too, she demonstrated a keen understanding of human nature. In her opinion, no one in his right mind would expect me to make a repeat performance immediately after being caught. Therefore, this was the one night when I could consider myself perfectly safe.

She filled another pail with coal and wanted me to take it home, right past the NKVD building again! This was more than I could take. At the risk of being disobedient for the first time in my life, I told Mother that this was simply beyond me. Mother acquiesced, but could not bring herself to let this golden opportunity slip through her fingers. Accordingly, she got the guards to absent themselves from a gate at a location far from the station house intermittently for a quarter of an hour, and then for another quarter of an hour, during which I hauled four or six pails of coal to our house. After my run-in with the NKVD, I no longer carried the bucket of coal through the main street, but instead went out through one of the gates, which would be left unguarded for the critical fifteen minutes necessary to do so.

I have no idea what the others in our building did for fuel. The natives, however, had two sources of supply. One was the dung of their animals which, when mixed with straw and dried in the sun, was used to fuel their stoves. Their other source was the cinders left over from coal combusted by the refinery and the locomotives. Residents would enter the grounds with sieves, sift the cinders to find unburned coal particles, and leave after having their sacks inspected by the guards who made sure that only cinders were removed from the factory grounds.

* * *

Working at the railroad had other, albeit minor, advantages, such as free rail passage both for workers and their families. This was no great concession, because the line ran only to Rossosh, and tickets for the 16-mile (25-kilometer) trip cost next to nothing. Still, it gave one the feeling of being privileged.

In fact, there was a good reason to travel to Rossosh. Every

A map of Russia showing our route
from Bialystok to Komi (eastward),
from Komi to Olkhovtka (southward),
and from there to Poland (westward).

(see Chapter 10: Relocated Again,
Chapter 11: Olkhovatka, and
Chapter 12: The Return to Poland)

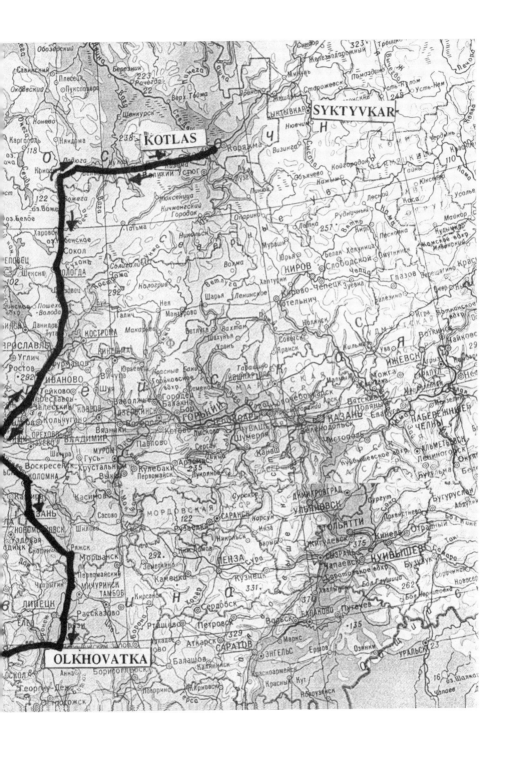

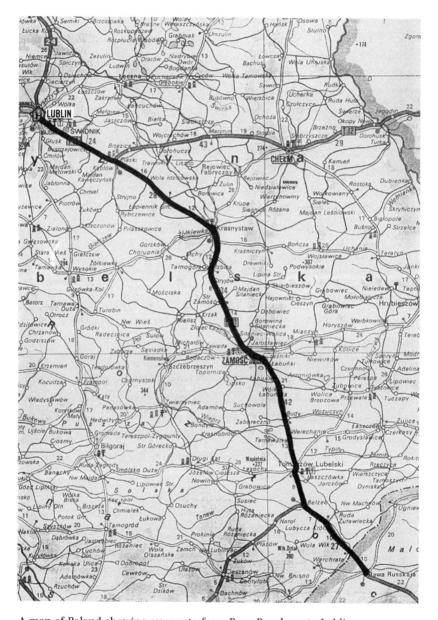

A map of Poland showing our route from Rava Russkaya to Lublin.

The Lublin Yeshiva.

A scene from the pre-war
Jewish quarter in Lodz.

Photograph courtesy of Beth Hatefutsot,
the Nahum Goldmann Museum of the
Jewish Diaspora, Tel Aviv, photo by
M. Raviv, Warsaw, provided by Marian Fuks

payday, refinery workers had the right to purchase a certain quantity of molasses for the official price of half a ruble per liter. At the time, molasses was selling on the Rossosh gray market for two rubles per glass. There being four to five glasses in a liter, this was a source of enormous profit, even if one had to pay a ruble per liter to buy someone else's allotment. The people in Rossosh would buy the molasses to produce bootleg vodka, known in Russian as *samogon* (loosely translated as "private label"). Inexplicably, although the NKVD was aware of the market, and even raided it periodically, most of the time it turned a blind eye to this illegal activity.

The distribution of molasses had another, quite fascinating, aspect. The refinery itself, like all other Soviet enterprises, had no cash of its own. It was supposed to put in the expected performance, for which it was supplied with the required raw material, while the State paid the workers' salaries. At times, however, the bi-weekly salaries were late in arriving. When this happened, the management would double the molasses allotment. This meant that workers could sell a larger-than-usual quantity of the commodity to get much-needed cash. In other words, most unconventionally, the refinery's management regarded workers as human beings with needs to be provided for—even if it entailed aiding an illegal trade. After living in the Soviet Union for four years, it was hard to believe: not only did the management treat us as human beings, but it even supplied us with a black market commodity to help us to earn some cash!

For some reason, very few of the locals engaged in this trade. Most of them were happy to give up their allotment in exchange for cash. We, the refugees, eagerly acted as middlemen. The logistics of this trade were not simple. One still had to show up at work in order to maintain whatever status he had. This rule was inviolate whether under the harsh conditions in Komi or under the much easier conditions in Olkhovatka. Consequently, the molasses trade could be conducted only during after-work hours or on days off.

The train schedule also caused problems. Everything usually ran smoothly on the Olkhovatka side. The trains would leave for Rossosh in the evening on schedule, arriving some time before ten PM (This meant that one had to find a place to stay overnight in Rossosh—no small feat). The goods were transferred in Rossosh to wide-gauge cars, and another load of raw materials (coal and beets) would be loaded onto them for the return trip to Olkhovatka. However, this transfer of goods frequently did not occur on schedule. Because the return trips were delayed, alternative means of transportation had to be found for getting back home from Rossosh. This was frequently impossible.

In any event, all these arrangements hinged on the extremely difficult maneuver of absenting oneself from work for a full day in the first place. These conditions narrowed the field of merchants to only the most enterprising, such as Mother. Mother also had no problem with getting back to work, since she regularly had forty-eight hours off.

Molasses was transported to market in sheet-metal jerrycans apparently left behind by the Italians, who had used them for gasoline. These were thoroughly washed so that no odor remained. In addition, their capacity was increased by filling them with water, closing the plug, and then heating them. Depending on the skill of the craftsman, a twenty-liter jerrycan could be blown up to twenty-five and sometimes even thirty liter capacity. After this treatment, though, the jerrycans acquired round "bellies," which, while adding to their capacity, made them difficult to carry. Mother was equal to the challenge: she simply slipped them into a sack to be carried on one's back.

People usually traveled to Rossosh with one or, at most, two jerrycans. For a while, we did too. (I usually accompanied Mother, who never thought of babying me.) Mother was convinced that we would need the money either while still in the USSR or later. Manual labor, however hard, was not something to be avoided. Eventually, Mother decided that it made no sense for two people to transport so little merchandise, at which point we became "wholesalers." We would travel to Rossosh first with four or five, and later, when proper arrangements could be made, ten or eleven jerrycans, each one weighing about sixty-six pounds.

We developed a regular routine for our new business. We would purchase molasses and store it in jerrycans in our house. When the day appointed for travel to Rossosh arrived, Mother and I would each slip a jerrycan into a sack, and take it down to the train tracks. Lea would accompany us on the first trip, and remain there to guard the containers. Mother and I would continue walking back and forth, carrying all of our wares to the tracks. By now the train would have emerged from the factory's gate and was ready to be boarded. There were usually several platform cars designated for carrying passengers the twenty-five kilometers to Rossosh.

Because Lea was too young for this type of "business trip," we had to leave her at home. Mother was sure that Lea understood the situation, and hence offered no explanation. Lea, however, took her exclusion very much to heart. She confided in her best friends, her rag dolls, that most probably Mother thought that she was bad, and hence did not take her along.

Not having Lea with us at Rossosh meant that we had no one to guard the jerrycans at the unloading end. When we started off in the molasses trade, Mother insisted that she carry the jerrycans into town one by one, while I stayed at the Rossosh railroad stations to guard the remaining ones. But I could not agree to this plan. We argued about it each time, with decreasing intensity on Mother's part because she knew very well that I would not let her do all the hard work.

The next problem to be solved was to find a place in Rossosh where we could stay, together with the molasses, till the next morning. As usual, Mother managed to cope. Somehow she found a lady in the town of Rossosh with whom we could store the molasses. I carried the jerrycans one by one to the lady's house, while Mother stayed at the station house to guard the remaining containers. When there were only two jerrycans left, we walked together to the house, each of us carrying one jerrycan. After a while, Mother found a lady who owned a hand-pulled two-wheeled cart, and then only three trips were needed.

Not wanting to risk being stopped while walking around with contraband, we would stay in the Rossosh station house until about midnight, when the town was fast asleep. Only then would I get up, pick up the sack with the jerrycan (or load the cart) and, with my heart pounding, walk out into the night.

I often felt that all of this was unreal. The solitary walk through the deserted streets of a strange town sometimes proved to be more than I could bear. I walked, as silently as I could, on the hard-packed soil of the streets of Rossosh, between rows of almost identical single-story whitewashed houses, a young boy alone in a moonlit world. From time to time, a dog started barking, filling my heart with fear. There seemed to be quite a few dogs in this town—what if some other dog, closer to me, were to wake up, smell a human being, and take off after me? Had this happened, I would have been at a loss as to what to do. Even worse, if enough dogs joined the fray, someone might wake up, look out the window, and call one of the town's NKVD agents. Even without the dogs, I could not discount the possibility that an NKVD agent might emerge from the shadows, and demand of me what on earth I was up to. If the NKVD were to detain me for even a few hours, Mother would have been devastated. Even if they had wanted to notify her, an unheard-of courtesy in such cases, they wouldn't know where to look for her. Later, when the two-wheeled cart became available, and I started ferrying a number of jerrycans on each trip, my fears were multiplied accordingly.

One may wonder how was it that we were able to openly load such quantities of molasses onto the train in Olkhovatka, yet fear being caught transporting them along the deserted streets of Rossosh. Looking back, I can only suggest the following explanation: Trade in molasses had long been a part of life around the local sugar refinery, and presumably not only in Olkhovatka. Furthermore, very little bootlegging apparently went on in our town—most of the activity being centered in Rossosh, for which our NKVD chief was grateful. On the other hand, the situation in Rossosh was just the opposite, and hence we feared that the local NKVD would be after us. And, of course, it is one thing to load jerrycans of molasses onto a train in broad daylight one by one, and another to transport them in bulk in the dead of the night.

The reader will notice that no policemen are mentioned here, only NKVD agents. This is because we simply encountered none—neither in Kortkeros nor in Olkhovatka. The NKVD, in contrast, were ever-present, primarily on the lookout for "enemies of the Motherland." Other small towns were probably no different, especially since actual crime must have been extremely limited during this time of war. Most of the able-bodied men had been drafted or otherwise displaced; and women did not, in those days, engage much in violent crime. (This phenomenon came considerably later in the century, at first in the West, with the advent of complete equality of women and the women's liberation movement.)

Before the cart joined our operation, it was very difficult for me to carry the jerrycans the mile or so to our final destination. So I devised a less taxing method: I would carry one of the cans from the railroad station to a half-way point, deposit it in the shadows of some house, and go back for another. When two or three jerrycans had been deposited, I would return to Mother and then we would both carry the remaining two jerrycans to our final destination, which was the shadows of Mother's "lady's" house. Then, with Mother staying there, I would go back to where I had hidden the initial batch of the jerrycans and carry them, one by one, to their destination.

At first, Mother opposed this procedure. She feared that someone would see me, and walk away with the jerrycans while I was making the trek back to the railroad station. I, however, was confident that no one would steal our merchandise. After all, we were operating in the middle of the night. One could leave anything anywhere without fear that it would be stolen. At this hour, everyone—including any thieves who may have resided there (and, as it turned out, the NKVD agents themselves)—were sleeping.

This tactic of leaving things unattended was actually something I came up with back in Kortkeros. There, after acquiring a desirable commodity like kerosene or butter from one of "Mother's ladies," I would leave the package in some shaded location, go on to another stop or errand, and then pick up the goods on my way back. Nothing was ever stolen.

By the time we were finished carrying the jerrycans to the house, dawn was breaking. We had to wait an hour or two before we could enter the house to store our merchandise, and then each of us would load a jerrycan on our back and carry it to the market place. Mother would stand there selling molasses, stuffing the rubles into the top pockets of her jacket while I wandered around, always on the lookout for a possible appearance of NKVD agents. Whenever this happened, and it did once or twice, we grabbed the jerrycans and ran. We never got caught.

A Jewish woman living in our town (who happened to be a full-fledged Russian citizen) did not fare as well. She supplemented her income by selling matches, a commodity then in short supply. Since the State held the monopoly on the manufacture and sale of matches, anyone selling them was simultaneously committing two unlawful acts: engaging in black-market merchandising and breaking the State monopoly. One day, as I was standing in the marketplace, the poor woman ran over to me saying that the NKVD was pursuing her. She asked me to please relieve her of the contraband. But just as I was about to do so, our own NKVD chief—that is, the one from Olkhovatka—appeared out of nowhere, gave me a knowing look, and took her away together with the supply of contraband matches.

* * *

Although Mother could stay in Rossosh a full day, it was not that easy to sell so large a quantity of molasses by selling it glass by glass (even if some of the customers purchased a relatively large quantity). At times, we were forced to leave some of it in storage, which neither Mother nor her local contact viewed as an ideal situation. To solve the problem, Mother decided to go wholesale. What was the most important use of molasses in the USSR? It wasn't cookies. She located someone with a still, who would take the bulk of the supply. This dramatically reduced the time spent standing in the market selling by the glass. It was also much safer, barring an NKVD raid on the distiller himself.

As I mentioned earlier, if the train was not on schedule, as often happened, getting back to Olkhovtka was a problem. First, one had to decide, after waiting in vain for a couple of hours, whether to continue waiting or to try some other means. This meant starting to walk along the road, which ran parallel to the rails but at least a mile away, in the hope that some passing wagon would offer one a ride. Sometimes this strategy worked, but by far not always.

Once Mother and I walked a good many foot-weary miles without anyone agreeing to pick us up. Then, after we had gone about half the distance, we discerned puffs of smoke appearing from behind a break in the hills. At first, we deluded ourselves with the thought that they came from the train headed to Rossosh, but soon enough a break in the hills permitted us a view of one of our familiar locomotives pulling the train *from* Rossosh home to Olkhovatka. If only we had waited!

As if this was not enough, yet another sight awaited us. The American lend-lease program was in full swing, and we were treated to a continuous parade of five-ton Studebaker army trucks traveling down the road—going our way. Their powerful headlights cut through the black of the night that had descended. We were miserable thinking of the comfort and speed that could have been ours if they had given us a lift. However, it was not to be.

I remember wondering what those army trucks were doing in our vicinity and whether it was not a violation of the lend-lease agreement that stipulated, or so I had read in the news-papers, that all equipment was supposed to be used for the war effort. We were certainly nowhere near the front.

Several times I had to travel to Rossosh alone. The open, platform-type railroad cars that usually served travelers made these trips especially difficult during the winter. At least when I traveled with Mother the two of us could huddle together against the bitter cold. I must acknowledge, though, that since everyone on the railroad knew Mother, I was given the run of the train on these solo journeys. Once, I used my privileged status to station myself on the walkway surrounding the locomotive, hoping to warm myself against its boiler. I soon discovered, however, that the boiler was rather well insulated. To add to my disappointment, I had to contend with the wind, since I lacked whatever limited protection was afforded by the walls of the open-roofed platform cars. Needless to say, I never tried that stunt again.

The money we earned put us in a comfortable position by local standards. Fortunately, Olkhovatka was not Kortkeros, and the end of 1944 was much different from our time in Komi. Indeed, when we arrived in Olkhovatka, there was a local Sunday market where one could buy milk, butter, eggs, and fruit. (The live poultry was of no use to us since our group lacked a ritual slaughterer.) For some reason, that market did not last long. Rossosh, however, where we sold our molasses, had a sizable market. It was a pleasure to count the money earned from our sales, and then walk down to the market and buy whatever we needed. Of course, it took a couple of months from the time we first arrived until we could afford this kind of shopping trip, and in the interim, we had to sustain ourselves on the daily bread allowance and corn meal. But once our income was established, we lived well.

Mother used to bake a couple of cakes every day, and would buy several liters of milk—we barely ate anything other than cake washed down with milk. Mother, being a city-bred lady, had never baked her own bread in her life, and bakery bread was still rationed. We would buy our ration every day, in order not to be conspicuous, but we either sold it or gave it away. At about this time we somehow obtained use of a small room on the ground floor of our building. Mother turned it into our own private "bakery." The room's wide, open shelves on one wall were lined with an assortment of cakes, which we would consume at mealtimes and at other times. All of Mother's cakes were delicious, but my favorites were her apple pie and her special corn-flour cake.

To be truly delicious, cake requires sugar, but this commodity could not be purchased on the open market. The refinery workers would not even try to pilfer it, since whatever bags they carried with them on the way home were carefully checked. To circumvent this inspection, a curious custom developed. People would come up to the storeroom foreman with pots or bowls of cooked fruit and ask him to sweeten it. They would ask the foreman (euphemistically) to "salt it please." And he would obligingly add a heaping measure of sugar to the compote. This clever solution worked for most people, but not for Mother, who wanted dry sugar for baking. Most likely Mother slipped him something or other from time to time, for the foreman did not mind pouring sugar into the cloth bags she brought. All that mattered to him was that she not be caught, since this would implicate him.

There were no body searches, though, upon leaving the refinery. As a matter of fact, there were no searches at all when leaving the refinery, except for a quick glance from the guard at the door, and the search through bags carried out the main gate. Accordingly, Mother would walk in wearing Father's woolen coat whose pockets, particularly the inner ones, could hold quite a bit of sugar without bulging. The sugar was "packaged" in white-cloth bags, specially sewn by Mother for this purpose. She would then walk through the factory grounds, enter the station house through one door, and leave through the other, just as with the bucket of coal.

＊　＊　＊

I took up school in Olkhovatka at just about the same place where I my studies had left off in Komi. There was nothing special about the school here, except that the caliber of teachers, while still quite high, was a bit poorer than in Komi. I continued doing all the homework in class where, again, I was the top pupil.

My final examination in history proved to be a test not only of my knowledge of history, but also of my ingenuity. When the class had assembled as usual, the teacher and a proctor from out of town walked in and deposited a tray the size of a file drawer on the teacher's desk. The tray contained slips of paper, arranged in file-fashion, each of which contained one major and two minor questions. Each student had to reach into the tray, pull out one of the slips at random, and answer the questions orally on the spot. There was some material that I knew well, and some I knew poorly—the sleepless nights in Rossosh had taken their toll. But since I wanted very much to succeed in the finals, I did some quick planning. I assumed that originally the slips of paper had been arranged in chronological order. And even if they had subsequently been shuffled, chances were that the first slip had escaped transposition. Following this reasoning, I picked the first slip at the front. (The astute reader will know from whose example I learned this kind of practical logic.) Sure enough, the question was about a period I knew well. I gave a perfect, almost verbatim, presentation of the material. My teacher was beaming, while the proctor was so overwhelmed by the almost word-for-word recitation that she stopped me in the middle of my answer. This was just as well, because her interruption saved me from answering the other two questions which, although minor, would have presented more difficulty. And so I was saved from disgrace.

Somewhere in the middle of 1945, a school was opened for the children of Polish citizens. Classes were held in the afternoon in our regular school building, their length depending on the season (since the school had no source of lighting other than the sun). We studied primarily the Polish language and literature. Polish was easy, and literature was fun. We read the works of famous Polish authors such as Mickewicz,[*] the Polish national poet, and classics by the likes of Sienkewicz. I liked even Mickewicz's long poems better than Pushkin's.

Although life in Olkhovatka was incomparably easier than that in Kortkeros, it had several drawbacks. The water supply was one of them. No matter how primitive the well bucket was in Komi, at least there was a well in every yard. Not so in Olkhovatka (and most towns of its size). Water had to be carried from the river, one bucket at a time, over an appreciable distance—about a third of a mile.

Another drawback: in contrast to Komi, where the authorities expected no more of us than to attend school, here in

---

[*] Mickewicz regarded Lithuania as his homeland and called himself by his Lithuanian name *Mickevicius*. In the complicated interaction between the Polish and Lithuanian peoples, Polish became the language of cultured Lithuanians, just as French was for years the sole language spoken by the Russian nobility.

Olkhovatka, we were told to go and work in the fields during the long summer vacation. It might be that Olkhovatka had many more fields than Komi or a longer growing season, but whatever justification there might have been, and even if they had presented an explanation to us, it still would not have made the work more enjoyable. The work was bad enough, but besides that, the fields were a good six miles out of town. We had to get up early in the morning, walk all the way there, and then put in a full day of backbreaking weeding— unless it rained. The hard work and the long walk wore us down. Still, I remember at least once lifting my eyes high enough to take in the beautiful view of seemingly unending fields of wheat, sunflowers, and corn.

Our agricultural assignment lasted only through the first summer. During the second summer we became student metal workers. We started by producing some kind of tool, mostly by using a file. The files they issued us were rusty and very dull, typical of Soviet industrial output. It took us the entire day to achieve what could have been done in less than an hour using a British product. Indeed, our instructor owned a good British file, and allowed us to take turns using it every once in a while. It wasn't hard to see and feel the difference. After completing that project, we were then supposed to learn how to operate a lathe. The more than ten lathes formally at our disposal were old-fashioned belt-driven machines powered by a single overhead transmission. The transmission itself was driven by some kind of gasoline or diesel engine that banged away in the basement. I can no longer remember why, but we never, in fact, got to operate a lathe.

It was here in Olkhovatka that we came face to face with death. Unlike Komi, where all the households were headed by women, here there were four Jewish families headed by men: an old couple, a widower with children, and two young couples. We also had the Neikron brothers with us. These two young married men were, like almost everyone else, employed at the refinery. Theirs was a special job: shoving hunks of chalk into an oven. The material itself was available on the refinery grounds. There was a wall of pure chalk standing there, and it was "mined" by simply hacking off chunks as needed. This chalk was used to generate a gas that whitened the sugar. The gas was lethal; inhaling it brought about suffocation and immediate death. People working at the oven were given instructions on proper precautions to be taken at all times. For unknown reasons, someone neglected to tell the two young workers that the oven doors must stay closed whenever the factory whistle was blowing. There was some kind of link between the two that I never fathomed. One day, when these two were working at the oven, they left the door open when the whistle blew to signal the noon break. The expected chain of events took place, and the two died.

Under the law, this constituted gross negligence on the part of the plant's chief engineer, for which he was liable to stand trial and be given a lengthy jail sentence. Actually, any long-term imprisonment meant being sent to a labor camp someplace in the frigid North, be it Komi or Siberia; local jails were usually intended for short-term offenses only. As fate would have it, the chief engineer was also Jewish, one of the two non-refugee Jews in town. (The other was his elderly father, head of the shoe repair workshop.)

As soon as the chief engineer learned of the tragedy, he came to our building to plead with the widows not to press charges, offering to compensate them for the loss. They accepted his offer. Before the funeral on the following day, two burlap-covered wagons full of produce drew up in front of the building. Their contents were rapidly removed, and everything was done to make it appear as if the wagons had come solely to take the deceased to their final resting place. After all, offering ransom for a crime was patently illegal, and the chief engineer hardly wanted to jump from the frying pan into the fire. There were heated arguments among us about whether or not the widows had done the right thing, but obviously no one could tell them what to do.

This was not the first time the refinery's chief engineer played a role in our lives. The first incident occurred during the Passover of 1945, prior to the tragic deaths of the two sugar workers. Just before the holiday, we were told that he was giving us a choice of the two days during which the grownups could absent themselves from work. The individual who appointed himself as our representative selected the first two days of the eight-day Festival. When this news was conveyed to the rest of the workers, one of the men objected, and rightfully so, that the seventh day should have been selected instead of the second, it being more important. But by then it was too late to change the plans. Apparently the finagling which the chief engineer had performed to allow such a large number of people to absent themselves from work could not be repeated. We were very grateful to him for making this effort. The combination of being allowed time off from work and having permission to conduct services brought back some of the holiday spirit we remembered from home.

This was not, however, the first time we held services. We had also gathered in prayer half a year earlier, on the two days of the Jewish New Year and on Yom Kippur, the Day of Atonement. Then, no prior arrangements had been made—people simply didn't show up for work. Although no punitive action was taken against us, nobody dreamed of attempting a repeat performance during Succoth, which follows Yom Kippur by only four days. It is quite possible that our chief engineer covered for our absence from work, without our knowledge. In light of what had happened then, he may well have proposed the Passover arrangements on his own initiative since he feared an unannounced disruption of work, which would have been hard to account for a second time.

Formal community prayer services require the participation of ten Jewish males aged thirteen and over. Since we had, by the previous count, only six grown men, it meant that boys over this age were an essential part of the quorum. I had reached bar mitzvah age in the summer of 1944, the first of our two summers in Olkhovatka. There had been no ceremony, no reception, no speeches—absolutely nothing, except that Mother managed to get me a pair of *tefillin*. This essential religious article, which boys begin using shortly before their bar mitzvah, was simply not available. The only ones to be found belonged to a few of the male refugees who had taken them along from Poland.

Remembering her father's statement from her childhood that he donned a second pair of *tefillin* for those who may be prevented from doing so, Mother inquired as to whether any of these men happened to have the extra pair. She was elated to hear that one of them not only had the extra pair of *tefillin* but was willing to sell it to her. Little did she know that the order in which the parchments are put into the head-piece compartments of the second pair is different than the order employed in the first pair, and for this reason the second pair conforms only to a minority Rabbinic opinion. Surely it would have dampened her joy if she had been aware of this. Still, it was definitely better than no *tefillin* at all.

I donned these every day until after the War. Then one morning in a synagogue, someone identified them as *Rabbenu Tam tefillin*—the secondary, less universally accepted version. It took me quite a while to understand what he meant, since I, too, was unaware of the distinction—not surprisingly, considering how much religious education I had received.

Mother had not neglected my Jewish education, however, however limiting our circumstances were. She and several of the other ladies hired an instructor to teach the children the Pentateuch (in Hebrew). This person lived elsewhere, and traveled to our town three times a week. Of course, he had to have one certain special "qualification"—he had to be retired, since otherwise he would have been prosecuted for not being gainfully employed. Our lessons came under the category of teaching religion, and, as such, were strictly forbidden by Communist law. However, the fear of the NKVD, all-pervasive in Komi, had somehow left us. Although we exercised caution, we felt quite confident that nobody would inform on our illegal activity. And, in fact, nobody did.

It is difficult to say now, from a distance of over fifty years, why we felt less restricted in Olkhovatka. This may have been because we were treated more like human beings and less like work animals. Or that it was because of the doubling of the molasses allotment, or the successful arrangement for holiday prayers. The availability of goods on an open market probably also contributed to our good feeling.

In Olkhovatka we were in for another surprise: it was possible to buy our felt footwear (*valenki*) at the workshop! This was a pleasure difficult to convey to a Western reader, who can have no idea what it means to be able to walk into a workshop set up expressly for the purpose of supplying mere non-Party residents of the Soviet Union with a much needed article of clothing. I remember going with Mother to the shop, located on the outskirts of town, and ordering three pairs of made-to-order *valenki*. On an assigned date we came to pick them up, paid in cash, and walked out with three pairs of brand new footwear that were treated with the same care generally lavished on a newborn baby.

Olkhovatka also boasted a town library (school libraries were unheard of), and I devoured all the books I could lay my hands on, particularly in summertime. My favorites consisted primarily of translations from Western languages. Books by Russian authors were of lesser interest, since we had many of them as required reading material in school. The Western literature included such works as *The Last of the Mohicans, Robinson Crusoe, Gulliver's Travels, A Tale of Two Cities, Prisoner of Zenda, The Adventures of Tom Sawyer*, and works by Jack London and Jules Verne, among others. I remember, in partic-

ular, trying to get hold of *Captain Grant's Children* by Jules
Verne. After a long search, I found someone who had it, but
he asked that it be returned within a few days. For some
reason, I did not start on the book until the last day. But I
managed to finish in time by reading through the night. I
couldn't keep the standard kerosene lamp burning since this
would have interfered with Mother's sleep. Instead I used the
local version of a bedside lamp, a slender-wicked glassless
kerosene lamp appropriately called *koptilka*, meaning, "sooty."
The next morning, Mother noticed immediately that my nos-
trils were extremely black—the accumulation of a full night's
soot from the lamp.

Reading books was one favorite pastime; another was
eating "fast food." We youngsters would get together in the
house of a friend to "fry" some potatoes brought by one of the
group. None of us had the patience to wait for the potatoes to
get cooked the regular way—in a pot, and, besides, that
wouldn't have been half as much fun. Instead, we would peel
the potatoes, slice them as thin as we could, and cook them in
the biggest frying pan we could find. In this way, they were
ready to eat in fifteen or twenty minutes.

In the distant background, the war was running its course.
The Germans were retreating; at the same time, the Soviet
military machine became increasingly powerful, making it
possible to bring some of the soldiers back home. They came
bringing war booty, including wristwatches, a commodity
almost impossible to obtain not only in Komi but also in our
new location. The average returning soldier brought back more
than one watch, and sold the extras. The joke went around
that the soldiers, who knew nothing of timepieces, priced
them by their size, asking a higher price for simple clocks than
for intricate watches. Mother bought me an Omega pocket
watch of which I was the proud owner for a number of years.

The chain of Soviet victories created an atmosphere of
happiness and, somehow or other, imbued us with a spirit of

partnership in the war effort. Of course, under the circumstances, the authorities had mounted an intensive effort to foster a desire to help the fighting men. Their pervasive propaganda even influenced me to contribute something to the Soviet fighting machine. I wrote a little skit about partisans in the Russian woods, and persuaded local officials to put the auditorium at our disposal, and even to let us use several rifles left behind by the Italians (and now in the custody of the town council).

The performance, designed as a fundraiser, consisted of two parts. One was our skit, performed by several of my friends, with Lea cast in a minor role. The other half consisted of several songs sung by one or two men of the refugee colony. The songs, well known to the adults, derived from the pre-War repertoire of the Jewish theater in the Polish language. I must confess that our skit was naive and rather trite, but at the age of 14, I thought it was spectacular. We raised 800 rubles from the sales of tickets and contributed the sum towards the purchase of a tank.

The imminent defeat of the German forces brought many changes with it, the most visible being the public celebration of the 1st of May in 1945, a few days before the fall of Berlin and the end of World War II (in Europe, that is—we knew almost nothing of the war in the Far East). The celebration consisted mainly of music broadcast through several loudspeakers mounted high on poles lining the town's main street.

It didn't take long for rumors to circulate that we, as Polish citizens, would soon be permitted to return to Poland. The children had heated discussions among themselves about whether it was better to take up residence again in Poland, or just use it as a way-station to Palestine. Most of the children were unaware that one could not enter Palestine without the difficult-to-obtain certificate, and I didn't want to be the one to spoil their fun by revealing this information. The adults were not overly concerned with what would happen once we left the Soviet Union. They were simply waiting for the moment when they would be allowed to say farewell forever to the Soviet "Garden of Eden."

THE RETURN TO POLAND

We left Olkhovatka in the winter of 1946, in just about the same way we had come—by a special train, reserved solely for refugees from Poland. There were, however, two striking differences: now it was winter, and each of the boxcars carrying us (again, as during the Kortkeros-to-Olkhovatka trip, devoid of the midheight berth) had a heating stove with some (but not enough) firewood. Also, for the first time during our travels, we shared the train with non-Jewish Poles. Since the train carried refugees from several neighboring locations, we shared it with people, both Jewish and gentile, whom we had not met before.

This second difference soon made itself felt. The closer we got to the Polish border, the more openly anti-Semitic these people became. Most of this activity was verbal, but at least one beating was reported. The instigators were warned that any future episode would be brought to the attention of the "railway police" (actually several officers assigned the task of bringing us safely to the Polish border). Fortunately, there were no repeat performances. I should note that the relations with our gentile Polish neighbors from Olkhovatka remained as cordial as before.

Our route took us through a part of Russia we had never passed through before. We were treated to astounding sights: majestic leafy forests, wide rivers with bridges above and constant boat traffic below, railroad stations with restaurants where people could order what they wanted (or so it seemed from afar), and other long-forgotten scenes. True, we were still rumbling along in the all too familiar boxcars, with one tiny window in each of the four corners. But at least we were free to keep the sliding doors as far open or closed as we wished. It was winter, so most of the time the doors remained shut, but we opened them when the air got too heavy to bear, or as soon as the weather allowed. During these moments, we could take in the scenes so reminiscent of my childhood years.

One day, as our train took us increasingly closer to our destination, it dawned on us that Lea had never attended a Polish school, and did not know how to read or write the language. These skills would be needed when we arrived, especially since no one had any idea when or if we would be able to leave Poland. I took it upon myself to teach her the Polish ABC's during our train journey. We had nothing—no books in Polish from which the language could be learned, no step-by-step workbooks or freshly sharpened pencils. All we had was our ingenuity and Russian newspapers, which provided the only "writing surface" available. Our pen was nothing but a nib attached to a small stick; our ink, boiled black sunflower seeds, like that used in the schools we attended in the Soviet Union. Nevertheless, by the time we arrived in Poland two weeks later, Lea had mastered the elements of the language and its grammar.

After some time, our freight car started running out of firewood. We decided that the next time the train stopped alongside a stand of trees, we would cut one down, chop it into pieces, and put them next to the stove to dry. I was against the scheme because I didn't believe that a newly-felled tree would dry fast enough, even next to a stove. The others felt differently and, in the end, I decided to join the wood-chopping party as an observer. So the next time we stopped for what looked like sufficient time to do the job, a number of us climbed down off the train and went over to a stand of trees close to the tracks. All we had was a hatchet. This meant that the entire tree had to be felled without the benefit of a saw. Before I knew it, I found myself with the hatchet in hand and everyone else looking on.

I was an experienced lumberjack, as the reader will remember, from my Komi days. Accordingly, I established the direction of the wind, made a V-cut on the leeward side, and then moved to the windward side and started hacking away at the tree. Soon enough, a cracking sound could be heard, and the tree started falling in the proper direction. All was proceeding according to plan when one of the onlookers panicked and started yelling at me to run. Thinking I had miscalculated, I ran. My path took me directly beneath the falling tree, but fortunately, it just missed me.

We were then faced with the problem of cutting the tree up into smaller lengths using only a hatchet. It wasn't long before we heard our locomotive's whistle blowing. We grabbed whatever pieces of wood we could, ran to the cars, and were again on our way.

We had to contend not only with the rapidly dwindling supply of firewood but also with scarcity of water. One day, after traveling nonstop over quite a long distance, we ran out of water completely. Our situation had deteriorated when suddenly the train stopped, seemingly in the middle of nowhere. Gazing out at the view, we spotted a well some distance away, which prompted a dispute as to whether it was safe to go for water, considering that the train might start moving again any time, leaving behind anyone who had gotten off. Mother thought it worth the risk. So I took a pail, and we both went to get water. We filled the bucket almost to the brim and headed briskly back towards the train.

Suddenly, when we were about halfway between the well and the train, the train started moving. We ran after it with the pail slowing us down considerably—even after half the water had spilled in the rush. Our legs were no match for the locomotive. To make matters worse, we soon came to a railroad bridge guarded by a soldier who would not let us pass. Every second spent arguing was precious—the train was picking up speed! Somehow, the soldier let us go; somehow, I have no idea how, we didn't fall through the spaces between the railroad ties. Fortunately, our absence was brought to the attention of the train police and the train stopped for us a distance beyond the bridge.

Our intermediate destination was the railroad station of the border city of Rawa Ruska. Here we had to change trains, because Russian train tracks are wider gauged than their European counterparts. Folk wisdom has it that the Czar, during whose reign the rails were laid, insisted that they be constructed differently so that his engineers would not be tempted to escape to the West together with the locomotives.

Since Rawa Ruska was the western terminus of the Russian railroad system and the eastern terminus for Polish trains, it had tracks of both gauges. As usual, we had to wait for the Polish train to come. With time on my hands, I went to the city market to buy some fruit. I was taking in the sights of the bustling market while loosely holding fifteen rubles when a boy about my age ran up to me and snatched the money from my hand.

At first it flashed through my mind that fifteen rubles were not worth running after. Then I recalled that in Rossosh, Mother had stood in the market with hundreds of rubles sticking out of her jacket pocket, and nobody ever tried to pull them out. Yet here some street urchin had the gall to snatch money out of my hand! Out of anger, I gave chase and soon caught up with the boy, who claimed that he didn't have the money. He claimed that he had given it to a second boy, whom he pointed out to me, who was also running away. I noticed, though, that there was yet a third boy, somewhat farther away, who was also running. Surmising that the second boy was only a decoy, I ran after the third one—and recovered my fifteen rubles. I then made my purchase and went back to the station to join Mother and Lea in waiting for the Polish train.

The train finally arrived and we boarded. After the standard three blasts of the whistle, the train started moving so smoothly as to be barely perceptible. Mother was ecstatic.

"Now I know," she said, "that we are in Poland. Here the engineer treats us like people; not like the other Russian trains where our boxcars got a sudden jerk after the third whistle, knocking the unwary off their feet." I had a different explanation: the Polish locomotive just didn't have enough power to give a big pull.

Be that as it may, we traveled some distance into Poland before coming to a halt at a tiny railroad station, little more than a flagman's booth. There we stopped for at least twenty-four hours. After a while, we discerned sounds of shooting in the distance, in the forest to one side of the tracks.

Later we were told that it was this shooting that had caused the long delay. It turned out that we had been the intended target of a sabotage attempt. During the German occupation, the Polish underground consisted primarily of two groups, the *Armia Krajowa*, or *AK* (the Land Army), and *Armia Ludowa*, or *AL* (the People's Army). The former was extremely rightist, whereas the latter operated under leftist auspices. When Poland was liberated (that is, from the Germans) and came under Communist rule, the members of *AL* became a part of the regular army. The *AK* members, in contrast, remained in the forests where they mounted armed opposition to the Communist regime. The *AK*, anti-Semitic like all Polish rightists, learned that Jews were coming back to Poland on our train and set out to interfere by force. (I have no idea what they intended to do with their fellow gentile Poles who were also on our train.) Their plans became known to the government forces, and the resulting shoot-out successfully routed the *AK* troops, allowing us to proceed to our destination.

As we moved farther away from the Soviet Union, it became increasingly apparent that the rubles in our possession would have to be exchanged for Polish currency. It was obvious that the black market was our only option. The thought of going into a bank and changing one currency into another didn't even enter anyone's mind because it was a foregone conclusion that the official rate of exchange would be highly unfavorable.

This, however, was not a problem we needed to solve. When we arrived at a major railroad station that had apparently seen traffic like ours before, a man was already waiting to take us to professional money changers who swiftly and efficiently exchanged our Russian rubles for Polish zlotys at a rate of exchange several-fold higher than the official rate.

Our journey continued. Each station and stop presented the same picture: rows of railroad cars with windows boarded-up by plywood stretching as far as the eye could see. This was the first depressing harbinger of the war's devastation, more of which we were to see later. It was especially depressing when we passed close to the town of Belzec, site of a German extermination camp. While still in Russia, we had learned about the tragedy that had befallen the Jewish people. But now, passing only a few of miles away from one of the death factories, the horrible reality was brought much closer to our senses.

Several tragedies of an altogether different magnitude were being played out on our train. There were several mixed couples aboard—gentile Russian girls who had married Jewish refugee bachelors. These girls had fallen for the lure of Jewish husbands, who, unlike many Russian men, were reputed not only to refrain from beating their wives but even to treat them royally! As we drew closer to the Polish border, these women became increasingly distraught, and the situation reached crisis proportions the deeper we moved into Poland. The women, some of them pregnant, suddenly realized that they were about to enter a strange country where they knew not a soul. They clung pathetically to their husbands, afraid to let them out of their sight.

The next major station on our journey was Lublin, the pre-war site of the world-famous Chachmei Lublin Yeshivah. When we arrived there early in the evening, an official announcement notified all passengers that the layover would last until midnight at the very least. This put an idea into our minds:

The elderly couple that had lived with us in Olkhovatka had owned a set of the Babylonian Talmud, which had accompanied them throughout all their travels within the Soviet Union. At the border, however, the Soviets had confiscated it under some pretext. Now someone in our car conjectured that most probably the yeshivah building housed abandoned sets of the Talmud, once used by its students. Since this property could now not only be regarded as ownerless, but was also probably not being treated with due respect, we would be doing a doubly good deed by going to the yeshivah and bringing back a set to replace the one that was confiscated at the border.

I joined the group headed for the yeshivah. I no longer remember how we located the building, but I do remember the eerie feeling I had while walking the streets of Lublin. The houses we passed were all intact, and the brightly lit store windows displayed an enticing array of goods. Prices were marked in zlotys. I had neither the time to look nor enough sense of the value of that currency to draw any conclusions about how good the local economy was. What did strike me, though, was the stark contrast between the windowless railway cars I had just seen, and the carefree appearance of the streets I was now passing through.

We reached the yeshivah building and found our way to the basement, where we saw an enormous number of volumes of the Talmud and other holy books. We immediately started trying to put a set together, but no matter how hard we tried, we couldn't manage to find all the twenty volumes from the same edition. Someone ventured a guess that the yeshivah's sets might be all the way at the bottom of the huge pile, and that the top layer was all individual volumes brought there after their owners had been taken away by the Germans. In any case, we did not want to start on the backbreaking task of moving thousands of books, many of them torn with front and back covers missing. We decided to be content with taking an assortment of volumes, irrespective of edition, and headed back for the train. The elderly couple was extremely thankful.

Our destination was Western Poland, which had been an integral part of Germany before the war. Over the centuries, Poland's borders had been in continuous flux. There were wars in the west and in the east and, as a result, there were constant claims and counterclaims for various pieces of territory. After World War II, the Soviet Union annexed a part of Eastern Poland, over half of what it had appropriated in 1939. But now that Poland was no longer a capitalist foe but a socialist partner, it had to be compensated for the annexation. There was no more obvious and easy way of doing this than to slice off a piece of Russian-occupied Germany (East Germany) on Poland's western border and hand it over to the Poles. Once the decision was made, the German inhabitants were simply driven from their houses to Germany without being allowed to take the bulk of their belongings with them.

This had created a kind of desert. Buildings were left "as is," with most of the property of the Germans in them. In many cases, this included stores and warehouses with their contents untouched. The Polish government was eager to settle its own citizens in these territories, and hence trains such as ours were directed to these virtually empty cities. A large number of people did indeed travel all the way there, where they appropriated the property abandoned by the original owners. On the other hand, those who did not wish to go that far west were free to settle elsewhere. These, however, could not expect any government assistance at all. This made the problem of finding suitable housing a major hurdle, for usually rent had to be paid in advance.

Mother, Lea, and I had no reason not to continue to the West. There was no point in returning to Warsaw. The apartment in which we had lived before the war had been a rented one and we had no claim to it. In any case, it was most likely reduced to a heap of rubble. However, it was not destined that we should travel to the West.

When our train reached the railroad station in Lodz, we were met by some people who suggested that we detrain there (incidently, these were relatives of the same man who, six years previously, had asked for cigarettes "for the baby"). These people told anyone willing to listen that Lodz housed several institutions, each known as a *kibbutz*. These provided free housing, food, and, eventually, assistance in emigrating (illegally) to Palestine. Children and young people lived in the *kibbutz* while older members of the family found lodgings wherever they could. When arrangements for the illegal border crossing were completed, the grownups were notified and joined the specific group of young people scheduled to leave.

Mother needed no additional incentives. We immediately detrained and hired a wide, flatbed wagon hitched to two horses. I even remember the price of our ride: 400 zlotys. The driver said "four zlotys." In terms of post-war currency, this was a mere pittance; an ice-cream cone cost five. What he really meant was "400 new, post-war inflated zlotys." To express his disdain for the valueless new currency, he cited the price the way he did.

The driver deposited Lea and me at a *kibbutz* whose address had been given to us at the train station. He then took Mother on to the "half-way house," a building at 16 Jakuba Street, which served as a hostel for singles—mainly people who were left alone after the rest of their families had been murdered by the Germans. One could stay there for a limited period of time while searching for more permanent lodgings.

The *kibbutz* consisted of an apartment with exceptionally large rooms. We were taught songs and Hebrew. Lea enjoyed being surrounded by so many children after the bitter isolation of the previous years. I was not very happy with the atmosphere in the *kibbutz*. I was especially troubled by the relegation of the majestic Sabbath to a mere day off. However, I naively assumed that this was a sacrifice we needed to make in order to reach Palestine, and hoped it would not take long.

After a day or two we went to visit Mother on Jakuba Street. It was depressing to see grownups sitting around without knowing what to do next. Many of them had lost any motivation for anything in life after the calamities they had experienced. We realized that in this respect we were more fortunate than everyone else, since at least the members of our immediate family were alive.

Unfortunately, the place on Jakuba street was full of unsavory characters as well as a number of poor souls who, having lost everything else, had also lost their minds. This, in the end, made it unbearable for Mother to stay there.

As soon as Mother took care of whatever arrangements had to be made, she came to visit us at our *kibbutz*. Quite by accident, she walked into the kitchen and found that there was no separation between meat and dairy utensils. That is to say, the food was not being prepared according to the laws of *kashruth*. When she discovered this, she left the place immedi-

The children in the Shomer Hatzair kibbutz in Lodz. Lea and I are in the top left corner.

ately without saying a word. A few hours later, she returned, and ordered us to pack. She had found other arrangements for us.

Later, Mother sat us down to explain herself. Obviously, with Father in Palestine, she wanted to get us all there as soon as possible. That was why the minute she heard about the *kibbutz* arrangement, she had decided to get us off the train. She knew that there were all kinds of Jews, some more religious, some less, and some not religious at all, but she had naturally assumed that in a public Jewish institution only kosher food would be served. She had never meant for us to stay there for any length of time, but merely wanted to leave us in a safe place while she looked around to see what other arrangements were available. When she saw that the food was not kosher, she explained, she hadn't lost a moment, but had whisked us out of there as fast as she could.

For Lea, Mother had found a *kibbutz* run by Agudath Israel, housed at 66 Zachodnia Street, the hub of post-war Jewish communal activity. The female residents there ranged in age from about fifteen to thirty, making Lea the youngest girl and the object of much doting. Mother left her halfway house and moved in with Lea. The *kibbutz* was always filled with young girls and women, many of them working at sewing machines in a room set aside for that purpose. Lea used to stand and watch, and when the seamstresses had finished for the day, she took advantage of the opportunity to teach herself how to sew. A new world opened up for her.

I was taken to 8 Nowomiejska Street, which housed mainly single men, all much older than I was. Most of them were widowers who had lost their wives to the Germans, although some were bachelors who, like us, had just now arrived from the Soviet Union. Both these residences were run under religious auspices, and being able to participate in the traditional Sabbath celebration enhanced our lives immeasurably.

Soon Mother was managing the kitchen where she and Lea

were staying, and she began to get her bearings. Little by little, she learned that travelling to Palestine was not a simple matter. Crossing borders illegally could be arranged only with tremendous difficulty, and there was a long waiting list, which meant that it might take months before our turn came. For reasons explained later in these pages, Mother decided to accept the position of housemother in an orphanage in the city of Bytom. Lea soon joined Mother in Bytom, while I stayed in Lodz, ostensibly only until some accommodations could be found in Bytom for me as well.

PART II

IN SEARCH OF A FUTURE

THE BYTOM ORPHANAGE

After the War, Bytom was one of the locations preferred by many Jewish organizations for their orphanages and youth hostels. It was located close enough to the Czech border to provide easy access for those who wished to cross illegally, yet was still far enough away to avoid arousing the suspicion of the Polish authorities, who were not eager to have their citizens, young people in particular, leave for greener pastures.

Mother had confided to us that she was not too happy at the Zachodnia Street residence in Lodz, so it came as no surprise to me that she jumped at the offer to serve (without remuneration) as the housemother in the Bytom orphanage. This institution had been established by Agudath Israel in collaboration with the *Vaad Hatzalah* and Mrs. Recha Sternbuch, a Swiss citizen renowned for her heroic rescue efforts during the War.* As I was to learn only many years later, there was actually a more powerful motivation behind Mother's decision.

While still in Russia, Mother had vowed that if she and her two children survived that "Workers' Paradise"—where so many parents lost their children to hunger and illness—she would repay her Creator by devoting herself to the care of His children. The housemother position thus seemed made to order for her. It was a mission of mercy that drew on every facet of her remarkable talents, energy, and character.

As it would turn out, all that Mother had accomplished until this point—from serving as a successful housewife and businesswoman in Warsaw to coping with all the excruciating challenges of the war—paled in significance compared to her achievements in Bytom.

---

* See *Heroine of Rescue* (Mesorah Publications) and similar books.

Young people at the Bytom train station awaiting a train that will take
them to the Czechoslovak border. At the top left of the picture one can
discern the small window, typical of this type of train car, alluded to in the
story of our trip from Bialystok into Russia. Courtesy Beth Hatefutsot, the
Nahum Goldmann Museum of the Jewish Diaspora, Tel Aviv.

The orphanage served as a way station for children who
constituted a kind of microcosm of the youngest Jewish survivors of the German war machine. The ravages of war and
genocide had left many Jewish orphans. Some of them, repa-
triated from the USSR by virtue of their Polish citizenship, had
escaped from Poland to Russia during the war together with
their parents, only to lose them there to the Russian cold,
starvation, and illness. These children were now scattered all
over Poland in all forms of temporary accommodations, some
staying with friends or relatives, and others in various gentile
orphanages, most of them affiliated with the Catholic Church.

Others had survived the war in Poland by staying with
gentile families. Jewish parents, who feared the worst for
themselves, had left their children with Polish friends, acquain-
tances, or former employees, hoping that if anything should
happen to them, at least their children would survive. Most
hoped that their relatives abroad would find the children after

the war and retrieve them from these families. Some most likely felt that, even if no one came forward to claim them, it was better that their child live among gentiles than die. Those who could, informed their relatives abroad of their children's whereabouts; others depended on the gentile family to do so when contacts with the outer world were re-established after the war.

Other children were left by their desperate parents in monasteries. Although it was unlikely that such institutions would ever part willingly from their wards, survival of their children was the parents' primary consideration. Even in these cases some parents harbored the hope that the children would eventually rejoin their parents—or at least their fellow Jews. Almost invariably, however, these guardians saw it as their "sacred duty" to keep the Jewish children among them.

The Jewish organizations established after the war to help survivors considered the reclaiming of orphaned children from non-Jewish hands as one of their most important goals. They offered information services to surviving relatives and concrete assistance in retrieving the orphaned Jewish children from gentile homes and monasteries. They recruited people to undertake this daunting task and armed them with lists, hints, and any other relevant information.

The *Vaad Hatzalah* was one such organization. Its agents scoured Poland's cities, towns, and villages in search of surviving Jewish orphans. They were also on the lookout for the many parentless children arriving from the Soviet Union.

The obstacles, both those anticipated as well as those undreamed of, were many and formidable. Most gentiles did not want to part with their charges. They had either become emotionally attached to the children, especially if they had none of their own, or they had a financial interest in applying for the status of adoptive parents, a status which entitled them to government support. Others could not bear to relinquish children whom they had baptized (thus, in their view, saving

their souls) and to whom they had given a full-fledged Christian education. These were some of the hurdles the rescue
workers had anticipated. Most unexpected, however, was the
reluctance of some of the children to leave their adoptive
parents. On the other hand, an occasional gentile family would
work intensively to reunite the children with their Jewish
relatives. In fact, one such impressive effort had led directly to
the establishment of the *Vaad Hatzalah* orphanage in Bytom.

Bytom is located in the Silesia district of Poland, about one
hundred and thirty miles from Lodz. Silesia was one of the
areas that were for many years a bone of contention between
Germany and Poland, and part of the territory later annexed
to Poland by Soviet order. As a matter of fact, before World
War II the city of Bytom sat on the border between Poland
and Germany. Its German name was Beuthen (pronounced
more or less as *Boiten*). Those who wrote the captions under

Photograph of members of a Poaley Agudah kibbutz in Bytom (Boyten in
Yiddish). Photograph courtesy Yad Vashem.

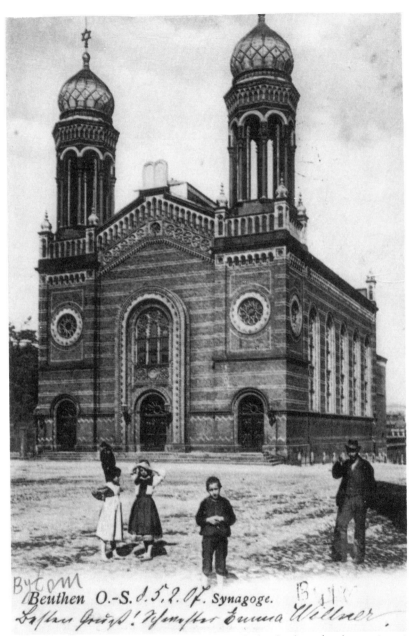

The (German style) synagogue in Bytom dating back to the times when it was a border town, administered jointly by Germany and Poland and known in German as Beuthen. Photograph courtesy Yad Vashem.

photographs appearing in various books (*Heroine of Rescue* among them) took its name from the hand-lettered banners in Hebrew or Yiddish that invariably appeared above the heads of people in group photographs. Since a poorly-lettered *T* or *M* in either of these languages can easily be mistaken for an *S*, and since any *B* can be also read as a *V*, Bytom became *Bisom*, *Bits*, or what have you, and Beuthen became *Voyten*. Nonetheless, the fact is that all the accounts of the Orthodox orphanage in the city with its various spelling refer to one and the same institution—the one where Mother so distinguished herself.

＊ ＊ ＊

The Bytom orphanage owed its existence to a remarkable individual, Avraham Yitzchak Winkelstein, and to a remarkable chain of events.

Avraham Yitzchak Winkelstein was born in Mariampol, Lithuania, a small town several dozen miles south of Kovno. Subsequently he moved to Kovno and was working there as an accountant when the Germans occupied Lithuania. He did not

Rabbi Winkelstein (second from right) at a festive occasion in Israel (much after the war).

differ in appearance from the Lithuanians among whom he lived. In fact, no one knew he was Jewish and, as a result, he was able to remain in Kovno without fear of being rounded up and slaughtered like the rest of Lithuanian Jewry.

An end to his peaceful existence came one night in a dream. His long departed father appeared before him and told him that the Germans were about to bring a terrible calamity upon the Jewish people and stressed that he, too, was a son of this unjustly persecuted nation.

For some time, he didn't know what to do. On the one hand, he was safe. No matter what fate awaited the Jews, he could keep on living in the secure haven of his native town.

On the other hand, his father had told him that he was part of the Jewish nation, which he took to mean that he should join his brethren and share their destiny. This meant leaving the safety of his non-Jewish ambience and joining his fellow Jews in the ghettos that had been set up in Kovno and in other Lithuanian cities.

He decided to enter the Kovno ghetto. When he started looking for a place to stay, someone suggested that he seek the company of Rabbi Mordechai Pogrimanski. Rabbi Pogrimanski was a rare genius with an incredible memory—one of the outstanding Talmudic scholars of the pre-war generation. Rabbi Pogrimanski invited Winkelstein to stay in his apartment, which he shared with Rabbi Mordechai Zuckerman, now living in Jerusalem, a family with three children named Kowalski, and another couple. Their communal apartment was part of a large four-building housing project built just before the start of the war.

For a while, life in the ghetto ran a normal course, with people working in shops and factories. Soon, though, with the westward advance of the Soviet armies, the Germans started liquidating the ghetto. Since it was initially thought that the Germans would make a house-to-house search and banish any Jews discovered to the death camps, everyone tried to secure some kind of hiding place. Winkelstein with the others in his apartment set up such a hiding place by building an additional room between the kitchen of their ground-floor apartment and the staircase. They did this by erecting a wall in the stairwell, which produced a narrow space between the original wall of the apartment's kitchen, which held the cupboards, and the newly built wall. A cupboard was moved, an opening was made in the wall, and the cupboard replaced, concealing the entrance to the hiding place.

Somehow the small space created in this manner accommodated all nine occupants of the apartment. They stayed there most of the time; at night, one of them would crawl out from the hiding place to peer through a window to see what was happening outside.

During one such foray, the group's lookout overheard one German soldier telling another that the entire housing project was slated for dynamiting the very next day. Fear gripped these desperate people as they tried to decide whether or not to flee. Finally, Winkelstein suggested—and everyone agreed— that they should all stay and pray for a miracle, since there was no way to leave the building without being detected. Needless to say, detection meant certain death.

The night passed and, indeed, the next day the Germans placed explosives around the four buildings and detonated them. But the miracle happened—the charges around their building failed to explode!

The Germans then set out on a thorough search of each apartment of the building. They went through the apartment occupied by the Winkelstein group room by room, including the kitchen, but failed to find the entrance to the extra room, even though the soldiers stood in the kitchen right next to the cupboard. The people in the hiding place held their breaths nearly to the point of suffocation, but the Germans left without detecting them.

That night, they resolved to escape. Again, it was Winkelstein who assumed responsibility for this decision and who became the leader of the group during all their trials and tribulations. When asked for his opinion, Rabbi Pogrimanski, despite his scholarly stature, deferred to Winkelstein, whose unbounded faith and trust in Divine Providence manifested themselves in everything he did and said.

Their building was located at the outskirts of the town with only a potato field separating it from the barbed wire fence surrounding the ghetto. Rabbi Pogrimanski, Rabbi Zuckerman, and Winkelstein crawled out first; the two families were to follow suit.

Very heavy rains had fallen previously, and the leaves of the potato plants had grown tall, shielding the escapees from the eyes of the Germans. When the three had made good headway, they decided that one of them should crawl back to tell the two remaining families that it was safe to leave. Just as one of the group turned around, he noticed a German soldier facing them, fast asleep. Although they must have passed him at close proximity on their way out, miraculously, he had not awakened, but they were afraid to run the risk of waking him now and therefore turned back. Hence, the two couples were never notified. The Kowalski family with their three children somehow managed to escape, eventually making their way to Israel. Nothing is known about the fate of the other couple.

In the confusion of the original attempt to return and the subsequent change of mind, the three lost contact with one another. Rabbi Zuckerman discovered that the strands of the barbed-wire fence could be pulled apart and crossed the fence in one place, whereas the two others crossed it in a different location. Without any contact among them, all three made their way to the river separating Kovno from its suburb, Slobodka, and crept along its bank at night, hiding during the day, until they finally met. A few days later, the advancing Russian armies routed the Germans.

As soon as he came to himself after the war and its or-
deals, Winkelstein set out to rebuild as much of the Jewish
religious community structure in Lithuania as possible. When
the Lithuanian government decided to expropriate the main
Kovno synagogue, Winkelstein wangled an audience with the
President of the country and, after almost an hour-long argument, was able to persuade him to rescind the order. When a
prominent rabbi was arrested for not having the proper papers, it was Winkelstein who intervened on his behalf and
procured his release from jail.

As a Lithuanian national, Winkelstein was entitled to a
passport. This valuable document enabled one to travel within
the Communist-bloc countries. Winkelstein intended to use it
to leave Lithuania for Poland, which, although under Communist control, was at least not a part of the Soviet Union. The
latter was viewed by everyone as an enormous jail to be
escaped by any possible means, whereas Poland was justifiably
regarded as a country that, sooner or later, one would be able
to leave for friendlier shores. When Winkelstein obtained his
passport, he did not use it for himself, instead, he handed it
to Rabbi Pogrimanski so that he could leave Lithuania. Now
without the passport, Winkelstein had to cross the Lithuanian-
Polish border illegally.

*　*　*

One day, while still in Kovno, Winkelstein learned of two
Jewish children whose lives had been saved by their parents'
Lithuanian maid.* He brought them to Bytom, where he established the nucleus of an orphanage. As a result of efforts of
similarly concerned people, the population of the Bytom
orphanage grew rapidly. Both the children and the staff regarded their stay in Poland as temporary, as a stop on a
journey that had not yet ended.

The children were housed in two locations: one for girls

---

* For their story see Chapter 21, "Snatched from the Vilno Ghetto."

and younger boys, and a second for older boys. Initially, the home catered almost exclusively to teenage girls, but soon after Mother took over it began to cater mainly to much younger children, with only a sprinkling of older girls. A separate orphanage was subsequently establish-

Mother surrounded by older girls in Bytom.

ed for teenage and older boys under the auspices of Winkelstein, who continued to participate in the administration of Mother's orphanage. The boys' institution gradually acquired some of the characteristics of a yeshivah.

Although most of the children had no parents, there were exceptions. Some parents placed their children there in the hope that they could leave Poland as part of a group.

Boys of the Bytom orphanage are at the left of the photograph. Rabbi Winkelstein is at the left at the head of the table. The group of older girls was brought over there to be photographed together with the sign proclaiming: "Bytom orphanage of Mrs. Sternbuch."

Three Jewish girls in a convent in Poland.

As soon as Mother arrived at the Bytom home, she immersed herself in the task of providing for the children's welfare. She poured her heart and soul into caring for them, to a degree no less than that of a natural mother.

Mother ruled the Bytom home with an iron hand, and the children loved her for it. Her policy was always: "The children come first!" After having had their childhood destroyed by war, they thrived on her firmness and on her attention to their proper nutrition and hygiene, to her insistence on a full night's sleep and exposure to plenty of fresh air. But most of all, they thrived on her overflowing love.

Mother supervised the shopping and all the housekeeping tasks for both the boys' and girls' sections, although she spent most of her time with the girls.

The shopping situation that Mother "inherited" ran contrary to her character; in fact, it was the antithesis of everything ingrained into her by her father. The two women who had been doing the shopping previously did not have the welfare of the children in mind. The standard fare at the orphanage was stale bread and other similarly inferior products, while the two women "helped themselves" to freshly-baked rolls and other delicacies each day. As soon as she became aware of this practice, Mother brought it to an end. Since she did not have the time to do the shopping herself, she delegated two of the older girls to do it each day in turn. The girls would be given a shopping list and a suitable sum of money. On their return to the orphanage, they were required to account for each and every penny they had spent.

The girls were housed in a large, rented apartment, with another smaller apartment across the hall. Children were packed into every room, but care was taken that each child should have her own bed. The only places where children didn't sleep were the kitchen, the dining room, and the tiny cubicle where Mother slept.

Lea came with Mother, and was treated just like the other girls, with one exception—the assignment of clothing. She would invariably be given only what was left over as unsuitable for the other girls. When she complained, Mother told her: "You have parents, so you don't need clothes."

An interesting sidelight was Lea's meeting with the four Blumenkrantz sisters, whom she had never met before. They eyed her with curiosity. Finally, one of them went over and asked: "Did you live in Olkhovatka? Did you once give a performance there?" It turned out that our little skit had made a greater impact than we had imagined. The Blumenkrantz girls were orphaned in Russia and, by a stroke of good fortune, assigned to a "show-case" orphanage meant to demonstrate to foreign visitors the care which the Soviet Union showered upon orphans in its charge. The food, clothing, and accommodations there were all better than in the standard Soviet orphanages. As another part of their privileged treatment, they were taken to see our little show in Olkhovatka with-

Two of these same three girls after Mother's "rehabilitation treatment."

out our being aware of the presence of special guests.

One of Mother's tasks was mending the children's clothing, something she was supposed to do in her free time while her charges slept. Since she had no free time, however, she often worked deep into the night. As a result of her super-human efforts, Passover eve found her sound asleep with the Seder about to begin. A heated discussion ensued between Winkelstein and the children. The "Rabbi" (as he was now known) understood that, no matter what, Mother must be up and awake for the Seder. The children, returning her love and devotion, insisted that it would be inhuman to wake her up after so many nights with so little sleep. Incredible as it may seem, the children's view prevailed and Mother missed that Seder.

It would be hard to imagine two more incompatible people than Mother and the Rabbi. The latter believed firmly that the orphanage's charges should conform to all the requirements of Jewish law, and was adamant that no leniency be allowed in this respect. Mother, on the other hand, felt that children who had just left a non-Jewish environment could not be expected to immediately adhere to every single rule and custom. She was convinced that only a gradual approach could solve the host of problems each child presented.

These problems were far from simple. Many children insisted on genuflecting and reciting Christian prayers; they continued wearing their crucifixes, and they even wanted to attend church services on Sunday. They missed their foster parents and friends, and were understandably miserable. These issues brought to the fore the difference in approach between Mother and the Rabbi. Mother was temporarily willing to overlook the persistence of Christian observance by the children. She felt that, given enough time and gentle prodding, these habits would dissipate by themselves. The Rabbi, in contrast, would have none of this. It was not surprising, then, that on more than one occasion a child would hear one piece of advice from the Rabbi and another from Mother.

Mother's association with the home at this juncture, the spring of 1946, lasted only a few months. Most of the children were "old-timers," i.e., brought there either by their parents or other workers before Mother's arrival. This situation came to an abrupt change, as we shall see later, when most of the children left Poland some time in August.

BIDING TIME IN LODZ

While Mother was hard at work at the orphanage in Bytom, I was in Lodz, suffering greatly from boredom. Because the residents of the *kibbutz* where I was staying were all so much older than I was, most of their activities did not interest me. During the day they were all busy, and in the evenings they would gather in groups to listen to a Talmudic lecture given by those among them who were capable of delivering one—a lecture that was way above my head. So whether in the daytime or the evening, there was nothing for me to do. To relieve the boredom, I would read several of the daily newspapers or take long walks in the city.

When I had the money, I would sometimes travel from one place to another by trolley car. Here my "news conditioning" of five and a half years in Russia caught up with me. In Russia, the news that reached us was about two weeks out of date, and its credibility was very low. Accordingly, when the Lodz newspapers announced that a certain trolley stop would be moved around the corner, it did not register with me. So, when I traveled that route the following day I stepped off the trolley when it slowed down to turn the corner, at the location of the former stop. I wasn't badly hurt, but the onlookers commented in unison: "Doesn't this boy know how to read?"

Most of the city of Lodz remained intact after the war, in contrast with Warsaw, which was subjected to intensive bombing and shelling while holding out against the Germans for three weeks, and was later almost totally razed during the Ghetto and the Polish uprisings. The Lodz borough of Baluty, however, was totally destroyed. Before the war, this district had housed the less affluent Jewish population of Lodz; the Germans made it the site of the ghetto. Nowomiejska Street, where our *kibbutz* was located, served as the dividing line between the two sections of Lodz. This street originated at the city's major square, Plac Wolnosci (Freedom Square) and ran towards the outskirts of town. Starting with the square, only six to ten buildings on each side of Nowomiejska were left intact. Past them stretched utter devastation as far as the eye could see. On either side of the road empty lots (from which most of the rubble of the destroyed buildings had been removed) alternated with shells of bombed-out buildings.

Nowomiejska Street stood in stark contrast to Plac Wolnosci itself and to Piotrkowska Street, the city's main thoroughfare, which also originated from this square and ran a good couple of miles to the other end of the city. Plac Wolnosci boasted two or three highly ornate churches. Neither these, nor the rest of the city, were touched by the Germans. The five-minute walk from the end of Nowomiejska Street to the square was like traveling from one planet to another.

The far end of Piotrkowska Street, which was in a neighborhood bordering on the city's suburbs, was home to a number of palatial mansions belonging to textile factory owners before the war. I found myself there one day because I had been asked to explore the veracity of an offer to "ransom" a Torah scroll. It was felt that with my perfect Polish, I would gain the would-be seller's confidence and, at the same time, get a sense of the price for which it could be purchased. I found him, but I was so untutored in the art of haggling that I could gain no information from him. He did, however, give me several fragments of a different scroll, which had been cut up into "decorations" of sorts, according to him, by the Germans, from whom he had rescued them. I was far from being sure that he had not produced the "artwork" himself. In any case, others went to him soon thereafter and ransomed the complete scroll.

Life in Lodz, although generally boring, had its beautiful moments. One of these was the Friday evening meal. We— myself and the several dozen men in my residence—would sit around a large table and partake of the Sabbath meal. The courses were interspersed with traditional songs, delivered with the fervor of people who, for the first time in many years, could sing them without fear of detection, imprisonment, or worse. We were not the only ones enjoying the singing. As soon as the first stanza reached a certain volume, the windows of the gentile dwellers of our apartment house would fly open one by one, and the ladies of the house would poke their heads out to listen. This audience would stand motionless at the open windows until we finished.

We sang traditional songs, except for one—the thirteenth Principle of Faith recited daily at the end of morning prayers. This statement of faith in the coming of the Messiah, whose melody was composed in one of the concentration camps and sung by many of those led to the gas chambers, was sung with a poignancy that befitted the closeness of the calamitous events and can no longer be duplicated.

During this entire time, I made no attempt to go to my home town of Warsaw. As previously mentioned, I was quite positive that the apartment we rented was in ruins. The same applied to the dwellings of both sets of my grandparents. The fact that Grandfather Lederman lived in an apartment building (on 3 Blonska Street) that he owned did not make a visit to its presumed ruins more alluring.

What changed this situation was a letter we received from Father. We had maintained a continuous correspondence with him from the time he was released from labor camp in Komi and he was aware of our doings and whereabouts at all times. In one of his letters he asked me to attend to some business in a Warsaw suburb. I no longer remember what I was supposed to accomplish, but I recall that I did what I was asked to.

I left for Warsaw in the morning and arrived only toward late afternoon because under post-war conditions there were no direct train connections between Lodz, Poland's second

A photograph of a Gensia Street sign (the correct Polish spelling, as shown, is Gęsia), taken after the war. There is no longer such a sign.

major city, and the capital. As a result, I had a two-hour wait between trains.

Once in Warsaw, I got off at the same main railroad station which, in better times, had taken me to the countryside. It was still located underneath the city's main street, Marszalkowska. I walked to the lodging which had been arranged for me at 2 Królewska, a street that passed parallel to the famous Saski Gardens and ran into the main street at a right angle.

The people with whom I stayed overnight were the Lifshitzes, the same people who had put me up on the night I got lost on my way to Kortkeros. Early the next morning, I set out for the suburb. There were no buses yet, so I made the trip in a truck that had benches installed along the sides. On the way back I traveled in a pickup truck that carried only three people: an elderly Polish man, a girl slightly older than

I was, and myself.

I got involved in a friendly debate with the Pole on some topic concerning Jewish religious observance. Upon learning that I was Jewish, the girl struck up a conversation with me. It turned out that during the War she and her parents had lived in the same house as my maternal grandparents—at 12 Gensia Street. She told me how she had witnessed their being taken away to one of the German death camps sometime in December, 1942. Although we had harbored no doubt that my grandparents on both sides had met this fate, hearing it from an eyewitness brought a storm of emotion to my heart. To this very day I regret not having asked her name and address so that I might have garnered additional details about my family.

Having successfully completed the errand for Father, I returned to Lodz and to my *kibbutz,* where the primary concern was finding ways to leave Poland. The religious among them had an additional concern—regenerating their communal religious life. At the moment, most of the activity which came under that heading was happening at 66 Zachodnia Street. As mentioned above, this address was a sort of community center. Not only was it the site of the girls' *kibbutz,* but it also housed the synagogue and the offices of religious organizations and served as the residence of a major rabbinical authority. Sadly, it was also the site of the inevitable "landmark" of recent Jewish history—a cellar with its mountains of torn and defaced religious books.

The rather large yard of this unofficial community center played host to receptions for two prominent rabbis: Rabbi Eliezer Silver, the Chief Rabbi of Cincinnati, Ohio; and Rabbi Isaac Herzog, then Chief Rabbi of Palestine and subsequently Chief Rabbi of Israel. The latter came to Poland to negotiate, among other things, the legal departure of several hundred Jewish children from Poland for the West. The personal involvement of an internationally known Jewish leader was required to effect this emigration because, at that time, the

Polish government was reluctant to let its Jewish citizens out. These arrangements also permitted the departure of all the children and teenagers cared for by the Bytom orphanage, a story described below.

While I was looking for something to do in Lodz, Mother had her hands overflowing with activity in Bytom.

Rabbi Silver accompanied by Mrs. Sternbuch and others during his journey to visit and aid Holocaust survivors. Photograph courtesy of Ginzach Kiddush Hashem, Bnei Brak.

Rabbi Eliezer Silver delivering a speech to a crowd of Holocaust survivors from a porch at Zachodnia 66 in Lodz. Photograph courtesy of Ginzach Kiddush Hashem, Bnei Brak.

A PAINFUL SEPARATION

Some time after Rabbi Herzog came to Poland, Mother asked me to come and live in her orphanage in Bytom. As the Rabbi had arranged with the Polish government, the children living there and in similar institutions were to leave for France. In order for make it legal for me to join them, I first had to be physically residing in the home. My sojourn in Bytom, which lasted about three weeks, proved even more tedious and uneventful than that in Lodz. Mother was too busy to pay any attention to me. I didn't even have a place to stay. I couldn't stay with the boys because they were far ahead of me in Jewish learning. On the other hand, there was no place for me in Mother's room; even Lea slept with the other girls. Since I was there only temporarily, I had to make do with sleeping on the dining room table!

When the day of departure finally arrived, we boarded a train that was to take us to Czechoslovakia, our first stop on our way to France. We were accompanied on this trip by Rabbi Herzog and his son Yaakov (who later became Director General of the Prime Minister's Office under Ben-Gurion). They attended to all our travel arrangements and were to travel with us all the way to Czechoslovakia. Two American rabbis, their status as US Army chaplains opening doors for them throughout Europe, were also on the train. Only much later did we learn that one of them, Rabbi Simcha Wasserman, was the son of the world famous Rabbi Elchonon Wasserman of Baranovich. (To tell the truth, even if we had known this at the time, it would not have meant much to us, since most of us, unfortunately, had never even heard of the senior Rabbi Wasserman.) The other chaplain was Rabbi Solomon Wohlgelerenter.

None of us children had any documents. We traveled on a

Youngsters boarding the children's transport organized by Rabbi Hertzog that took them from Poland to Czechoslovakia. Photograph courtesy Ginzach Kiddush Hashem, Bnei Brak.

group visa, simply a list of all the children's names, which also served as our passport. We arrived at the Polish-Czechoslovakian border as night was falling and were stopped by passport control. There was little that the border police could do to check us except to line us up and take a roll call. But either they were too lazy to do this or the inadequate lighting prevented them from dealing with a group of over six hundred children. Whatever the case, they skipped this step. They had less difficulty, however, in dealing with the adults among us.

Since this was a children's transport, there were not supposed to be any adults on it except for the previously mentioned rabbis who served as chaperons. We were allowed a certain number of counselors, who, by definition, were supposed to be teenagers, and, of course, Mother, who was officially responsible for all the children.

Despite these restrictions, a Mrs. Springer, who worked in some capacity at the orphanage, had joined the transport together with her two obviously grownup sons. Apparently she had deluded herself into thinking that she and her sons would be taken for teenagers. Furthermore, there were already more teenagers on the train than we could reasonably pass off as counselors, and even some boys over the age of twenty. To make detection by the police more difficult, the children had been instructed to sit on the boxcar floors in a position close to prone so as to make the presence of the grownups as unobtrusive as possible.

The police, however, were not fooled. Nevertheless, they were lenient concerning the number of counselors, but they drew the line at Mrs. Springer and her elder son Yaakov, who were told to disembark. Her younger son somehow blended in with the children and stayed on the train.

Mother, of course, needed a proper document. For some inexplicable reason, though, she was given a passport belonging to someone else. Mother to this day feels that this was due to negligence by those responsible for the trip's technical aspects. In fairness, though, those people later insisted that there had been a delay in issuing Mother's passport and so they had handed her one belonging to another person, knowing that this might be Mother's last opportunity to leave Poland legally together with her two children. They naively hoped that the police would not be too inquisitive and that she would consequently be allowed to leave with the children.

(According to another version of this mishap, albeit one that does not fit our understanding of the events, no passport application had been filled out since it was assumed that Mother would stay behind to continue her work. Only when the children adamantly refused to travel without her, was it decided that she must go too, and by then it was too late to apply for a passport.)

Be that as it may, the ruse wasn't a very clever one. Mother did not look much like the woman whose photograph appeared in the passport. To improve her chances of passing the police inspection, Mother tied a scarf over her face as people used to do when they had a bad toothache, covering as much as she could, and proceeded to do plenty of moaning and groaning. This stratagem might have worked, except that one of the children called her "Mrs. Lederman" in the presence of the border policeman who was just then inspecting her passport. This time no miracle happened; Mother was taken off the train. Lea and I were travelling in a different car and didn't see this happen, but we were told immediately.

Mother at the Sheinfeld wedding in Bytom. Mother was given Mrs. Sheinfeld's passport for her journey out of Poland.

What to do now? Should we follow Mother off the train or continue our journey with the other children? Suddenly the decision fell upon my shoulders. I was fifteen and had never before decided a matter of that magnitude on my own. By comparison, the decision not to run back when we had crossed the border illegally in Malkinia seemed much easier. First of all, then I was absolutely sure about what should be done. Secondly, I had Mother right there beside me. I convinced her that I was right, but she took responsibility for the decision. Now I had only Lea, just twelve years old, to consult.

Lea strongly favored getting off the train. Emotionally, I agreed with her. But reason demanded that I weigh two other factors: I was certain that Mother would prefer to have us outside of Poland even if it meant a separation; in addition, the appearance of her two children at the police station might further compromise her situation. For all I knew, we might enter the police station just as Mother was in the middle of heatedly denying the charges and insisting that she really was the recently married owner of the passport. As I was weighing the two alternatives, the train started moving, thus taking the decision out of my hands.

-1-

Wyjazd z Polski.

-I-

Wyjechaliśmy z Bytomia 22/VIII-1946 Do Katowic jechaliśmy autem jechaliśmy nie spokojnie. Bo Bolek spóźnił się z powrotem z Warszawy gdy on wrócił wgrodziliśmy się do sanitarnych wagonów. Zatrzymali nas przy granicy po Polskiej stronie Tam stało się wielkie pierwsze nie- szczęście. Na drugi dzień zdjęli z wagonu moją mateczkę, za to że nie miała paszportu. Przez ten wy- padek zatrzasnęli nam drzwi i ja zemdlałam, a reszta zalewała się gorzkimi łzami. Na sobotę zdjęli nas do hotelu „Pałac" w Ostrawie - Murawskiej. Sobota przeszła szczę- śliwie. W sobotem wieczorem o 11 g. wyjechaliśmy do Pragi. jechaliśmy całą noc i nie spaliśmy.

First page of Leah's diary, describing Mother's being taken off the train, our stay in Moravska Ostrava and departure for Prague.

TEMPORARY ORPHANS

Our train rolled into the Czech city of Moravska Ostrava from the east as the Friday afternoon sun started setting in the west. Whoever had planned our journey did not (or perhaps could not) take into account the fact that trains, particularly in a post-war period, are likely to be delayed. Perilously close to the Sabbath, the call went out for us to board a convoy of trucks lined up next to the train. These carried us from the station to several of the city's hotels, where lodgings for us were hastily arranged. These hotels were empty, most probably because they were undergoing restoration after the war, and were suitable only for such undemanding guests as we were.

We spent a miserable and uncomfortable Sabbath at the hotel, with hardly even a thing to eat. (Since we were unexpected guests no one had cooked for us—we were lucky enough to get beds.) We left at eleven o'clock on Saturday night and continued the journey to our next stop, a former detention camp at the very edge of a little town, Diablice, just outside Prague. This leg of the trip passed uneventfully. We got off the train at Prague and were received with flowers and speeches (which had been kept "in storage" since Friday, our expected date of arrival). Then we were taken by trucks to our accommodations—barracks consisting of several large rooms, each lined with rows of army cots. Once we settled down, we met children from other orphanages and a relatively small group of adults.

Our stay in Diablice lasted exactly five weeks. The two American Army chaplains remained with us for the duration, and then for most of the journey to France. We were given pocket money, which some of my friends and I utilized for several trips to the strikingly beautiful Czech capital, Prague.

Rabbi Hertzog at the Prague train station addressing the children whom he took out of Poland. Lea, wearing a white cap, is right behind the sign. Photograph courtesy Ginzach Kiddush Hashem, Bnei Brak.

Rabbi Hertzog visiting the children during their temporary stay in the Diablice camp, near Prague. The tall man to his right is his son Yaakov. To Rabbi Hertzog's left is Rabbi Wohlgelerenter. Photograph courtesy Ginzach Kiddush Hashem, Bnei Brak.

The city did not display any war damage, at least as far as we could see. We naturally wanted to visit the famous Prague synagogue but somehow never managed to get inside. I also visited the Jewish Community offices several times to inquire about Mother. I couldn't learn anything officially, but I did meet a woman there who gave me some encouraging information. Although she couldn't supply any details, she told me that Mother was not in jail.

Lea and I at the Diablice camp grounds.

Even the local currency fascinated us. The colorful bills were tiny and in near-mint condition, never folded. Our several trips to the city gave us a kind of fairy-tale feeling.

In 1946, the Jewish New Year was celebrated on Thursday and Friday. This was the first time since our Warsaw days that I prayed with a congregation resembling those I remembered

Waiting to board the train from Prague to France. Photograph courtesy Ginzach Kidush Hashem, Bnei Brak.

Boarding the train from Prague to France; note the Torah scrolls and the flags. Photograph courtesy Ginzach Kidush Hashem, Bnei Brak.

from before the War. It was also the first time since then that I heard the blowing of the *shofar*. The holiday was followed by the Sabbath, after which trucks rolled up almost immediately and brought us to the train station once again to start the second and, for the present, last leg of our journey.

As on the first leg of our journey, we now joined a special transport of Jews who had been allowed to leave Poland. Here, our group, who all had some sort of religious background, came into contact with young people in their late teens and early twenties who were entirely non-religious. Every once in a while, we were subjected to emotional stress as a result of some of their attitudes.

Memorable about that journey towards the free Western world was our first taste of ready-to-drink canned cocoa. The cans had something like a candle sticking out of them. We would light the candle, wait for it to burn out, and then open the can and drink the hot cocoa. We had never seen anything like this before. How could we have? It came straight from the warehouses of the US Army Quartermaster General!

The trip was otherwise uneventful, except that our route took us through Germany and our train stopped in Nuremberg on the very day the specially convened court sentenced the Nazi war criminals to hanging. Until we heard the newsboys calling out their wares, we children were not even aware that such court proceedings were taking place. It did seem strange to me at the time that the German newsboys announced this event with such fervor. Of course, to them it was an excellent way of selling newspapers, and apparently, little more.

We traveled on for a week, with groups of children disembarking at pre-arranged locations. Ours was the last group to get off—on Yom Kippur eve, October 4, 1946. We had arrived at the French town of Aix-les-Bains, located close to the junction of the French, Swiss, and Italian borders. We were obliged to wait a while before being picked up by a bus whose driver was a young religious man with a trimmed beard and a French beret. We had never seen such a sight before. A religious Jew wearing a beret like all other Frenchmen! And driving a bus on top of it! This bus was the only vehicle at our service, so it took several trips to take the approximately three hundred of us to the Beau Site Hotel, located next to the town's park and only a stone's throw from the baths which gave the town its name.

We were served a proper meal by the hotel's waiters, and then assigned rooms. Following the afternoon prayers, we re-assembled in the dining room for the special meal which precedes the twenty-five-hour fast of Yom Kippur, the Day of Atonement. It reminded us of similar events in our now-distant past. Indeed, it was a sight never to be forgotten. More than three hundred children, many of whom had gone through virtual hell, now sat at tables in a first-class hotel in one of the world's most famous resort towns and partook of the traditional pre-Yom Kippur meal. It was almost as if nothing had happened, as if there had been no Holocaust, as if most of them weren't orphans who would never be able to visit their parents' graves.

The event was supervised by several ladies who clustered in one of the corners of the huge dining room, all dressed in the customary white worn by Jewish women on the Day of Atonement. Every once in a while, they gave instructions to one of the

Doctors and nurses from Denmark who volunteered to provide us with medical services.

waiters. To my distressed imagination they seemed to be angels descended from Heaven to comfort us and heal our wounded hearts.

Directly after the fast, arrangements were made to get our lives organized. Accordingly, boys aged fifteen to twenty-one were moved to a nearby location, and I had to leave Lea with the girls and younger boys in the old Beau Site, about half an hour's walk away.

Twenty-five of us boys made the move. We were housed in premises previously occupied by another orphanage. There was a spacious *sukkah* waiting for us there, and we celebrated the holiday with as much joy as we could muster.

The younger boys in Lea's hotel also built a *sukkah,* but then told the girls not to dare enter it. Lea was so upset by this prohibition that she got the girls to build a *sukkah* for themselves. The boys responded to this by threatening to wreck the girls' *sukkah,* claiming with childish illogic that since girls are not obligated to use a *sukkah,* therefore they mustn't be allowed to have one. The girls countered this threat by having two of them watch their *sukkah* in two-hour shifts around the clock for the entire holiday.

Some time that winter we were relocated to Villa de Richemont, on the outskirts of town. The Villa was a beautiful house set in a lovely, sweeping garden surrounded by a fence. It boasted a basement kitchen (from which food could be raised to the ground floor by a dumbwaiter, operated by pulling a rope), three enormous rooms on the ground floor, a number of smaller rooms (including several under the gabled roof), a large bathroom, and many other accoutrements of comfortable living. It was (and still is) situated high up on the face of a mountain, commanding a view of the city and its lake, Lac du Bourget.

We had a lot of catching up to do in our studies, primarily our Jewish studies. Because we had been deprived of a Jewish education for about six years, this now became the immediate concern. The people in charge divided us into nine groups according to our levels of achievement. For quite a while, however, all of this was only theoretical due to the shortage of teachers. Essentially, two people were guiding us: the director, Rabbi Simon Segal (currently Executive Director of the Kamenitzer Yeshivah in Boro Park), and a main instructor, Rabbi Shmuel Meyer Miller (until recently the Rabbi of Amidar, Bat Yam in Israel). The two of them could not possibly handle nine classes all by themselves, but as a result of their efforts in canvassing the area surrounding

Sisters of two of my friends in front of the Beau Site Hotel.

Aix-les-Bains, the teaching staff was supplemented by another four, and then five, members. The postwar situation being what it was, however, teachers came and went, many staying with us only briefly.

Assisting the teaching staff was Samuel Lemmer.

Lea and I in front of the Beau Site Hotel. The sign proclaims that the hotel houses refugee children.

As one of the older boys in our group, Samuel had had the chance to gain a broader Jewish education as a child than we had. He volunteered to tutor those of us for whom a teacher was not available, and spent countless hours imparting to us the knowledge we were so sorely lacking. He was also one of the very few older boys asked by the administration to serve as our leaders.

We were also especially privileged to have a "resident scholar" among us, in the person of the previously mentioned Rabbi Mordechai Pogrimanski of the Kovno ghetto. When Mrs. Sternbuch heard that Rabbi Pogrimanski had arrived in France, she asked Rabbi Miller to go and welcome him. Rabbi Miller did just that, and also managed to persuade him to come and stay with us.

The stature of this scholar towered above anything we were capable of grasping, but somehow we sensed this. At the outset, Rabbi Pogrimanski studied by himself, oblivious to everything that went on around him. Most of the time he stayed in his room, but from time to time he could be found sitting in the garden, fully engrossed in his studies. On one occasion, however, he joined the boys on a rowing trip that took place on a minor holiday. Strangely enough, a storm hit the usually peaceful lake during the outing, almost capsizing

Rabbi Pogrimanski.

the boats. The boys were panicking, but Rabbi Pogrimanski

remained calm even though they really were in extreme danger. Finally, they were rescued by the man who operated the boat rental concession, who came and ferried them to safely in his motor boat.

While our administration was struggling to put together a teaching staff, the girls and the younger boys were inundated with educational personnel. Nonetheless, someone decided that reinforcements were needed, and arrangements were made to bring in a number of educators from Palestine. One of these was Yitzchak Levy, then still a bachelor, whose son Rabbi Gavriel Yosef Levy married Lea's eldest daughter many years later. Mr. Levy was not sure that hand-baked matzos, which he was accustomed to use for the Seder nights, would be available in post-war France, and he was unwilling to compromise at all in fulfilling this mitzvah. Accordingly, before he left Jerusalem he had a quantity of flour (ground from wheat grown specifically for this purpose) put in a metal container, which was then soldered shut to prevent moisture from entering. (In this way the flour was absolutely protected from accidentally becoming leavened.) He had no idea where he would find the proper facilities for producing kosher-for-Passover matzos out of this flour, but apparently he trusted

Lac de Bourget.

the Master of the Universe to help him solve that problem. Mr. Levy found it remarkable that although he had to pass several border-control checkpoints on his way from Palestine to France, the guards always accepted his claim of harmless perishable goods and never insisted on opening the mysterious box.

Rabbi Pogrimanski's first request from Mr. Levy was to allow him to put on his *tefillin*; he believed that they conformed to a higher standard than his own, since they had been produced by a first-class Jerusalem scribe. Given Rabbi Pogrimanski's concern for the proper performance of Torah law, it was only natural, then, with Passover soon approaching and Rabbi Pogrimanski becoming increasingly concerned with finding absolutely kosher matzos, that he discuss the problem

חיי תורה באיקס־לה־בין

איקס־לה־בין, העיירה היפה, שיושבת בין ההרים במורדות האלפים, ע״י אגם, נהפכה למחסה זמני לילדי ישראל. בע־ יירה הזאת התרחצו הרומאים העתיקים, ומי חשב שגם בהיסטוריה היהודית ייזכר פעם שמה ? היום היא מלאה חכ־ מים, יהודים ישרים וילדי ישראל, שני־ צלו לשמחתנו מהשמד הנורא.

יש בה מוסדות חינוך החל מגן ילדים ועד ישיבה. ב,,וילה רפאל" נמצאים כ־40 ילד (כ״י) קטנים, ואחדים מהם כבר משתתפים בשיעורים אצל הילדים הגדולים. במלון ,,בר־סיט" גרים כ־250 ילד כ״י מגיל 5 עד גיל 18, שחלק גדול מהם יתומים, בלי אב ואם. הם מקבלים שם חינוך יהודי ברוח ישראל סבא. המלון דומה בחיצוניותו למלון ,,המלך דוד" בירושלים, אבל בפנים מרגישים על כל צעד ושעל את עקבות הגרמנים. המוסד מוחזק ע״י ועד ההצלה באמ־ ריקה. הילדים מחולקים לקבוצות לפי גיל וידיעתם, ולומדים 5 שעות ביום לימודי קודש אצל מוריהם שבאו אתם עוד מפולין, ושמתמסרים להם כמו ליל־

ديהם, והשיגו במשך חצי שנה ללמד ילדים מא״ב עד התחלת לימוד הגמרא. תינוקות של בית רבן אלו, שלא טעמו טעם חטא מימיהם, ושסבלו יותר מכל בן אדם אחר בירצות סיביר בערבות אסיה התיכונה, בבונקרים בפולין וב־ מחנות השמדה, לבך עולץ, כשאתה רו־ אה את חשקם ללמוד, את ידיעתם הרבה בלי־ מודי הקודש. הילדים עומדים /תחת הנהלת המורה שפירא זינגר חברה במו־ עצת החברות שע״י ה , ,ות האירופאי של פועלי אגודת ישראל. מפורות ,בית יעקב" מפולין, שהצילה בעצמה הרבה ילדים, ומשמחנכת את ילדותיה ברוח ,,בית יעקב ו..בתי־ה".

למוסד גדול זה שלחה עכשיו פא״י שנים לשליחיה הארי״י, יצחק לוי ויצחק יודלין, כדי להכין את הילדים לחיי הארץ, ובמיוחד לחיי התורה בארץ. נוסף עליהם עוד חבר פא״י משווייץ. בראש המוסד היפה הזה עומד ד״ר לבל מתלמידי יח״ל, שהתחבא בזמן מלחמה בסביבות אקס־ לה־בין, ושמתכוון להקים שם עוד מוס־ דות כאלה לתפארת.

אבל גולת הכותרת של חיי התורה באקס־לה־בין, הן שתי ישיבותיה, הרא־ שונה, ,,ישיבת חכמי צרפת", נוסדה תיכף אחרי גמר המלחמה, ולומדים בה בעיקר בחורים מצרפת עצמה, מצפון אפריקה וגם יחידים מפולין, סי״ה כ־60 כ״י. בראש הישיבה עומד הרב חיי־ קין, בן ישיבת רדין ועוזרים על ידו הרב יצחק ויינגרובר ועוד רבנים. הלי־ מודים הם בצרפתית בעיקר, והבחורים האלו הם אולי היחידים בעולם, שמש־ תמשים במלות הלועזיות של פרש״י. בני ארצם של בעלי התוספות חדשו את נעוריהם, וישבים שוב על התורה כמו לפני כמה מאות בשנים.

הישיבה השניה ב,,וילה רישמונט", עומדת תחת הנהלת הרה״ג ר' מרדכי פוגרמנסקי שליט״א, וכמה מבני ישי־ בות ליטא אומרים את השיעורים. רוב הבחורים בדעתם להמשיך בלמודם בא״י.

הרי לפניכם תיאור קצר של חיי התורה באקס־לה־בין, שרק מביא את העובדות הובשנות ואת המספרים הי־ בשים. אבל כאן כל ילד וכל בן ישיבה הוא עולם מלא, וא״א לספר על באו״א אפילו בספר שלם. וכולם רוצים לעלות לארצנו. האם הכינונו מקום בשביל כולם ?

An article in the She'arim newspaper describing the educational activities in Aix-les-Bains.

with Mr. Levy. To his delight, he discovered that the solution was close at hand in the metal box Mr. Levy had brought. Rabbi Pogrimanski proposed a deal: Mr. Levy would contribute his flour, while Rabbi Pogrimanski would travel to Paris (where the only matzah-baking oven in France at that time was situated) and bake the matzos. The suggestion was well received, and the problem solved.

* * *

We were residing in one of the most beautiful spots in Europe, perhaps in the world. We lived in a spacious building whose windows gave us a gorgeous view of half the town. The other half—which boasted baths, park, hotels and the 5000-foot Mt. Revard, reachable by cable car and bus, could be viewed from "downtown," with its tree-lined main street, colorful shops, and leisurely traffic. (The very mountain on which Villa Richemont was situated blocked our view of this side of town.) We could go rowing on the lake on Friday afternoons—if we chose not to ride around town on bicycles, which we could rent very inexpensively. But with all this, we were far from happy.

Perhaps our unhappiness stemmed from our lacking a

sense of permanence. We knew that our stay in France was temporary, yet we had no idea where we would go from there—or when. Maybe we were longing for something with which to connect, something that would give us a feeling of being on *terra firma*.

Friday afternoon recreation time in Aix-les-Bains.

Perhaps this is why one day (the 1st of May, I think) one of the boys suggested that we get together during the afternoon break for a group singing session, the repertoire of which consisted entirely of Russian songs. First, we assembled in one of the attic rooms but, as it became crowded, we threw caution to the wind and regrouped in one of the larger rooms next to the office. Soon we were extolling the charms of the Volga, the beauty of wheat fields sown by the free and happy Russian people, the majesty of the country's mighty rivers, the strength and bravery of the Red Army, the might of the Soviet artillery, the prowess of Soviet tank drivers and the accuracy of their turret gunners in routing the Japanese, and the daring Revolution-era exploits of the horse-drawn *tachanki* machine guns. We sang of soldiers of the Revolution who walked untiringly through hilly steppes, daring cavalry regiments led by Budenny through thick and thin, fearless submariners slipping quietly away on secret missions, and so on. The hardships, the ever-present hunger, the uncertainties of the times during which we had learned these songs had vanished, leaving only the flowing beauty of the melodies and lyrics to give us the illusion of life in a never-never land. Given the chance we would have most probably gone through the entire repertoire, which each of us knew by heart and which included dozens of songs. But this was not to be. In the midst of our camaraderie the door suddenly flew open to reveal a very agitated Rabbi Miller. "Do you have to bring Stalin here all the way from Moscow!" he shouted. This effectively terminated our spontaneous cultural event.

Another factor contributed to our unhappiness. It is said that an army travels on its stomach; for us too, after years of hunger, food was a major issue. Our meals, which had been tolerable at our "midpoint house," now became a problem here in the Villa. We were assigned a cook of our own, a French woman, but she insisted on native French cuisine. This included salads and, quite frequently, vegetable soup—mainly split pea. We couldn't communicate with her since she only spoke French, so once we spoke to the cook's husband, who spoke German, about what we called "cooked grass" only to be told, "but these are cooked vegetables." Of course, there was always at least some bread spread with jam straight out of large cans. But this could not really satisfy a bunch of Polish-born youngsters with healthy appetites to whom vegetable, in the form of salads or in any other form were at best a side dish, and who were looking forward to going back to their previous fare—plenty of bread and butter, eggs, hot milk, meat and potatoes for lunch, and similar substantial foods. We couldn't understand why we had to sustain ourselves on what to us was nothing more than "grass." Lunch, supposed to be the main meal, frequently also consisted of salads—leaving us as hungry after eating as before. To our dismay, our complaints got us nowhere.

One day we decided that only a hunger strike would solve the problem. We went to the garden and plucked handfuls of grass which we placed on the tables in empty jam cans. We stood there, all twenty-five of us, yelling, "We want food! We want food! We don't want grass!" Rabbi Segal came downstairs and told us that he would see what he could do about it, but did not promise anything. He insisted that we wash our hands for the meal and eat—which we did.

Our complaints continued to the point where several members of the supervisory body came to see how we were being treated. The cook was told to prepare a regular meal, meaning one that is served daily. Since, however, the cook's main concern was showing that she knew how to cook, she served the supervisors, who were sitting in the office upstairs, a full four-course meal, the kind that was served only on the Sabbath!

Needless to say, we were very upset. Again we assembled in the dining room, which was situated directly beneath the office, and yelled, "Why was the commission given fish, meat, cake, and dessert?" We repeated this slogan over and over, not sure if they could hear us upstairs. Nevertheless, for all our efforts, any subsequent improvement in the food was marginal.

Rabbi Pogrimanski was not the only star to join our educational staff. One day Rabbi Miller learned that a friend of his from his yeshivah days in Poland, Rabbi Aharon Kreiser, was in Marseilles, together with some of his fellow students from the Mirrer Yeshivah. Almost all the Mirrer students had escaped Lithuania at the last minute and spent the war years together, as a yeshivah, in Shanghai. Now they had been given permission to leave China and were making their way to the United States. Some of them were in France, trying to find a way to get into Palestine. Their efforts (illegal, of course) had not yet borne fruit, and they were stranded in Marseilles. Rabbi Miller pleaded with his good friend Rabbi Kreiser, and, through him, the rest of the group, to stay with us in the meantime and help alleviate our shortage of teachers. To our great good fortune, they agreed.

With their arrival, the teaching situation changed overnight. Not only were there now enough teachers, but the most outstanding boy among us had two of them, one for each half of the day. These young scholars had just completed six years of intensive studies, uninterrupted (I'm sorry to say) by visits to home and relatives who were no more. They were eminently overqualified, yet they knew how to reach down

A group of Mirrer Yeshiva students in France. From right to left: Rabbis Kreiser, Horowitz, Shapiro and Grushko, who subsequently joined our teaching staff. The fifth person is Rabbi Shmuel Orlanski, presently in Bnei Brak.

to our level. Rabbi Pogrimanski was finally able to have a real study partner, Rabbi Yosef Horowitz (currently a senior lecturer in a major Israeli yeshivah) with whom he had long discussions lasting into the early hours of the morning.

Front view of Villa Richemont.

Side view of Villa Richemont facing the lake.

Our villa, Richemont, was the last building on a mountain road, giving us a sense of isolation. One evening, a heavy rainstorm broke out. It thundered heavily, and bolts of lightning following one after the other. The downpour seemed to threaten to wash our building down the mountainside and into the lake—and then the lights went out. Some of the boys became frightened, and one even began crying. Rabbi Kreiser, who was with us then, sized up the situation (our instructors, excepting rabbis Segal and Miller, resided elsewhere) and knew just what to do. He found a candle or two, gathered us around the dining room table and regaled us with stories about Shanghai. He taught us several melodies, too, which we sang together. Everyone gradually relaxed and soon cheered up. By the time the storm subsided and power was restored, we were relieved, but sorry the enchanted evening had ended.

Now that more grownups were available to supervise us, we were taken on more trips than ever before. We went up Mt. Revard several times, both by cable car and bus. In the winter we went skiing. In the summer we took more rowing trips on the Lac du Bourget, and once we even went on a full-day boating excursion there.

Lac du Bourget has all the trappings of a fairy-tale. It is a

large lake with several landmark buildings along its shores. At the time, at least, these included a picturesque monastery, situated further north from Aix, on the other side of the lake. It could only be reached by boat. So, during the Passover Holiday, an excursion boat was cha-

Younger children disembarking from the excursion boat in Aix-les-Bains.

rtered for the young residents of Beau-Site and Richemont. We spent the day hiking in the hills in the vicinity of the monastery, while enjoying the view of the forests on this, the unpopulated side of the lake, and the panorama of the lake itself with the town of Aix-les-Bains in the background.

The indefatigable Rabbi Kreiser joined us on this outing. He organized the Richemont boys into a group and prodded us to climb one of the rather steep paths that abounded in the vicinity of the monastery. He climbed ahead of everybody together with a young Jewish soldier

A group of boys from the yeshiva at the peak of the Mont Revard (elevation 1550 m). The person with his hands clasped is Rabbi Simon Segal. The woman is our French cook, with her daughter next to her. I am the second boy from the left in the seated row.

serving in the British army, whom he had "procured" in some mysterious way. The Rabbi, together with this tall, slim,

freckled-faced young man in uniform, took the hills without any apparent effort, while we were soon exhausted, and protested that we could not keep up. Rabbi Kreiser urged us on with the promise that he would teach us a new song —something appropriate for Passover. When no longer able to continue, we

Climbing the mountains near the monastery at Lac de Bourget. Rabbi Kreiser is in the rear.

sat down for a rest, and the Rabbi proceeded to teach us a song in Russian, an extended translation of one of the songs of the Passover Seder. To this very day, this song is the highlight of my family's Seder night.

Rabbi Segal was intent on deriving the maximum benefit from the presence of Rabbi Pogrimanski in our midst. He thus persuaded this Torah luminary to present the opening lecture of the older boys' new semester. The Rabbi agreed, although for him it was like teaching kindergarten. He opened the volume, quickly took in the full Talmud page—which he hadn't studied for over twenty years—closed the volume, and went on to present a lecture on a full page of the Talmud—from memory! His discourse included the commentaries, which

Class conducted on the porch of Villa Richemont. I am third from left; Rabbi Samuel Krybus is the teacher.

he quoted verbatim. To put it mildly, we were very impressed

—precisely what Rabbi Segal had intended.

Rabbi Pogrimanski was also well known for his talks on ethics (*mussar*), and Rabbi Segal persuaded him to deliver some of these, too. His first talk overwhelmed us, and those of us who had sisters excitedly transmitted the news to Beau Site. The news reached the administration there, and it was decided that next time the rabbi spoke the older girls would be invited to hear him too, along with their teachers. We set up chairs for the girls in an adjoining room on the day of the Rabbi's next talk. Although Lea was too young to participate, there is no doubt as to the powerful impression he made on the older girls, and in particular on the girls' teachers, several of whom were graduates of the famous Cracow Beth Jacob Teacher's Seminary, established by the renowned Sarah Schenirer.

Some time later, Rabbi Miller married one of the teachers in Beau Site. As a result of his wife's efforts and those of the other teachers, many of the Beau Site children are leading a full Jewish life today.

The entire operation, which included the maintenance of all the children in Aix-les-Bains (there were others besides us)

Rabbi Miller, his bride and her friends.

was managed by Dr. Moshe Lebel. (Dr. Lebel, who presently lives in Telz-Stone near Jerusalem, was also the founder of the Aix-les-Bains Yeshivah for French-speaking boys.) He had been one of the co-founders of our school, together with Mrs. Recha Sternbuch. The renowned Mrs. Sternbuch visited us twice, staying with us for dinner and treating us to Swiss chocolate bars. The connection between Mrs. Sternbuch and Mother being known to our administration, I was assigned the duty of

---

ועד ההצלה ב"ה

VAAD HATZALA REHABILITATION COMMITTEE

2 NASSAU STREET • **NEW YORK CITY** • **Telephone REctor 2-4862**

January 6, 1947

Dr. Leybel
Hotel Bryant
54th Street & Broadway
New York, N. Y.

Dear Dr. Leybel:

There is a very definite agreement between us and Rescue Children — an affiliate of Vaad Hatzala. Rescue Children are to provide physical necessities and funds for the care of orphans in your homes and elsewhere. Vaad Hatzala is responsible for the educational program and religious upbringing of the children.

We have discussed your program at length with you and are satisfied that you are giving a fair proportion of religious learning and secular education to bring these orphans up as good Jews and useful citizens.

We will thank you to mail us the exact program of your daily activities.

Should you desire to change your program, or should we desire to change it, this shall be done by direct correspondence with the New York office.

Sincerely yours,

VAAD HATZALA
RABBI ARON KOTLER

IRVING BUNIM

IMB:LS

Photostat of a rare letter, signed by Rabbi Aharon Kotler and Mr. Irving Bunim, pledging continuous support of Dr. Lebel's "French operation," of which we were a part.

waiter each time she came in order to parade me before our patron. The other boys were jealous of this distinction.

* * *

Father started corresponding with Lea and me as soon as he was able to locate us. Since our pocket money didn't amount to much, I asked him for some assistance. He responded by placing a one Palestine pound note (worth about three American dollars) into each of his subsequent letters. The money went primarily for buying film for my camera, stamps, and similar items. After a while, I noticed that a letter mailed from Palestine on Tuesday would invariably arrive on Friday. Father agreed to my request to arrange our correspondence thus, so that every Friday would be "letter day." Indeed, I would stick my hand into the mailbox to retrieve his letter (and the one-pound note) with the same certainty that a person reaches for an item he himself has previously put in a particular place. This went on as long as I stayed in Aix.

* * *

Of course, all this time we missed Mother exceedingly and, even more so, were worried about her fate. We knew that she was not in jail—that much I had heard from the lady I met in Prague—but nothing else. Of course, the question of Mother's fate and whereabouts was put to Father in our first letter to him. His answer was enigmatic: Mother would be joining us as soon as she possibly could. We simply couldn't get any elaboration out of him, no matter how frequently we tried.

We were left to conclude that Mother was still somewhere in Poland and that, at least for the time being, there was no way to communicate with her, and little hope that she would ever be able to join us. We finally got resigned to the fact that we might not see Mother again. We consoled ourselves with the knowledge that although Mother was not with us, she was still alive—a fate much better than that which had befallen the mothers and fathers of most of our friends.

Mother, on her part, was extremely afraid of jeopardizing her status. She feared that any letter she might send abroad would be interpreted by the authorities as a preparation for leaving Poland, which could be done only illegally. As a result, whatever news that came from her to Father arrived in a roundabout way.

* * *

One day our group was informed that Rabbi Segal, together with Rabbi Miller, had decided to entrust our education to the Beth Joseph Yeshivah, which was opening a special branch for us near Paris. Those of us who had sisters or younger brothers in Beau Site took tearful leave of them, of our entire teaching staff, of the beauty that was Aix-les-Bains, and headed for our new destination in the vicinity of Paris.

Little did we know, but our departure signaled the beginning of the end of the sojourn in Aix-les-Bains for all the children. For some time after our departure, life for the girls in Beau Site continued as before. The charms of the place did wonders for Lea and others, all of whom had been deprived of a normal childhood. The girls used to go swimming at a secluded beach at the Lac de Bourget. Lea used some of money Father sent through me to rent a bicycle, and would ride for hours (giving her friends a turn, too). For the first time in her life, she was part of a group of children her own age. She had a special relationship with the previously mentioned Yitzchak Levy, with whom she corresponded extensively after he returned to Palestine, concerning topics in Jewish thought and philosophy. Her days were filled with all the normal pastimes girls her age enjoy: studies, group activities, stage productions, and memorable Sabbath afternoons spent with peers and their counselor.

After some time, the entire children's home was transferred to a luxury hotel in St. Pierre—a famous resort city in the French Alps. The children ate delicious meals, attended classes, learned Swiss embroidery and art, and went on chaperoned mountain climbs which lasted two or three days. All this indulgence helped the children recuperate from the ravages of war and from the sense of uncertainty which resulted from constantly being moved from place to place.

Lea and I corresponded all the time, primarily by way of postcards, and thus I learned of her decision to follow her Beth Jacob teacher, a student of Sarah Schenirer, who took a part of the group to Henoville, near Paris, to form a Beth Jacob school. This move, based as it was on ideological motives, resulted in a drastic reduction in the girls' standard of living. The accommodations were poor, the girls slept on mattresses on the floor, the meals were a far cry from those in Aix or St. Pierre, and the girls were very much on their own.

Matters became even worse when most of the girls left with that teacher for the United States. Lea had no intention of going with them. Palestine, by now Israel, was the place where she wanted to be. She longed to be among Jews and of course, with Father. However, no matter how bad things were before, they got even worse. When the majority of the girls left, the place lost its official status and was no longer sup-

The hotel in Grenoble where Lea lived after leaving Aix-les-Bains.

plied with food. For a while, the several remaining girls bartered clothing left by their friends for food. Fortunately, on the Sabbath at least they were invited for meals by refugee families near by them, who cooked and took their meals together. Her contribution consisted of checking carp heads for worms, enough heads for the entire group, every Friday. During the week she survived on strawberies that she picked in a nearby forest and cream, for which she bartered clothing.

At some point, Lea recalled that we had relatives in Paris, and traveled to them. It was no small task for a young girl, inexperienced in using public transportation alone, to navigate her way through the metropolis that is Paris. She located the relatives, but they turned out to be non-observant, making her stay with them extremely difficult.

When she told them of her desire to go to Israel, they gave her the address of the Agudath Israel organization in Paris. That office, however, could only give her a train ticket to the port city of Marseilles where a group of young people was gathering to sail for Israel.

Lea, a "skinny fourteen-year-old," as she puts it, took the train to Marseilles knowing only that she must somehow make her way to the port. The person at the train station's information booth started explaining to her how to get to her destination by bus. When she indicated that she was out of money, she was told that "all she had to do" was to follow the coastline to reach the port. On this sagacious advice, she embarked on a six-hour walk amidst a torrential downpour, accompanied by howling winds.

Yet Lea succeeded in reaching the port, and in joining up with the youth group: boys and girls of a notoriously antireligious movement. After a two-day wait, a laughably small vessel arrived, and she boarded together with the group. Because she was observant, Lea was completely ignored; not a single one of the youths or accompanying adults concerned themselves with her welfare or even spoke to her. The boat

was in such extremely poor condition that the journey stretched out for weeks. The storms did not help any, almost causing
the boat to turn back. At one point, the fuel ran out, and they
had to make an unscheduled stopover. Not surprisingly, all
this resulted in intense and continual seasickness.

When they finally reached the waters of the Haifa port, it
was the Sabbath. Everybody began climbing over the sides of
the ship into smaller boats that would take them to shore.
Knowing that this was forbidden on the Sabbath, Lea refused
to budge. The party representatives who boarded to greet the
newcomers attempted to persuade her: "Religion", they said,
"is for the Diaspora—here in Israel everything's allowed." Lea
was not convinced and, in the end, she was removed by force.

By the time the entire group had been processed by the
authorities, it was well after the end of the Sabbath. Together
with her group, Lea was transported by bus to a non-religious
kibbutz (collective agricultural settlement) in the vicinity of
Binyamina. The nature of the kibbutz became apparent almost
immediately—she was particularly appalled by the decadence
of relationships between the young people. This situation set
her thinking about how to get out, but she soon realized that
she would not be able to talk her way out by explaining to the
officials that she had been placed there by mistake. Indeed,
Lea soon became aware that she was one of many religious
children who were victims of such "mistakes," or attempts to
integrate them into anti-religious communities where every
effort would be made to convince her that "here in Israel
everything is allowed." So one day she simply walked off the
kibbutz and set out alone to find Father in Tel Aviv. After she
had walked for a long while, a kind soul took pity on the
young girl trudging down the road and gave her a ride the
rest of the way.

Tel Aviv was an unknown city to her, but after finding her
way through Paris and Marseilles, she managed there too.
Soon she was standing in line for the Number 4 bus, which

she had been told would take her to Father's address, which she had written on a slip of paper. As the line crawled for-

ward, she realized that she didn't have a penny to her name and couldn't pay the bus fare. She turned to the person behind her and asked for a loan of the bus fare—as well as his address. She explained that she was on her way to meet her father, who would return the money. The person gave her the fare and assured her that she need not worry about repayment.

Lea stood next to the driver to make sure he didn't forget to call her

Lea at the time of her arrival in Israel.

stop. She walked the remaining blocks to the apartment and, with her heart beating increasingly faster, knocked on the door. A man, looking only remotely familiar, opened it and looked at her. After several moments' silence, Lea said tentatively, "Tatusiu?" Almost simultaneously, Father cried out "Lilka!" He embraced her, and then both burst out in tears which subsided only after a long while.

They sat down and talked until the early hours of the next morning, each trying to tell the other about all that had happened during the years they had been separated. They finally fell asleep at dawn, only to resume their tales next morning after breakfast, and for a number of days after that.

* * *

Château Bois du Rocher, where the Beth Joseph Yeshivah, headquartered in Brooklyn, NY, had set up a branch for us boys, was a former ducal residence, pressed into service as a residence for refugees, perched on a mountaintop between Paris and Versailles. Actually, it was less a mountain than a slope rolling downward from a plateau that served as storage for what seemed like hundreds of aircraft, probably military, put out to pasture after the war. This airfield was separated from our new residence by a short strip of forest, which surrounded our place on all sides, and a tall, heavy mesh fence. We stood at this fence often, trying to catch sight of an aircraft taking off, but, alas, we could only see propellers starting to turn and then stopping. Apparently this was a maintenance procedure—to keep the engines from getting rusty. Vehicles could reach our château only by traveling through this airfield, but this required top-level authorization. Otherwise, we could be reached only by a climb along a dirt path up the slope from the bus or train that ran in the valley below.

Our yeshivah occupied the only empty space left by the other refugee occupants: the grand ballroom. It was a very large room, with mirrors on every square inch of wall not taken up by windows. A huge chandelier hung down imposingly from the middle of the ceiling. For furniture, we had several large, heavy wooden tables with benches, and army cots. This room served as our synagogue, dining room, classroom, and bedroom. Com-

The boys at Château Bois du Rocher. I am the third from right in the back row. The person in the rabbinical garb is Rabbi Y. L. Nekritz, the son-in-law of Rabbi Abraham Yaffen of Novhardok.

pared with Aix-les-Bains, ours was now a pauper's existence. The lack of privacy added to our discomfort. And the oversize bulb glaring down from the otherwise non-functioning chandelier made it impossible for anyone to go sleep early.

As soon as I got my bearings, I set out to deal with this problem. Apparently some war activity had taken place in the woods surrounding the château and field-telephone wires lay around there in abundance. We procured a length of such wire and strung it between the two longer walls of the ballroom. Then we got hold of some surplus army blankets and hung them on the wire, thereby creating a partition. Somehow, without suitable tools or materials, we were able to move the light bulb to the other side of the room, which we designated as the "non-sleeping" section. Richemont it was not, but at least we had some modicum of privacy. We still prayed, ate, and studied in that one room, but now, at least, we could sleep undisturbed.

Father's letters to me continued as before, but somehow now we couldn't fine-tune the mails to arrange for Friday arrivals. With the High Holidays nearing, I asked him for a set of prayer books. The New Year's set arrived in due time. The prayer book for Yom Kippur, the Day of Atonement, arrived at 10 AM of that very day, a little too late, especially since receiving mail isn't permitted on that day. But we had a non-Jew at the Château to whom I handed the package without a word, and who had the good sense to open it and bring it to me.

The plan had never been for us to stay in France indefinitely, even though not everyone had the same destination in mind. The Beth Joseph administration was eager to get us to the United States, to join the mother yeshivah. For my part, I hoped to be able to get to Palestine. For either, we needed a passport (or other travel document), which none of us possessed. So one day all of us took a trip to a little town in the Versailles district. The mayor, who apparently doubled as police chief, was persuaded (possibly by the sight of large-denomination banknotes) to issue travel documents to a sizable group of boys, all of whom had their identity confirmed by two of their own teachers in a language other than the mayor's own. Under the circumstances, however, he was quite willing to accept an interpreter's rendering. The applications went to Versailles where they were properly stamped and returned, and then delivered to us.

In the meantime, our administration sent a list of our names to the United States in order to obtain student visas. These had the advantage of being exempt from the quota

— 1 —

FRANCE

TITRE D'IDENTITÉ ET DE VOYAGE

N° ▬▬▬▬

Nom du titulaire : LEDERMAN

Prénoms : PAHVEL BOLEK
Lieu de naissance : VARSOVIE
Date de naissance : 19. 7. 31
né de :
et de :
Nationalité : ORIG POLONAISE
Profession :
Résidence de fait : Chateau Bois du
Résidence antérieure : Rocher Joury au Jorof

Le détenteur du présent titre n'a pas qualité pour obtenir un passeport français.

— OBSERVATIONS —

Stateless-person's passport issued to me by the French authorities. Note the (misspelled) double first name.

limitations imposed on immigrants. We had no inkling that these visas allowed only a limited stay.* One day we were joyously informed that the arrangements for a first group had been completed; we would soon be asked to go to the American consulate in Paris to take care of formalities. I was among those to whom the congratulations were due—and the only one not excited about it.

 I had no intention of going to America. Father was in Palestine, and that was where I planned to go. Our director, however, thought differently. He called me over and explained that, as of now, there was no way for me to get into Palestine. He also reassured me that should such an opportunity present itself in the future, the United States government would not stand in my way. I allowed him to convince me.

The day of sailing for the US was set for January 23, 1948. Special arrangements were made by our administration to allow the truck that was to take us to the train station in Paris to drive through the otherwise off-limits airfield. The train stopped directly at the French port of Le Havre, where we were processed through customs and passport control. I have no idea what the customs officers expected to find among our belongings, which, for the most part, were packed in rather small *papier-mâché* valises that had to be protected from excessive moisture. They nonetheless went through the contents of each valise very thoroughly. Each, that is, except for that belonging to one of the older boys, who hadn't heeded the administration's admonition to get his underwear washed. Apparently the smell was not to the custom officer's liking because, as soon as the boy opened the valise the officer thundered "*Allez!*" ("Go!") and slammed the valise shut. He looked very relieved as the poor boy moved out of sight.

We traveled in style on the S.S. Ernie Pyle, a former troop carrier which had been reincarnated as a refugee transport

---

* Later, special provisions were made in the United States immigration law allowing us to apply for permanent residence and citizenship.

vessel. The families among the travelers were assigned officers' quarters, whereas the rest of us were quartered in the troops' compartments. The comfort provided by these accommodations was more or less of the quality of our Rocher lodgings, so we had nothing to complain about. Still, all of us became seasick, some for longer and some for shorter periods.

The food situation proved extremely problematic, and we had to be content with what we deemed kosher even without certification—mostly bread and butter, eggs, and tea. Little did we know that the first two items require rabbinical supervision: back in Poland, these did not. We were not the only ones aboard unhappy with the situation.

The ship's cook was very upset by our unwillingness to touch his delicacies. He knew what the problem was even though none of us spoke enough English to articulate it. So one day he came in, together with the waiters, beaming at having found food that was definitely kosher: chickens fried in butter. When we refused to touch it, he was beside himself. "But these fly!" he protested, flapping his hands like wings.

I had several dollars on me, remnants of the Palestine pounds that Father used to send every week, and was thus induced by one of my friends to buy an American beverage better than anything we had ever tasted—Coca Cola. The privilege cost something like 40 or 60 cents (for a 5-cent bottle of Coke), and the stuff proved to be totally unacceptable to my digestive system. To make matters even worse, my seasickness came back.

I really should have spent the several dollars to resole the only pair of shoes I possessed, as these had rather large holes. Yet the very idea seemed to border on blasphemy because I was on my way to America where I would be shod, dressed, and outfitted from head to toe. And if it rained on the ship, well, I would just stay in the cabin. Or so I imagined.

We were only a few days out of port when we ran into a major storm. The ship rolled violently, spray deposited veritable layers of water on the deck, and, of course, the rain kept falling. Those of us who were getting over seasickness suffered something of a relapse. I, like many others, sought comfort on the exposed deck, thereby providing a convenient inlet for some of the water straight into my shoes.

The storm raged for a couple of days, extending our scheduled journey from nine days to two weeks. As soon as the storm passed, the captain ordered full steam ahead, and we entered New York Harbor before dawn on Friday, February 6, 1948. We were treated to a grand view of the Statue of Liberty's torch and of Manhattan's skyscrapers. At dawn, our ship was boarded by US Immigration officials who set up shop in the dining room and processed us so swiftly and efficiently that our papers were checked and stamped by the time we alighted at one of the piers.

The elevated highway along the Hudson River, a major thoroughfare, was our first glimpse of New York and I couldn't stop marveling at the unending stream of large, relatively new cars passing by. In Paris we had seen cars of every vintage and manufacture, most of them small or medium-sized, and old. But here it seemed that everyone was driving a big, new, or almost-new car. This vision of affluent America was shattered almost immediately by the sight of porters, some of them Yiddish-speaking, bending mightily under heavy loads. I found it impossible to comprehend how the affluent American Jewish community, with what I imagined to be unlimited funds to spend on Jews all over the world, was unable to assist these poor souls.

We were met by people from the United Service for New Americans (USNA) which was a division of the American Joint Jewish Distribution Committee (AJDC), known to Jews the world over as "The Joint." They took us to the Hotel Marseilles, at the corner of West 103rd Street and Broadway, where our American dream suffered another blow. On Friday evening (and subsequently on the Sabbath morning meal) we were offered a choice of fish or meat, but not both.

Saturday night, after the end of the Sabbath, seemed like the best time to acquaint ourselves with the city, and my friend Boruch and I started by purchasing a street map of Manhattan. Lo and behold, we found that on the other side of the George Washington Bridge there was a place called Englewood Cliffs. This was a major discovery because Boruch had an aunt living in America, and now we had the information we needed to locate her. Or so we thought.

In fact, all six of Boruch's father's sisters had long before immigrated to the United States, and one lived quite nearby: in Englewood, New Jersey. Boruch had even written to the family telling them that he was coming, but he had only been able to give an approximate date of arrival. We had no doubts that New Jersey was a section of New York State, so it made sense that it might be located on the other side of the Hudson. We excitedly drew the conclusion that Englewood Cliffs and Englewood were one and the same. We also decided that Washington Bridge was probably a major thoroughfare that would surely have a terminal with buses to Englewood.

We dropped our nickels into the turnstile, hopped on the local IRT uptown subway, whose cars looked prehistoric compared to those of the Paris metro, and soon found ourselves at the Washington Bridge station. We got out and started walking in the general direction of the bridge, until we came upon a fish store whose owner looked Jewish enough for us to speak to him in Yiddish. He confirmed that there was a bus terminal (little more than an open-air affair then) and gave us directions to reach it. We started walking, but soon got lost. Just then we were approached by a middle-aged Jewish couple who perceived our plight. Fortunately, they were also on their way to the terminal. They generously brought us to the bus going to Englewood (not Englewood Cliffs), and asked the driver to let us off at the stop closest to our destination. He did, and deposited us at about 9 PM in the middle of a snow-covered town.

We looked around for something to guide us further, and noticed a well-lit store with the name "Hoffman" written in huge letters above the display window. "Hoffman? He must be Jewish," we reasoned, and headed for the store. It turned out that while "Hoffman" was actually an advertisement for a popular soft drink, the store was, in fact, owned by a Jew. To our pleasant surprise, he told us that he knew the family: not only did they live just around the corner, but they had been in his store only a short while before. (We didn't have their phone number, and never dreamed of getting it because the convention of calling before visiting was not something we had ever learned. Besides, without knowing English, putting through an inter-city call, which then could be done only with an operator's assistance, would have been beyond us.)

As we walked up the path to their house, I asked Boruch to enter first, since I had no intention of being mistakenly hugged by his relatives. As he appeared in the doorway a cry went out in Yiddish, "The green one is here!" (This Yiddish term for a greenhorn seemed particularly appropriate in this case, since Boruch was wearing a green coat and cap.) They gave us a joyous welcome, replete with the anticipated hugs, etc. Soon we were treated to the bounty of the New World. The family delighted in offering us fresh fruit—"These are oranges, that other thing is a banana"—and showing us the wonders of modern technology—"The light goes on when you flip this switch on the wall," "There is a thing called a toilet inside the house that has to be flushed." (These people had left their tiny Polish town in the twenties and thought that these were novelties only to be found in America.) We slept over, and returned to the hotel the following day.

We utilized our free two-week hotel stay for newcomers—courtesy of the USNA—to see the city. On the second Friday night a nice fellow came to invite us to join the morning prayers at the synagogue of the Grand Rabbi of Bobov, then located at West 86th Street, off Broadway. He pointed out that we had already experienced one Sabbath at the hotel, and that we had everything to gain and nothing to lose—even if it did require a seventeen-block walk down Broadway. We accepted his invitation and never regretted it (especially Boruch, because it turned out that the Rabbi had known his father). This walk brought us face to face with another American phenomenon: kosher delicatessen stores open on the Sabbath. We didn't know what to make of it.

Our second week drew to a close, and the time came to take up permanent residence in the Beth Joseph Yeshivah. However, the visit we had made there some days previously had not been an overwhelming success. This, coupled with the constant encouragement of our Mirrer Yeshivah teachers back in Aix-les-Bains to make every effort to enter the Mirrer Yeshivah, had its effect. Hence, on Thursday morning I contacted someone at the Mirrer Yeshivah who rented a room for me with a family (since no dormitory existed at the time). That evening, I accompanied him to the synagogue of the Mirrer Yeshivah for evening prayers.

The yeshivah was then located on Ashford Street in the East New York section of Brooklyn. Its entire physical premises consisted of the rented synagogue and a rented dining room in the basement of another house of prayer, fourteen blocks away. Only dinner was provided; breakfast and supper, as well as lodgings, had to be paid from the USNA allowance given us.

The first evening prayer was an experience such as I had never before encountered. The one hundred and twenty students present prayed as one. Everyone was seated as the two introductory lines were recited. A pound on the lectern by the prayer leader brought everyone to his feet. He intoned the *Borechu* ("Bless G-d," the call to worship which begins the Evening Service), and the congregation responded in unison. Then everyone sat down together in a manner that would not shame a well-disciplined army. A second of quiet hung in the air just before the *Shema* prayer—punctuated only by the buzzing of a fly—and then a thunderous *"Shema Israel"* issued simultaneously from the mouths of one hundred and twenty people united in praise of the One Above. It rent the air with a force that stays with me until this very day, over fifty years later. Then and there I knew that I wanted to be a part of this yeshivah.

A new era dawned in my life.

*   *   *

After a somewhat difficult adjustment period I became a full-fledged student of the Mirrer Yeshivah. I "wandered" with it from East New York to Flatbush, Brooklyn, where it first was housed in a small building on Ocean Parkway; then to other temporary quarters on East 9th Street; and finally to its present location on the corner of Ocean Parkway and Avenue R. After offering a great deal of resistance, I finally succumbed to Mother's entreaties and undertook a high school correspondence course. This involved burning the midnight oil in the yeshivah's basement after a full program of Torah study. Evening college courses followed, eventually leading to an engineering degree from what was then known as the City College of New York.

In 1959 I went to Israel where I had the good fortune of meeting and marrying Yonah Berkman of Kfar Avraham, a suburb of Petach Tikvah. We returned to the States for another five years to allow me to graduate from engineering school by attending late afternoon and evening classes. We finally moved to Israel—re-joining our families—in 1965, and have been living in Bnei Brak ever since.

Rabbi Feldman, the Mashgiach of the Mirrer Yeshivah in Brooklyn, speaking at the farewell party for me; Rabbi Samuel Brudny is at my left.

PART III

PICKING UP THE PIECES

The unparalleled fury of the Second World War shattered the lives of its survivors, especially those of Jewish children. Mother's rescue work involved removing them from homes and institutions which had harbored them during the war, but which were not always willing to return them to their people when the war ended. But even more so, it involved returning the children to normality by nourishing them back to physical and emotional health with loving care. A small sense of appreciation of what transpired in the lives of these children can perhaps be obtained through the personal stories of some of those whom she restored to normal life.

MOTHER AS RESCUER

As the reader will recall, Lea and I lost contact with Mother when she was arrested and removed from our train on our journey out of Poland. For a long time we learned almost nothing about her fate, although at least we knew she was alive. But eventually, we heard the whole story: While Lea and I continued our train journey westward out of Poland, Mother was released by the police, who apparently were content with having prevented her from leaving Poland illegally. Mother made her way back to the nearly deserted apartment in Bytom. Several children remained who, for one reason or another, had not been able to make our train. Among them were a brother and sister, children of their newly designated "mother," Mrs. Sarah Rubinstein.[*] The passage to freedom had been allowed only for children and their counselors. Mother, the only person with a passport, was the sole adult supervisor permitted for the entire contingent. Mrs. Rubinstein, who had no travel documents, could not come along, and her children refused to go without her. Mother now had Yaakov Springer, the young man who was taken off the train together with her, to assist her.

Mother firmly believed that her unsuccessful attempt at leaving was dictated by Providence. She felt that she was taken off the train for the express purpose of devoting herself to rescuing more Jewish children from their gentile guardians, and she even knew where to start.

Two of the girls in the orphanage, Fela Safian and Ruzia Halzband, had brothers in a monastery.[**] The girls did not want to leave Poland without their brothers, but were per-

---

[*] See Chapter 21, "Snatched from the Vilno Ghetto."

[**] See Chapter 22, "Two Brothers, Two Sisters."

suaded to leave with our transport on the promise that an immediate effort would be made to extricate the brothers and reunite them with their sisters. When the promise was given, nobody believed that it could be implemented, because unsuccessful attempts had already been made several times using the "I am a relative" ploy.

The only other alternative in such cases was the time-honored method of bribery. Mother, however, had no idea if her budget would be sufficient to achieve the release of the two children. In addition, she didn't feel that she could simply appear at the monastery and offer money straightaway—in particular, since this was her first attempt at this kind of work.

So she hit upon a plan. She went to the Jewish Coordination Committee and persuaded them to issue her an identity card in the name of Sarah Safian. This card did not constitute a legal document, and was used primarily for receiving various kinds of assistance. Still, it was better than nothing.

I have little doubt that Mother's plan included fervent prayers, because otherwise it is difficult to explain why the abbot of the monastery accepted her document as genuine and let her have the Safian boy. Mother told the latter to get his things together and to wait, with his friend, Ruzia's brother, outside the office. Mother then spent some time with the abbot, discussing the manner in which the orphanage was run, the kind of schooling that the children received, and a variety of related topics—until she felt that she had gained his confidence.

At a certain moment, she opened the door slightly and closed it again. "I see," she commented, "that this boy has a friend who is inseparable from him. He is even with him now." The priest nodded, but didn't utter a word. Mother's heart started racing. She was about to put down her stakes for the second boy, well aware that in doing so, her credentials as an aunt might be questioned. So she switched the topic again. She said to the priest, "You know what, you were so good to the boy, here is some compensation." Upon saying this, she pulled out a large wad of bills and placed it on the table.

The priest was beside himself with joy and thanked her profusely. Another wad of bills was pulled out. "And this," Mother said, "is compensation for the expenses of the second boy. They really will be miserable if separated." Having said this, Mother got up, bid a hasty good-bye, and flew out of the office. She took the two boys by their hands, and walked out with them as fast as her feet could carry her. The abbot stood there, rigid as a statue, stunned and unable to utter a word.

Mother was overjoyed. She regarded her success in this seemingly impossible task as a clear sign from Heaven that she had been entrusted with the sacred task of bringing "lost" Jewish children back to their faith. Buoyed by this achievement, she set out to seek them out wherever they might be located.

This work required extensive and very tiring travel. Her missions usually started with a train journey that could last a good part of a day (or even more) with long intervals spent on wooden benches waiting for connecting trains in what were sometimes deserted and always unheated railroad stations. At times, the only way to reach a destination was to arrive in the evening, and board a train the following morning, necessitating an overnight stay. Mother was afraid to go to a hotel since this would involve presenting documents and the risk of being questioned about her intentions.

But whatever the discomfort involved, she never refused a request to rescue a child. Mother had to use a great deal of cunning and was exposed to far greater dangers than her predecessors in this sort of activity, since the more accessible children had already been rescued. Also, as the shock of war and occupation wore off, the traditional Polish anti-Semitism had started to reassert itself with increasing force.

True, Mother had certain things in her favor. With her light chestnut hair and blue eyes, she looked every inch a member

262 THESE CHILDREN ARE MINE

of the Polish city-bred aristocracy—and her perfect Polish strongly reinforced this image. These, however, could not ward off a police interrogation regarding the purpose of her travel to certain destinations. A vagrancy charge could be easily pressed against her with all its severe consequences. There was also the danger that the family who had custody of a child whose aunt or other relative Mother was pretending to be, would question her for details known only to them, details which she could not supply and which would thereby expose her.

There were other dangers, too. Mother traveled to villages by horse and wagon over unpaved roads without anyone to help her if something went wrong. She was a one-woman organization. Nobody knew where she was going, how long she expected to stay, and so forth. Had anyone wanted to kill her and bury her in a nearby forest, they might have done so and never been found out. It would have been impossible even to find her grave.

Once, even Mother's irreproachable gentile appearance failed to shield her. She was taking a bus to the city of Czesto-chowa, from where she planned to hire, as usual, a horse and wagon to reach a hamlet where yet another Jewish child unknowingly awaited his return to his people. These were times when anti-Semitism had reached such a peak that a Jew identified as such on inter-city public transportation was liable to be quickly disposed of by being simply thrown off the moving train or bus as it passed through an uninhabited area. On this journey, a priest, who apparently suspected Mother of being Jewish, asked her if she knew on which side of the highway the statue of the Black Madonna was located. This famous Catholic shrine is a landmark that greets people arriving at Czestochowa much as the Statue of Liberty once greeted immigrants arriving in the New York harbor. It was inconceivable that a true Pole could not answer the priest's question.

Since she hadn't the faintest idea of the correct answer,

Mother took a guess. "Are you sure?" the priest responded.

Uncertain, Mother switched sides—and immediately real-ized that she may have made the mistake of her life. Thinking quickly, she then switched sides several more times, and finally exclaimed, "Well, you know, I went through a war, and my memory just fails me." Fortunately, the priest let her off at that.

Another time she was on a train conversing with someone when a group of people entered the car, searching for Jews to throw off. Mother continued talking as if nothing had hap-pened, and the search party did not give her a second look.

Mother's rescue work was sometimes made even more difficult by obstacles created inadvertently by the parents who had left their children with gentiles at the beginning of the War. Some people went to great lengths to insure that not only would their children eventually return to their people, but that they would be returned to one specific person. To this effect, they left instructions with the Gentile surrogate parents not to release the child to anyone except a certain relative.

These well-meant arrangements sometimes backfired. Years later, Mother would tell of one case where a gentile with whom a girl was left had been instructed by the child's father to release her only to someone sent by a cousin named Schtrauch who lived in Haifa. Somebody informed on the gentile, accusing him of harboring a Jewish child, and he had to run away. His house was torched, together with all his possessions. Despite all this, faithful to his promise, when Mother came to him, he insisted that she first locate Schtrauch or else he could not give up the child.

When Mother failed to rescue a child, she would refuse to eat that day. She regarded the money spent for her food as compensation for rescuing children, and when she could not do so, she felt she was not entitled to compensation.

Mother's tactic was to approach families known to be holding Jewish children and to claim that she was an aunt or other close relative, or that she had been sent by relatives abroad to retrieve them. These fictional relatives were usually from America, were invariably "very rich," and were willing to pay the family handsomely for all the trouble they had gone to in raising a Jewish child, shielding him from the Germans, etc. Mother's foreign currency translated into seemingly enormous sums of the highly inflated Polish currency—usually enough to induce families to part with the children.

Still, Mother had to make sure to stay within her budget since the funds available to her were not unlimited. In some cases, she felt that the story of the rich relatives would result in unreasonable demands, and might even raise doubts about her motives. She also had to contend with people who knew that thousands of inflated Polish zlotys were only one hundred American dollars. In such cases, she took other approaches, as the account in the following chapter illustrates.

THE HEIRESS COWHERD

Gisella Shuldberg was the only child of extremely wealthy parents, Michael and Nellie Shuldberg (who were relatives of the Wissotzky family of tea magnates). Michael and his three brothers managed the famous Dubeczno glass factory, owned by their aristocratic mother, Olga. Michael, the youngest, served as the chief engineer. Over 3000 workers, many of them Jews, lived on the Shuldberg estate and worked in their factory in the Wlodawa district.

Michael Shuldberg had met his wife in Paris while studying at the university there, and brought her home to the family estate where he lived with his brothers and mother. Life couldn't have been smoother for the entire clan.

Gisella was born in October, 1936. Michael and Nellie took up residence in their palatial apartment in Warsaw before the birth so that this event could take place in the capital's exclusive private maternity hospital. Even after Gisella was born the Shuldbergs continued to alternate between Warsaw and Dubeczno, spending several weeks in each location. The couple did not want to miss out on the social life of the capital; yet on the other hand, given Mr. Shuldberg's role as the glass factory's chief engineer, he could not absent himself from Dubeczno for too long.

In the late summer of 1939, with rumors rife about impending war, Gisella's parents left Warsaw for the family estate at Dubeczno. When Gisella was only three years old, the Germans marched into town. One night she was awakened by pounding on the door.

"Machiek!" she heard one of the factory workers cry out to her father. "The war with the Germans has broken out!"

Within hours the Shuldbergs were digging trenches against the German invaders side by side with their workers. But they soon realized the futility of their efforts and the precariousness of their situation: several of their own German factory workers burst into the family's home to shout at and curse its Jewish owners. A few months later, their former manager, a German, took over the factory, and Gisella's family was forced to move into one of the worker's quarters.

Like many others who deluded themselves, Gisella's father confidently insisted that the Germans would never harm him because of the invaluable contribution he was making to the economy. "No one is as expert as I am in understanding the different chemicals in this factory," he declared. "The factory can't run without me!" His words held some truth, for he was never selected in any of the various German round-ups of the local Jewish population. Twice, though, he had narrow escapes, one involving jumping out a back window to avoid capture.

Dubeczno was located a mere six miles from the Sobibor and Majdanek concentration camps, in whose direction long trainloads of Jews streamed constantly on their one-way journey. The Jewish population of Dubeczno walked a thin tightrope between survival and dread of death. Gisella's mother began selling the family's rugs, furniture, and clothing just in order to survive. She was also forced to suffer all kinds of indignities at the hands of the new German owners. For instance, they made her serve as their personal caddie to pick up tennis balls on what used to be her own tennis court. They later made her work in the factory, which meant leaving Gisella alone for many hours each day. The girl's former non-Jewish friends refused to play with her.

One night, Gisella's grandmother suffered a fatal heart attack. The many workers, Jew and gentile alike, for whom she had been an exemplary boss, mourned her deeply. Her bier was carried over six miles so that she could be buried in a proper Jewish cemetery. She was warmly eulogized for the many kind deeds she had done, such as giving the workers free fish, caught by her own private fisherman from her own pond, for the Sabbath. What a pity, people thought, that her son Michael hadn't fled over the Russian border with his brothers when he had had the chance. At the time he hadn't wanted to abandon his elderly mother. Now she was gone, and he and his family were trapped.

The round-ups of Jews continued throughout 1942. When the transports to Sobibor and Majdanek failed to contain the requisite number of Jews, SS soldiers spread out through local towns to round up children to fill the quotas. On one occasion, Gisella was saved by hiding in the attic. Another time, her father hid her with a forester who lived in a small cottage in the woods not far from Sobibor.

It was at this point that the Shuldberg's gardener, Dominicznik, recalled a kindness Gisella's grandmother Olga had done for him. His wife had once been deathly ill, and Olga had taken her to the hospital, and personally cared for her until she recovered. At the time, the gardener said he would one day repay Olga for her kindness; now he decided to fulfill his promise. He had a sister who lived deep in the forest, far from other villages, and asked her to take custody of Gisella. Gisella was sent to this sister, but she cried so much that the peasant family had to send her back. When she got home, Gisella saw that her bed had been folded up and put away. "Were you so happy to get rid of me?" she cried.

One day, the Germans ordered all Jews still in Dubeczno to leave for the ghetto in nearby Wlodawa. Michael knew that deportation to Sobibor would follow immediately. That night, Gisella was told by her father to call Dominicznik. The gardener came to the house and spoke with Michael in whispers. Later that night, Gisella's mother took her for a walk and told her that she was now to change her name to Halina.

Early the next morning, while it was still dark, Halina's mother kissed her good-bye. Her father took her by the hand and led her outside the factory to where Dominicznik's teenage daughter was waiting. The six-year-old was told by her father that she had relatives in Switzerland to whom she should go after the War. His parting words were, "Eat whatever they give you and be happy!" He left her and returned to take his pregnant wife into hiding in the home of the local priest. This was the last time that Halina saw her parents.

Halina was miserable. She was again taken to the wooden house in the forest where she was given a lukewarm welcome by the Wajdzik family, who well remembered her hysterics two months earlier. Halina knew, however, that this time there would be no going back. She cried, but this time, silently.

The Wajdziks had agreed to hide Halina because Michael Shuldberg had promised them half the factory if his daughter were to survive the war. Without money as an incentive, there is no doubt they would never have let Halina set foot in their house. Halina, with the maturity forced upon all the children of that era, intuitively understood her precarious situation. She tried her best to make the family happy with her. She played with the Wajdzik grandchildren, and made sure to keep out of sight of the teenage son, who would beat her whenever he got the chance.

Sometime after this arrangement was made, the German occupiers issued a decree that anyone caught harboring Jews would be killed along with his entire family. Stories began to circulate about entire Polish families brutally murdered for violating this order. Mrs. Wajdzik panicked.

When she imagined that Halina was out of earshot, she gave vent to her hysteria. "This little girl even looks Jewish. Let's get rid of her before all of us are killed!"

But her husband refused to listen. "We are so far out in the forest—who will find out?" he replied. Halina was standing quietly nearby and heard every word.

Several days later, the Wajdziks decided to take strict measures concerning Halina. She was forced to spend the entire day up in the attic or in a bed under several layers of thick blankets. The house had three bedrooms and a kitchen, connected by a corridor. A ladder in this corridor led to a trapdoor in the roof. Sometimes Halina had to climb the ladder and spend hours sitting in absolute silence on the roof. To use the outhouse, she had to creep unseen through the darkness. Halina had no choice but to accept her forced imprisonment and uttered not a word of complaint.

Alone in the world, child of a nation hunted and hated, Halina drew her own conclusion: She no longer wanted to be a Jew. She approached the Wajdziks and told them that she wanted to convert to Christianity. They were pleased with the idea of bringing salvation to a Jew, and immediately took her to the priest. Halina was baptized and, within weeks, had mastered the Christian prayers and recited them enthusiastically. She begged the Wajdziks to tell her Catholic legends and stories about Catholic saints. To her mind, being Jewish meant only death and torture, and she wanted to live. She was certain she had done the right thing when one day she overheard the priest telling the Wajdziks that they must not think of giving her up to the Nazis now that she was a Christian.

The months crawled by, and the summer of 1943 arrived. The Germans relaxed their grip on the area somewhat, since all of eastern Poland was *Judenrein* (purged of Jews) by that time. The Wajdziks felt sufficiently safe to let Halina out of her attic prison. They concocted a story about her being a cousin from Warsaw whose house had been destroyed in the bombing. True, Halina still looked Jewish. But she was safe because people weren't looking for Jews anymore. Halina was given the responsibility of taking the cows to pasture. Accompanied by a dog and her own special lamb, she walked long miles every day. It was hard work—she had to be sure the cows didn't wander into the neighbor's fields and eat the wheat stalks—but she loved the silence and beauty surrounding her. Halina helped her new family gather wood, dig up potatoes, and do other chores around the house. In a few months, the little heiress had completely adapted to her new role as cowgirl and maid.

By the summer of 1944, advancing Russian troops had reached the area. Halina now had nothing to fear from the Germans. Also, having lived with the Wajdziks for two years, she considered herself a carefree Polish Christian girl whose future lay with her adopted family. She began school. With the approach of winter, though, she had to forgo this pleasure since she lacked shoes for the walk. The long winter nights were spent in the Wajdzik family circle, talking, playing cards (at which she was an expert) and joining the general activity. There were a total of four books in the Wajdzik home, which she read avidly. She read and re-read the accounts of Napoleon's wars, the Crusades, and stories of nuns and Polish saints, until she knew each page by heart, word for word.

Since 1943, Jewish partisans in the area knew that Halina was staying with the Wajdziks and had once warned the Polish family that they would pay a heavy price if anything happened to the child. During one visit, a partisan entered the house and picked up the blankets to verify that Halina was still alive. He whispered to her that her cousin Roman was alive and well. Yet, since that visit, years had passed with absolutely no contact between Halina and her people.

In 1945, when eastern Poland was completely in Russian hands, Jewish partisans came to the Wajdzik's home to demand that the Jewish girl be given over to them. Halina, though, adamantly refused.

"I'm a Catholic now!" she answered defiantly. "I go to church every Sunday. I want nothing to do with Jews!"

This was only the first of several futile efforts to reclaim the little girl, who was old enough to realize that the calamity which had befallen her family stemmed from their being Jewish. She preferred the hardships of her small-village existence to the dangers of being the daughter of a hunted people.

Although the danger to herself had passed, she was quite aware of the active hatred of Jews that permeated the neighborhood. The area was—and remains—one of the most anti-Semitic in all of Poland, a country that continued to hate its Jews even when most of them were not alive anymore. Bands of Armia Krajowa (AK) militants roamed the countryside, always ready to pounce upon a Jew who had somehow escaped the Nazis. Indeed, they did not hesitate to threaten to kill Halina, who was known to be Jewish, if the people in the village would not shelter the militants in the event of police raids.

Meanwhile, Halina's cousin, Roman, thirteen years her senior, had spent the War as a soldier in the Red Army. When he received a month's furlough in 1946, he headed straight for Dubeczno to see if any of the family was still alive.

Walking through the town, he met Polish villagers he had known as a youth. They told him that every Jew in town had been killed, and that if he didn't get out fast, he would soon suffer the same fate. With a heavy heart, he made his way back to the train station. A man sitting opposite him noticed his dejection and asked, "Why are you so sad?"

"I just found out that everyone in my family was killed," the soldier replied morosely.

"Who are you?" the stranger continued to probe.

The soldier muttered, "Shuldberg."

The stranger was momentarily startled, but then he spoke up. "No! Not everyone! You have a cousin who is still alive! She is living in my in-laws' house!"

Roman jumped out of his seat in astonishment. The two left the train station, and the stranger led Roman straight to the Wajdziks.

Halina was out with the sheep and cows when one of the Wajdzik children came running to call her back to the house. When she entered, she looked up and saw a stranger in a Russian uniform towering over her. She wondered what he could possibly want from her.

"Gisella, it's me! It's me—your cousin, Roman!"

Faint memories stirred within her, happy memories of a warm family life and a safe, comfortable existence. Halina threw herself into her cousin's arms. They spent an hour talking together, after which Roman left, promising to keep in touch. Halina had no idea that Roman wanted to take her away from her Polish foster family. In the meantime, a steady stream of presents, including books and material for a coat and dress, began to arrive for her.

Roman contacted the Central Jewish Communal Council in Warsaw for assistance in retrieving Gisella. The Council, an official Jewish organization sanctioned by the state, was not too keen about taking Jewish children away from their Polish foster parents. They believed that the children should not be uprooted, and, moreover, that the Polish families should be compensated for all their expenses. However, there were exceptions, particularly when the request came from next of kin. In such a case, the relative would receive the full cooperation and legal backing of the authorities to acquire custody of the child.

Nowhere was this more needed than in the Wlodawa district, where it was highly dangerous for a Jew to set foot outside the town of Wlodawa itself and venture into the villages in the neighboring countryside. In this rabidly anti-Semitic area, the Council turned for assistance to the Wlodawa police chief, whose authority extended over the secret police too.

The police chief wielded total power here because of the swarms of Armia Krajowa that infested the area. Being in charge of such an area made the police chief a virtual warlord. He could do what he wanted without answering to anyone.

In June 1947, a team of local policemen descended on the Wajdziks. Without asking Halina how she felt about it, they forced her into their truck. Another Jewish girl, Jadzia, who had been staying in a different village, and who also had a living relative who wanted her to leave the Polish family, was also picked up. The pair were kept under guard in Wlodawa until arrangements could be made for their cousins to take custody of them. One day, the two girls were taken by their guards to a swimming pool. Suddenly, the police dog accompanying them fled, and one of the policemen ran off in pursuit, leaving only one guard to watch the two girls. Shortly afterwards, an ammunitions dump near the town exploded. The noise, fire, and smoke were so intense that everyone, including the lone remaining guard, went running to see what happened. In the commotion, Halina and Jadzia seized the opportunity to run away, back to their foster homes. Neither of them wished to exchange her assumed Polish identity for her real Jewish one.

The Wajdziks spirited Halina to their daughter's home in a different village. When the policemen came looking for her, they feigned innocence and declared that Halina had never returned. Two weeks later, Halina was back at the Wajdziks, confident that she would not be sought again. Apparently, the police never bothered to inquire about Jadzia, who also returned to her Polish "family."

But Roman was determined to rescue his last surviving relative, even against her will. He heard that a Mrs. Lederman who ran an orphanage in Bytom specialized in extricating Jewish children from the most difficult environments and promptly went to appeal to her for help.

Mother agreed to try to reclaim Gisella. Roman had failed to apprise her, however, of the unsuccessful "police kidnapping" and of the dangers specific to the Wlodawa area.

The winter of 1948 was unusually cold, but Mother unhesitatingly commenced the arduous train journey to eastern Poland, arriving in Wlodawa a day later. At the station, she hired a horse and wagon to take her to the Wajdzik's place, a peasant's hut at the edge of town. It was not only the last dwelling along the unpaved street, but was located at a distance from all the other houses, making the situation even more precarious.

Mother knocked and was ushered in. Mother did not look Jewish, and impressed the family as a cultured, aristocratic lady. She made the usual overtures to the family, saying that she was a relative and had come to reclaim her sister's daughter. Naturally, she added, she was willing to pay them for their kindness.

Initially, the Wajdziks were adamant in their refusal to even consider giving up Halina. At some point, though, they relented and agreed to give her to Mother for the princely sum of two thousand dollars. Considering the state of the Polish economy and the value of the dollar in those days, it was far too much to pay for a single child, so Mother got up and left. Of course, she had no intention of giving up on the girl.

Somehow, Mother "discovered" the police chief. (Apparently when she reported her failure to Roman, he then told her about the police chief who had been so cooperative and suggested that she contact him.) Mother was reluctant to seek the help of any official Polish authority. She reasoned that it was one thing for him to extend himself for the Council, but a totally different thing for him to do some "dirty work" for an individual. Still, on the hope that he was approachable, she decided to try.

Mother walked into his office and laid down several one-hundred zloty bills. This wasn't too much by current standards, although it was more than enough to land Mother behind bars had she miscalculated the chief's motives. But the chief apparently didn't need any encouragement. He listened patiently to Mother's lament that the girl was the only child of her deceased sister, and that although she herself was a poor woman, she was spending her last penny to get her out. The chief then agreeably dispatched several policemen, all of whom Mother treated to a few hundred-zloty bills.

The Wajdziks heard an unexpected knock on the door, and in burst several Polish policemen. Gisella knew immediately why they had come, and she quickly got into bed and faked a high fever. The policemen charged into the room only to see her feigning illness under a pile of blankets. In a hoarse voice, Gisella told them that she had a burning fever and couldn't move. The sympathetic policemen glanced at each other, and finally left. Gisella knew that the act would gain her only a little time.

"Please take me to your sister's house!" she pleaded with the Wajdziks. "They'll be back for me soon!"

However, the winter being particularly severe, with temperatures dropping far below zero, the Wajdziks were reluctant to travel to another village that night and persuaded themselves that it was unlikely that anyone would come again so soon in this weather. They had not reckoned on Mother.

Later that day, Mother appeared at the police chief's home. "Do you have the girl?" she asked anxiously.

"I couldn't get the girl out today," the chief said bluntly. "I'll get her out tomorrow. But do you know that there's another Jewish girl in a different town in this district? You can have her too."

Mother's eyes narrowed in suspicion. After all, it might be a trap. "Look," she told the man, "I came here because I want to take my niece. What do I need another Jewish girl for? I'm a poor woman. What would I do with her?"

The chief started trying to convince her. "Okay, you really are a poor woman—but I have an idea," he smiled. "I'll get the child for you, and then you can take her to the Jewish Communal Council. They're looking for Jewish children and will pay you lots of money for her." With the chief continuing to press, Mother let herself be "convinced." To prove it, she slipped some more bills into his palm while declaring that she was parting with the last money she had in anticipation of a reward for bringing the other girl to the Communal Council.

Mother did not know that the other girl also had a cousin in the Soviet Army who had already visited the police chief and urged him to help get his cousin out in any way possible, despite the failure of the first attempt. The police chief had been sufficiently impressed by the army uniform to promise that he would do everything in his power to assist him. He was pleased now at this opportunity to make good on his promise.

Another day passed, with the Wajdziks congratulating themselves on not acting in haste. They were reassuring Gisella that she had nothing to fear when suddenly they heard a truck drive up. This time the policemen paid no attention to what Gisella or anyone else had to say. When the Wajdziks vehemently protested, the policemen started beating everyone in sight.

Gisella fought. She screamed and yelled, bit and kicked at any policeman who dared approach her. She shouted that she wouldn't go, but they grabbed her and forced her into the back of their canvas-covered truck. Mrs. Wajdzik ran to the truck and tearfully handed the girl a silver crucifix. "Here, Halina, this is so you'll remember us," she said. "I'm sure you'll soon forget that you're a Christian and you'll become a Jew again!"

"No, I won't!" Gisella answered, resolving that this would be her personal promise to Mrs. Wajdzik. And for a long time, Gisella kept her word.

In the frozen darkness of the back compartment of the truck, Gisella fumed. The policemen made a short stop to pick up Jadzia, who was deposited next to Gisella. The two girls shivered in the cold truck for long minutes, and when they felt paved roads beneath them, they understood that they had reached the district town of Wlodawa.

Soon the truck came to an abrupt stop. The canvas flap was lifted, and Gisella recognized the home of Wlodawa's police chief. They entered the warm house and were given a

A synagogue in the town of Wlodawa. Photograph courtesy of Beth Hatefutsot, Photo Archive, Tel Aviv.

gruff welcome from the chief.

"This time," he told the two girls strictly, "you're not going anywhere!" He told them to take off their shoes, which he proceeded to confiscate, leaving the two girls standing in their stocking feet.

Gisella and Jadzia were furious at the turn of events and schemed of ways to escape. Suddenly, the lights went out. It was only a blackout of the kind that frequently occurred in the Wlodawa district, but the girls screamed in fright anyway.

A sudden knock on the door ushered in a woman who could not be seen in the dark, but whose commanding presence could be felt. It was Mother. Gisella hesitatingly approached the strange woman and ran her fingers through the soft, plush fur of Mother's coat. It was real fur, the kind Gisella faintly remembered her mother wearing. Gisella could feel Mother's warm smile, even in the darkness. Mother told her that she was her mother's sister, and that she had come to take her. Gisella looked at her in surprise, unsure if this total

The interior of Wlodawa synagogue. Photograph courtesy of Beth Hatefutsot, Photo Archive, Tel Aviv.

stranger was telling the truth.

Gisella and Jadzia spoke with Mother, who took out her "equipment"—an assortment of candies and Swiss chocolates—and gave them treats just like a real aunt would. She told them that she would be taking them back with her the next day.

Mother and the girls spent the night at the police chief's home. Gisella and Jadzia, of course, wouldn't go to sleep without first offering their prayers. Jadzia had been sheltered by a family of Baptists, a small minority group in the predominantly Catholic Poland. The girls got into a heated argument as to which religion was better, and then fell asleep.

Actually, it was the Sabbath, a day on which Mother would never ordinarily have traveled. Yet she knew that as long as she remained in Wlodawa, she was in grave danger from the Wajdziks and their entire clan. The Wajdziks, accompanied by some militant friends, might make an appearance any minute, and Mother could not be sure of the police chief's reaction to such a turn of events. Mother was also well aware that the two girls were there under compulsion, and they would do everything in their power to escape. She therefore decided that under these circumstances, Torah law obligated her to travel back to Bytom immediately.

A policeman was delegated by the chief to accompany the three to the railroad station. While walking, Mother treated the girls to another mound of candies and Swiss chocolates. In addition, she promised them that when they got to Bytom, she would purchase each of them a pair of rather exclusive "mountaineer's shoes." It brought a momentary respite, but Mother's problems were far from over.

Gisella was the more stubborn of the two. Even though she was positively inclined towards Mother, she still longed for the only family she could clearly remember. The train moved farther and farther from Wlodawa, but Gisella could not come to terms with the fact that an infidel Jew was taking her away from her Christian home. Suddenly her anger flared, and she started kicking and scratching Mother. She demanded to be allowed to go home. All of Mother's reasoning and promises of goodies were to no avail.

Finally, Mother asked her, "Is there anything in the world you want?"

Gisella abruptly stopped raving. She was silent for a moment, and then she looked up at Mother and said, "Books!"

"Books?" Mother repeated. "Let me tell you something: In my house I have whole walls lined with books!"

Gisella's resistance collapsed.

The threesome stopped overnight in Warsaw. Leaving the train station, they passed the ruins of the Warsaw Ghetto, and saw the tremendous destruction and mounds of rubble. Only the following day did Mother finally reach the Bytom orphanage—with the two girls in tow.

Gisella grew angry again when she learned that her "aunt" had no home of her own and, even worse, didn't own a single book! Gisella's fear of being forced to live as a Jew reasserted itself, and she made plans to run away. (Needless to say, it would have been quite a feat for a nine-year old girl to divine how to travel back to the other side of Poland.) Mother realized just how delicate the situation was, and gave strict orders to keep the orphanage's door locked at all times. Still, Mother stood by her word, and took Gisella to the local public library the very next day—something that did not meet with Rabbi Winkelstein's approval. Gisella made the trip to the library a daily ritual and her thirst for books did much to assuage her unhappiness at returning to live among Jews.

Mother had her hands full with Gisella. Both she and Jadzia were closely guarded until it appeared that they could be integrated with the others. Appearances proved deceiving, however, and one day she and Jadzia ran away. Their flight somehow went unnoticed for several hours. The girls planned to travel by train, each to her previous home. The money was to be obtained by selling the silver crucifixes they still had on them. Their first stop was thus a jewelry store, where they exchanged their crucifixes for Polish zlotys. Then they ran to the train station to make a fast escape. It turned out, however, that the money they had just received sufficed for only one of them. In an act of magnanimity, Gisella gave her share of the money to Jadzia (who promised to send money to her friend from home). Soon a search party from the orphanage found Gisella sitting alone on a bench in the train station, and promptly brought her back to the orphanage. Jadzia has not been heard of since.

Gisella was inwardly torn. Mrs. Wajdzik's parting words to her had affected her deeply. She also remembered other comments the Wajdziks had made to her, such as "Oh, you'll probably end up going back to being a Jew." She felt that she owed it to them to remain faithful to Christianity and their way of life. And she dreaded the idea of living as a Jew. At the same time, she had to admit that life in Mother's Bytom orphanage wasn't all that bad. She enjoyed her daily visits to the library, and there was a certain chemistry between her and Mother that gave her a feeling of safety and security.

In fact, she loved Mother, and, like all the orphans in Bytom, appreciated her tremendous warmth and the encouragement she handed out so generously. And the undeniable sincerity behind Mother's approach—heavy doses of love interspersed with tactfully worded remarks concerning improper behavior—helped her succeed in gaining the girls' trust.

Gisella slept in the dormitory room that held all the young girls aged eight to eleven. These girls were deemed too young to attend more than a few classes a week. Although several classes were at one time taught in Polish, these were soon abandoned in light of the girls' awakening interest in the explosive happenings taking place in the Middle East, which aroused a desire in them to learn Hebrew.

In addition to enjoying all the fun activities provided for

them, the girls were kept busy helping with the many chores in the home. They also used this time for long talks and patient listening among themselves about all they had gone through, an unscheduled activity that did much to speed the healing process.

When Mother met Gisella, she was in need of complete rehabilitation. Not surprisingly, young Gisella, who later adopted the Jewish name Ruth, had negative feelings about Judaism, adults, and life in general. Mother took her along with the other girls on outings to parks, on boating trips, and to a myriad of equally enjoyable activities. She had one goal in mind: to help the girls overcome the traumas of war and return to a normal life—to the fullest extent possible. By all standards, she succeeded admirably.

The momentous events taking place in the Middle East, which crested in 1948 with the declaration of the new State of Israel, proved to be a turning point for Gisella. She, together with all the other residents of the orphanage, sang and danced when the State of Israel became a reality on May 15th. Soon the home resounded with endless, passionate talk among the girls about leaving Poland for Israel. Thoughts of emigrating to America were now abandoned, and *aliyah* to Israel became the only future interest.

In Gisella's case, however, the journey was not direct. After stealing across the Polish-Czechoslovakian border in the fall of 1948, Gisella reached Austria, where she joined a transport of sick children on their way to Switzerland. There, a sickly, elderly great aunt awaited her. It wasn't until two years later, after attending a private Swiss school, that Gisella achieved her goal of arriving in Israel, where she settled in a kibbutz, married, and raised three children.

Until this very day, Gisella (now named Ruthie) maintains contact with her friends from the Bytom orphanage. In previous years, whenever she visited Tel Aviv, the Lederman-Eisikowitz cafe on Aliyah Street was a never-to-be-missed stop.

Mother would welcome her like one of her own children, and treat her (and any children she brought along) to some of the cafe's delicacies. Summing up her relationship with Mother, Ruthie commented: "I loved Mrs. Lederman, I felt tremendous warmth and encouragement emanating from her, and I could feel it was sincere. If she made a decision about something, I accepted it right away because I knew she cared about me.

"She was the first person I met after losing my family that I felt I could trust and rely upon. I was in a rebellious frame of mind, but she knew how to convince me; she helped me stabilize emotionally. I had negative feelings towards Judaism and adults, and was filled with bitterness over my fate. By taking all of us out to parks, boating exped
tions, and many other pleasant activities, she helped us overcome the knots in our existence that prevented us from returning to normal life. She will always be in my mind as the paramount educator."

FOR THE SAKE OF A DOLL

To all who knew her, Mother was a bulwark of strength, a figure larger than life with the determination and follow-through to accomplish whatever in her opinion needed to be done. Yet when it came to the children, she took a gentle, kindly approach—especially when it came to allowing them to return to Judaism gradually. Her approach, typified by Masha's story below, proved itself time and time again.

Masha Merkretz was five years old in 1942. The blond-haired, blue-eyed child and her parents lived in Pantolowice, a town in Galicia, Poland. On the day that changed her life, she was too young and too preoccupied with her play to notice the tear-streaked faces of her anxious parents. Neither could she perceive the grimness that gripped the town and the sense of impending doom.

Galloping hoof-beats were heard coming down the street, slowing and finally stopping outside Masha's house. Masha's parents watched silently from their window as the rider, a grizzled man in his thirties, dismounted. He knocked on the door, but waited for no answer before entering. Masha's parents stared at him, and then silently nodded. Masha's mother bent down, picked up her beloved child, and gave her a tearful good-bye hug and kiss. Masha's father pulled out a small bag of items he had prepared, and then he, too, gave the little girl a hug.

The bewildered girl clung tightly to her mother, frightened by the strange man and the intense atmosphere, unsure of what was to follow.

"Masha, you must now go with this man." The child heard the uncertainty in her mother's voice, and immediately burst out crying.

"Mama! No! No! I don't want to go with this man!" She

clung to her mother with all her might and refused to let go. Her parents found it all but impossible to control their emotions.

Masha's father pulled a small piece of paper out of his pocket. "Drabic," he addressed the stranger in a choked voice, "here are the addresses of our relatives in America. If this terrible war ever finishes and our daughter remains alive, please contact these relatives and tell them to come and take Masha."

The rider, who was actually the village postman, nodded his head and accepted the bag of belongings and the piece of paper. Masha, her pudgy fists clenching the folds of her mother's dress tightly, continued her battle to remain with her parents.

"Masha, sweetheart," her mother stroked her head, trying to calm her.

"I don't want to go with that man!"

"Masha...."

"Why are you giving me away?"

"Masha... if we are going to die... we want you at least to live...."

Masha's father quickly scooped her up and briskly carried her outside to the waiting horse. Drabic followed and hoisted himself up. He then turned to take the frantic, screaming girl into his hands and, holding her tight, galloped away. He left her two heartbroken parents behind, wondering if the fate to which they had entrusted their precious daughter would be any better than their own.

A few hours later, a new little girl called Maryshia joined the Drabic family in Jaworzyna Slonska, a village near Pantolowice. The child, Mrs. Drabic explained to one and all, was the daughter of her brother who had died young. Since the child's mother was no longer able to take care of her, the Drabics had decided to adopt her. The Drabics' daughters, Andzia, also five, and Zosia, eight, accepted the new arrival with equanimity. They harbored suspicions about this new "cousin," but had the good sense not to say anything. The Drabics' local cousins and relatives kept the secret well. Maryshia, too, was thoroughly drilled in the story about her father dying and her coming to live with her aunt.

Young Maryshia, blessed with an easy-going disposition, had no trouble adapting to her new circumstances. She soon felt at home in the small, impoverished dwelling which the Drabics called home, and they, for their part, willingly shared with her the little they possessed. In no time at all she was calling them *Wujciu* (Uncle) and *Cocia* (Aunt) with all the enthusiasm a child feels for a blood relative. Maryshia's presence, though, did attract a certain amount of attention from suspicious villagers. For this reason, Cocia, ever on the alert, did not let the child attend school. She explained to the neighbors that Maryshia had a delicate constitution that made her susceptible to a wide variety of ailments. Surprisingly, if anyone had cared to notice, the child was usually well enough to be sent with Zosia and Andzia to take the pigs to pasture.

On the first Sunday of her stay in the new house, Maryshia attended church with her new family. The high ceiling, spirited singing, and impressive decor made a favorable impression on the girl. She began to learn how to recite the Catholic prayers, and eagerly looked forward to returning the following week. It didn't take long before her faint memories of the Sabbath, kosher food, and other Jewish practices vanished. She was soon as used to the standard fare of bread, potatoes, onions, and pork as those who had been born peasants.

On her third Sunday, as Maryshia was walking out of church with Wujciu and Cocia, a strange woman sidled up next to her.

"You are an orphan now, poor child!" the stranger whispered in her ear.

Maryshia looked up, startled, but the significance of the words evaporated in the happy inner child's world in which she was engrossed. The woman's words implied that she knew that Maryshia's parents had been killed because they were Jewish. This, of course, meant that the Drabics were harboring a Jewish child. This particular woman was trusted by the Drabics, but the fear of being reported to the Germans was so pervasive that, as an extra precaution, Cocia often sent Maryshia to her sister in a distant village for long stretches of time, until it seemed safe to bring her back.

Their fears were not imaginary. Once Cocia spotted a German soldier walking towards the house. Instantly and unceremoniously, Maryshia was stuffed into a closet while the soldier went snooping through the house. "No, there is certainly no one staying here with me," she could hear Cocia saying indignantly. "Whoever accused me is just a malicious troublemaker!"

It took three years for the dust of the guns and tanks to finally settle, happy years for Maryshia, who felt part of a close family circle. When the War ended, Cocia dutifully pulled out the paper entrusted to her and wrote to Maryshia's relatives. For months, the Drabics waited in vain for a reply. "I guess no one is alive or else they just aren't interested," Cocia told the unconcerned eight year-old. "You'll stay with us and be our daughter for good."

It was only in 1947 that a letter of response finally arrived. Maryshia's relatives were alive, the Drabics read in surprise, and they would like to see Maryshia.

One fall day a tall, elegant-looking lady exuding confidence, warmth, and concern arrived at the Drabic home. She looked very different from the local villagers and it was obvious that she had come from afar. Maryshia didn't pay much attention when the strange woman sat down to speak with Cocia.

After a lengthy conversation, Cocia called the child over. "Maryshia, this lady wants to take you to your relatives."

Maryshia's disinterest was immediately replaced by grave

concern. Somewhere from the distant, obscure past she recalled a similar unpleasant scene, one she most definitely did
not wish to repeat.

The strange lady with the twinkling eyes flashed her a
warm smile. "Maryshia, your relatives asked me to come and
get you, and to bring you to them."

"No! I don't want to go!" she said, and sullenly turned
away.

There was nothing left for the mysterious stranger—Mother
—to do but exchange some pleasantries with the Drabics and
leave.

Naturally, Mother did not let this initial setback stop her.
On her subsequent visit, she was greeted cordially by the
Drabics, but with much animosity by a suspicious Maryshia.
This time, however, Mother came fully equipped. She wasted
no time in producing her magic bag, out of which poured forth
all sorts of candies, topped by bars of Swiss chocolate, something no one in that village had ever set eyes on.

Eager for the sweets, the child nonetheless warned Mother
emphatically, "But I am not going with you!"

"Where I come from," Mother said matter-of-factly, "this is
the daily fare."

The girl remained adamant. She knew the Drabics were
not her real parents, yet they had been good to her. She saw
no reason to leave them to go with some unfamiliar lady, no
matter how kind or "sweet."

Mother, at her wit's end, finally asked the girl, "Is there
anything you want very, very badly?"

"Yes," came the immediate answer. "A doll. A big, big
doll." Maryshia spread her hands wide showing how large a
doll she wanted.

Armed with the knowledge of this potentially powerful
bribe, Mother traveled to Walbrzych, the nearest large city, to
purchase the doll. When she returned, doll in hand, Maryshia
went with her willingly. Together they traveled back to the

orphanage in Bytom, Mother keeping close guard over her new charge, who was holding the big, beautiful doll—and a large silver crucifix given to her by her "uncle and aunt" as a going-away present. Maryshia had been delighted with their gift and assured them that she would treasure it always. Mother, ever the lady, had promised Mrs. Drabic visiting rights, and indeed, the woman consistently made the grueling trip every three weeks to see the girl.

The pair began their long trip to Bytom with a bumpy wagon ride over the rough, unpaved country roads until they arrived at the nearest town with a train station. There they had an overnight wait for the next train. Once aboard, they spent several hours until they reached Bytom.

Mother led Maryshia, now called by her real name "Masha," through the doorway of the orphanage. The murmur of children's voices could be heard from the hallway, and it didn't take but a minute for the two dozen girls in residence to stream into the dining room, excitedly shouting with glee, "Mother's come back!" Masha's initial discomfort at being the object of so many stares was mitigated by her trust in Mother, with whom she had already developed an emotional bond. The many warm hugs and kisses Mother showered on Masha— as on every child—gave ample reassurance that she was in good hands.

Masha insisted on sleeping in Mother's bed, where she proceeded to kneel under the quilt and recite Catholic prayers, clutching her crucifix.

The weeks went by and Masha adjusted to the Bytom home. She was upset on those days when Mother would set out on a new journey, but Mother told her candidly: "Masha, I have to bring more children like you, so that they will have a good life and so they will be able to return to their families."

One winter's day, Masha became quite ill and spent the next several days tossing and turning feverishly in bed. When the fever broke one morning, she noticed that something was missing. That something was the crucifix. She cried out to Mother in alarm, "It's gone!" Every good and decent Pole wore one, of that she was certain, and she felt almost sinful not to have hers.

Mother sat down next to the bed, her presence itself a comfort. "You know, Masha," she began sympathetically, "it was probably the Polish maid who comes to clean every day. She probably saw that pretty necklace and took it for herself. But don't worry, I'll buy you another one." Masha missed her crucifix terribly. Every few days she would come over to Mother and ask pitifully, "Did you buy another one yet?"

Mother understood the girl's feelings—a mixture of sentimental attachment and a desire to be *good*. She avoided a direct confrontation about religion, preferring to wean her of her non-Jewish habits as painlessly as possible. "I went to the store to buy a new one, but it had just closed," she would answer Masha. Or, "They didn't have any in stock," or, "They said they would have it next week." Naturally, each disappointing answer frustrated the little girl. Yet, as time went by, she forgot all about the crucifix.

Masha gradually began to feel drawn to the other girls, and, wanting to be with them, moved out of Mother's room. She studied Hebrew with the others and learned to recite Jewish prayers. Teaching arrangements were such that the older girls in the orphanage taught the younger girls Jewish studies, while Polish teachers came from outside to teach Polish and other basic subjects. Masha enjoyed the delightful excursions to parks and resort areas led by Mother. The atmosphere of camaraderie inspired by Mother made the girls' stay in Bytom pleasurable, and Masha became an enthusiastic member of the happy group. She began to identify with her Jewish companions, and so began the return home to her rightful place among her people.

In 1948, Masha crossed into Czechoslovakia illegally with another ten girls from Bytom. They continued traveling overnight to Bratislava (known to many Jews as Pressburg), where they stayed in the homes of local Jews for several days. The group eventually made its way to Italy, and from there embarked on a miserable and prolonged voyage aboard a freighter headed for Haifa. From Haifa, Masha was sent to Beit Asher in Rishon LeTzion, where she met Lea.

Her attachment to her Bytom friends was so great that when her American relatives supplied her with all the papers needed for obtaining a visa to come to the States, Masha preferred to stay in Israel. She married at the age of eighteen, and settled in an agricultural village where she lives until today.

"It was very hard for me to abandon Christianity and to feel I was a Jew," Masha, now a grandmother, recounts. "Even after I became fully observant, even after I was married and had my own children, I always wondered whether perhaps a mistake hadn't been made; perhaps I had been switched with someone who was Jewish. After all, my blond hair and blue eyes weren't typically Jewish."

Many years later, after the Six Day War, Masha's aunt from the United States came to visit her. During her stay she shared with Masha her many memories of Masha's parents and relatives. It was only then that Masha felt truly and indisputably Jewish.

Masha raised a beautiful family, and is now reaping the joy of seeing her grandchildren continue in the path of their ancestors as observant Jews.

JUMPING THE TREBLINKA TRAIN

Estherka Bornstein was born in December, 1933, to a traditional Jewish family who lived in the country town of Sobolev, about sixty miles from Warsaw. Her father was a professional tailor who sewed quality suits for the Polish gentry, her mother a warm and devoted homemaker who lavished all her attention on Estherka and the two younger boys. It was a close-knit family: Mr. Bornstein's parents lived in the same house, and Estherka enjoyed happy visits to her maternal grandparents, the Bravermans, who lived in a farming hamlet about fifty miles from Sobolev, and to cousins in Zelechov, about thirty miles away.

A few short days after the onset of the War, when Estherka was almost six years old, the Germans began their advance on Sobolev. Estherka's mother fled with the children to the cousins in Zelechov, while her husband remained in Sobolev to protect the house and hide the family's valuables. When the Germans entered the city, he was caught in a massive round-up, and detained for a time in the local church with the rest of the men. The timing proved to be remarkably providential, for when the family's home subsequently received direct hits by bombs and went up in flames, no one was there.

Mother and children returned to Sobolev and the shaken Bornstein family searched for a place to live, a task exacerbated by the flood of refugees from areas already conquered by the Germans. Conditions swiftly deteriorated as the usual restrictions and punitive measures were applied against the Jews. Estherka's father was more fortunate than most in one respect: the landowner for whom he had worked in the past gave him small tailoring jobs to do, in an attempt to help ease his plight.

Estherka's parents were afraid to leave the house and

rarely did so, yet staying at home did not provide absolute protection. Once German soldiers came looking for her father and dealt him a terrifying beating. As the fall of 1940 approached, the little girl watched helplessly as her father grew ill and died. Estherka's mother, all alone with three small children to protect, tried to find some way out of the noose tightening around their neck. She sent the oldest boy to the cousins in Zelechov, where it was hoped he might be safer. Estherka was sent to a non-Jewish farmer known to the family, called Florentine. Before the girl was sent away, her determined mother sat down the little seven-year old and repeated to her the names of all her relatives.

"If you remain alive," her mother told her resolutely, "you will know whom to look for."

Estherka remained with the Florentine family for three months. It was a time of constant anxiety and worry, both for her mother's safety, and her own. She knew that if asked, she was supposed to say that she was Polish. At the same time, she knew very well that all the neighbors were acquainted with her family and knew that she was Jewish.

As anti-Jewish measures increased in frequency and intensity, the Florentine family started to worry about the risk of hiding a Jewish child and began to talk of sending Estherka away to relatives who wouldn't know she was Jewish. One night as Estherka lay in bed, she caught a fragment of a conversation. The words were chilling: "They've brought boxcars to take away the Jews."

The sizable Jewish community of Sobolev was going to be rounded up and transported that very night. Estherka fervently hoped that because her mother lived on the outskirts of town near the countryside, she would be spared. With an adult sense of reality beyond her years, she realized, though, that things might turn out otherwise. Since being with her mother, no matter what fate awaited her, held more appeal than trying to survive on her own, Estherka ran away from the Florentine household that very night to re-join her mother.

Early the next morning, a non-Jewish friend of the Bornsteins drove up with a horse and wagon. Mrs. Bornstein had
made this arrangement long ago as a measure of last resort.
This true friend had heard, as had everyone else, about the
waiting train and had quite correctly surmised that this was
the right time to show up. Estherka and her younger brother
helped their mother load a few linens and blankets on the
wagon before escaping with the friend. The threesome hid in
the Pole's silo while most of the town's Jews were carted away
to their doom.

Since it was too dangerous to remain in the silo, the family
hid in the nearby forest, returning under the cover of darkness
to get food. They might have been able to continue this way
but the harsh Polish winter caught up with them. Snow fell,
and the bitter cold accompanying it made surviving in the
open an impossibility. The Germans issued announcements to
the effect that all Jews who had avoided the previous train
"journey" could now come out of hiding and settle in the
ghetto. They promised that no harm would befall anyone who
"came in from the cold," and that there would be no more
transports. Jews began to emerge from their hiding places,
grateful for a roof over their heads and for having been spared
the fate of those who had been shipped out.

The crowding in the ghetto was indescribable, yet people
went to great lengths to make room for everyone and adjust
to the conditions as best they could. The Bornsteins found a
room, which they shared with a young couple and their baby.
Estherka joined the small group of children who crept under
the ghetto fence to barter possessions for food and medicine.
On one such foray, she saw a German grab a child about her
age and kill him! She stopped in her tracks and ran back in
panic through the fence to the relative safety of the ghetto.
After that incident, Estherka's mother refused to let her go out
of the ghetto again.

No one had any illusions about the end awaiting the ghetto's inhabitants. More than once, Estherka heard her mother and other adults wondering out loud when the next roundup would take place. They did not have long to wait. One night the sleeping ghetto was awakened to shouts of, "*Raus*! *Raus*! Out!" All Jews in the ghetto were beaten and driven out to the waiting train, desperation and hopelessness written on their faces. Despite the madness of adults and children being savagely pushed into freight cars, Estherka's mother succeeded in pulling her two children along with her into the same car. When the mass of human cargo was too tightly packed to admit another body, the doors were shut and locked.

The suffocating air inside the car made breathing almost impossible. Those who had been pushed in first quickly succumbed to the bodies pressing on them and to the lack of air. Estherka's youngest brother, only three years old, was one of the first victims. Estherka and her mother tried desperately to stay on top, knowing it was the only way to stay alive. One man in their car had escaped from a concentration camp only to be rounded up again. More aware than most of the train's final destination, he was determined to get out. Using a tool he had smuggled in, he pried open the small window at the top of the boxcar. Fresh air flooded in through the opening, bringing a measure of respite. The man peered out the window and suddenly spotted a road sign: "5 kilometers to Treblinka."

"This is it! We have to break out now or we'll soon be dead!" he cried.

He lifted himself up and jumped out. One person after another stepped on the bodies of those underneath and did likewise. Shots began to ring out as the German guards caught sight of the escapees and tried to shoot them down.

"Estherka, you must go out!" her mother urged her.

"No! I'm not going unless you go first." The little girl was afraid her mother would stay behind.

"You go first!"

"No!"

"Estherka, if we manage to escape from this alive, go to Osiny, to Grandma's farmhouse. If we ever get separated, we'll try to meet there."

There was no time for further talk or indecision. Estherka's mother pulled herself up and threw herself out onto the snowy embankment. The train continued its race down the tracks. More shots were fired. The person next to Estherka grabbed her and held her up to the opening. The terror-stricken child clutched the bars on top and gazed at the snowy terrain whizzing by. Gripped by fear, she froze.

"Let go!" bellowed the man underneath, but Estherka couldn't move. The man pried her hands off the bars and pushed her out. Estherka tumbled onto the snowy slope, white fluffs of snow dusting her face and coat. Shots rang out near her and, sure that she had been hit, she lay still. After slowly realizing that she was still among the living, Estherka scooped fistfuls of snow into her parched mouth and thirstily gulped them down. At last she stood up. She clearly understood that her first task was to find her mother.

Estherka traced her way back along the tracks searching for her mother. Precious time had passed between her mother's jump and her own, during which the speeding train progressed around a third of a mile down the tracks. Along the way back, Estherka discovered several bodies, victims of the shots, but not her mother. She was walking alone on the road near the railroad track when a group of children returning home from school came along. She joined them for a short way, and then knocked at the first door she came to and asked for water. The person inside peered at the little girl and replied sharply, "Go away! We don't want to get into trouble!"

Estherka continued wandering through the village until someone told her to go to the Polish policeman. He, too, sent her away. She tried knocking on another door only to be told by the agitated Polish inhabitants, "There are Germans here! We can't keep you here! Try the house at the end of the village."

The little girl walked to the last house in the village where she found an old lady living alone. This elderly widow took pity on the little girl. She let her come in to sit down and warm herself next to a heater. Confused and frightened, Estherka found herself relating the day's horrifying events.

"There was a woman here who came looking for her daughter," the old lady revealed when the girl had finished. "She left a short while ago. You can still see her footprints in the snow. I will let you stay here overnight. Tomorrow you can go on your way, following those footprints."

The next day Estherka followed the footsteps. They were large imprints of the sort made by rubber galoshes. This was a hopeful sign. Estherka remembered that her mother had been wearing galoshes. The footprints in the snow soon led to the road, where they could no longer be seen. Estherka had no choice but to keep walking, not knowing what the next hour would bring, petrified of meeting up with a German. She clung to one small straw of hope: that she would be ignored because she was so small.

She continued to walk on and on, endlessly. She didn't know where she was going, but she knew her goal was Osiny, the place her mother had told her about. When it began turning dark, she stopped and knocked on a door. The Poles who opened the door listened with compassion as the child bravely told them she was on her way to Osiny. They said they would help her get there, but first warned her that the Germans had launched a search for partisans in the forest that very night, and they couldn't keep her in their house because of the danger. They told her to go to the barn; perhaps she would even find a blanket there. Estherka left the warm house for the frozen night and headed for the barn. Under a pile of hay she found a small depression with a blanket folded inside. She wrapped her frail body in it and numbly fell into a troubled sleep. Shootings coming from the nearby forest punctuated her consciousness and added to her dread. Towards morning, she heard footsteps. Terrified, she listened as they headed in her direction. Suddenly a voice cried out, "Who's there?!"

Estherka was so frightened she could not move. A hand stretched out over her hiding place and lifted the blanket. "Who are you?" the strange man asked her.

"I am a Jew," she mumbled. When the man didn't react, she realized that he, too, was Jewish, and that she must have slept in his hiding place. She told him her story and, with dawn, set out again on her own, remembering that her mother had told her not to stay with Jews because she'd have a better chance of survival as a child alone. She returned to the Polish family, but they explained that they could not hide her because the Germans were always on the lookout for Jews. It would be too dangerous both for her and for them. But they did provide her with food, money to buy a train ticket to Osiny, and instructions on how to get to Sielc, the nearest railroad station.

Estherka set out on her way, grateful for the help. When she had almost reached the train platform in Sielc, fear got the better of her. She suddenly realized that an eight year-old traveling all by herself would look suspicious. So instead of turning towards the train depot, she kept walking down the road. Another footsore day of walking was soon behind her. Fearful in anticipation as night closed in, she knocked at another stranger's door. The inhabitants took a look at her, and in their eyes she could read their thoughts: "Here is a Jew." Still, they gave her food and a place to sleep overnight. In the morning, she left their house for another day of wandering. The next night, the Polish inhabitants of the house she knocked at would not let her in without a note from the mayor. She went to the mayor's house to request the authorization. Remarkably, the mayor's compassionate wife scribbled a note for her. She returned to the family, who sat her down to supper and began to question her. By now Estherka was afraid to say she was a Jew. She tried to make up a story, but the Poles saw through it immediately.

"You're lying," they told her. "You're really a Jew."

Caught, Estherka lowered her eyes. "Yes."

"I think we should bring her to the police," the man of the house declared. Yet the hour was late, and the one-man police station had already closed for the night. They decided to leave the girl with a neighbor of the policeman along with strict instructions to deliver her to the police station first thing in the morning.

The following morning, before turning her in, the neighbor coached her. "Don't say you're a Jew and I won't either!"

He brought her to the policeman, telling him that he found a child and didn't know who she was. The policeman took Estherka into an inner room of the police station, shut the door, and began asking her one question after the other. "What's your name? Where are you from?"

To Estherka it seemed foolhardy to try to deceive this intimidating policeman, so she began to tell him the truth. "I am a Jew," she said simply.

The policeman looked upset. "Don't ever say you are a Jew again! Take a Polish name."

Could it be? Was he really going to help her?

The policeman spoke to her earnestly. "Everywhere you go, be sure to cross yourself! Here, watch how I do it. Do you see?" He demonstrated, and insisted that Estherka repeat his actions. "No, no! That's how the Russians do it! Poles do it beginning with the other shoulder!

"And one other thing. Don't ever say 'Good morning' when you meet someone! Say "Niech bedzie pochwalony..." (may... be glorified...). This was the standard way Polish peasants greeted each other; Estherka had herself seen it many times before. She tried repeating the words a few times. The police-man, satisfied, let the little girl out of the station by way of a side door. He thrust in her hand directions on how to reach Osiny, and Estherka went on her way. She reviewed his in-structions, and thought about a Polish name for herself. She finally decided upon Theresa, which sounded enough like her real name Esther to be familiar. For a surname, she chose "Wisniewsky," a name she had heard mentioned with pride, for it was the surname of a Polish partisan leader fighting the Germans. The name had no Jewish connotations at all, and she hoped it would serve her well.

It did. It was a long time before she again told someone she was a Jew.

Estherka trudged onward another few hours and then stopped, exhausted, and knocked on a peasant's door. This time, the little eight-year-old girl had a new story to tell: Her parents were Polish partisans, Wisniewsky by name, she had lost them, and she was on her way to her aunt in Osiny. The strangers stared silently at her, as if debating the truth of her tale. In the end, they gave her some food and sent her off with directions to Osiny. The next day was a good one for Estherka: She got a free ride on a horse-drawn wagon. She felt a difference now that she had a good story to tell. The heavy burden of fear and desperation seemed lighter, and she dared hope she might survive. By sunset the following day, she arrived in Osiny. She turned to the old farmhouse that her grandmother had once owned and where she had spent many happy hours in carefree play. The farm was now owned by friends of the family; she even remembered some non-Jewish friends of her mother's who still lived in the district. She knocked on the farmhouse door. Her fingers and toes were frozen solid, and she appeared to be on the verge of total exhaustion. The door opened and familiar faces came into view. Her heart pounded and she hoped the next moments would not prove she had made a mistake.

"You know me, don't you?" she said as she looked up into the faces. The woman looked at her sharply and then said, "You look like a Braverman—are you?" Their suspicion turned to shock as they realized the little girl had come to them all alone. Estherka's head began to swim and weakness swept over her. "How did you survive, child? How did you ever make it here!"

They quickly brought her into the house and gave her a warm drink and some food. She could see they were torn between concern for her and concern for themselves, lest they be found helping a Jew. Estherka understood that her mother had failed to reach the house. Her fondest wish, the hope that enabled her to persevere, had been dashed.

After a quick consultation, the family decided to try and keep her. As a precaution, they arranged to rotate her among several of her mother's non-Jewish friends in the district. Each family took the girl for a day or two. Thus Estherka survived the next four months until spring arrived.

Then one night a meeting of the village council was held. The father of the family where Estherka was staying returned home from the gathering in a somber mood. "It is impossible to keep her here any longer! We have *Volksdeutsche* living in the village and they know that a Jewish child is being held in the area. All of our lives are in danger!"

He turned to Estherka, "You must go! Do you have anyone to go to?"

She looked up at her hosts with sad eyes. "I guess I can go to Sobolev, to the family where I stayed three months last year."

Without further ado, the family sent Estherka on her way the next morning. Her steps were heavy as she unwillingly set off again for the unknown. Her thoughts turned to the family in Sobolev, and she remembered that they, too, had been afraid to keep her any longer. What good would it do her to go back there? They had suggested to her that she move to relatives of theirs who lived far away. Maybe, she wondered, she should go straight to those other relatives. No one in that district knew her family, and if they had been willing to take her in then, perhaps they would still oblige now.

She took a deep breath and decided to head for this un- known family. Once again she found herself standing in front of a strange door, ready to knock, her heart in her mouth. When the door opened, the family quickly pulled her in. As they looked at the worn, helpless child standing before them, they remembered the story of the young girl they had been asked to take in the year before.

Estherka could see the ever-present fear in their eyes. Would they take her in?

"We must do something," the woman whispered to her husband. Finally, they told Estherka that while they them- selves could not keep her, they would arrange for her to be a mother's helper in a family with young children, on the condi- tion that she keep her Polish name and identity.

Estherka was sent to a family living about twenty-five miles from Sobolev. They were told that she was the daughter of a famed partisan leader and had become separated from her family. Her new hosts took pride in the patriotic activities of the little girl's supposed parents and gladly took her in. They hoped that at the war's end they would be rewarded hand- somely for their kindness.

Estherka never breathed a word of her true identity. She watched the cows and fed the ducks, and played with the small children in the home. Her new family treated her well. They wouldn't let her attend school since they feared this would reveal her presence to the Germans, who were always on the lookout for partisans. Several times, when danger seemed imminent, she was forced to hide.

As a matter of course, Estherka was taken to church, like all good Polish children. But the whispering behind her back made her very uncomfortable. Indeed, she felt alone in the world. Still, the will to stay alive helped her keep up her act. In church, she often prayed that she be saved from the fate that had befallen the rest of her family. Sometimes, while out in the pasture with the cows, she would glance around in all directions to make sure she was alone, and then look up at the heavens. "I am a Jew!" she whispered over and over. With time, she concealed her secret more and more deeply, not to be confided to a living soul.

In fact, Estherka was not really sure that she still wanted to be a Jew. She felt torn between her real identity and survival. A year passed, 1943 slipped into 1944, and fall arrived once again. Estherka was gathering mushrooms with her young friends in the forest when, suddenly, they heard music from afar. They ran excitedly out to the road, and beheld a completely novel sight: soldiers marching down to the road to the accompaniment of musical instruments. They watched wide-eyed as row upon row of troops passed by. The soldiers, they realized in delight, were Russians—liberators! Their arrival heralded the end of fighting between the Germans and the Polish partisans. Peace had come to their district. The Polish villagers warmly welcomed the Russians, thankful that the heavy German yoke had been removed from their neck. Their joy diminished somewhat, however, when the Russians ransacked the town, carting away large quantities of food.

The autumn of 1945 found Estherka a lovely eleven-year-old child still with her Polish peasant family. Her twelfth birthday was fast approaching, and she knew that meant confirmation, when she would have to confess to the priest. She was nervous about it, because even years of attendance in church hadn't given her any idea what she was supposed to tell the priest in the confessional booth. She called aside a friend who was also about to turn twelve.

"Let's pretend," she suggested. "I'll be the priest, and you come to me and confess."

The other girl contritely confessed to some sin as Estherka

carefully observed her. Later, in privacy, she practiced to make sure she wouldn't stumble when her turn came. When she eventually found herself opposite the priest, Estherka lowered her eyes and penitently told him, "I lied." Her plan worked and she seemed to have passed yet another test successfully.

The war had ended months before, but Estherka remained a lost Jewish child with no plans for the future. Indeed, following her confirmation, Estherka's host family arranged for her to take private lessons from the priest in both Christian dogma and regular school subjects. One day, the priest started questioning Estherka about her past. In short order he realized that she was a Jew—a far cry from the daughter of a Polish partisan. He smiled at her and asked, "Is this the lie you told me about during confession?"

The incident frightened Estherka, and prompted her to look for a more permanent place to stay. She approached her present foster parents (who were still unaware of her true identity) and told them that years earlier her own parents had entrusted her to a different family, and she was thinking of returning to them. They agreed, and sent her off to the Florentines, whom she had not seen since she was seven. The Florentines received her with great joy, pleased to find her still alive, and expressed a willingness to adopt her. Estherka felt she had found a home.

Mr. Florentine had a brother who had saved a young Jewish girl, and later married her. When this woman heard that Estherka had turned up, she came to visit and sought out a moment when they could speak privately.

"Estherka," she said in a voice tinged with melancholy, "I had to marry my husband, and I now have a child. For the time being, I must stay here." But you," she continued with genuine emotion and concern, "you should go back to living with Jews. I know Jews I can send you to."

"I don't want to go back to living with Jews!" Estherka answered fearfully. "I only want to go to relatives!"

"Don't worry!" the woman told her. "You have nothing to be afraid of with Jews!"

This woman got in touch with the Vaad Hatzalah, and one day, two men came to the Florentine residence. One of them, a man by the name of Warshavsky, told Estherka that he knew her family, and was a distant relative. He gave Estherka certain signs, which she recognized, to prove the truth of his words. He treated Estherka like a true uncle, to the point where she felt confident enough to agree to travel to Warsaw with him. Yet once they were in the train station, doubts began to surface. Should she really go back to the Jews? Would her life be endangered once again? Would they care for her as the Florentines had done?

She couldn't afford to take any chances. She looked around cautiously and began to slip out of the station house. Mr. Warshavsky reached out and tapped her on the shoulder. "Estherka, where are you going? The train is almost here."

The girl turned around and sat down on a bench in defeat. Would she regret going with these men? she wondered. Only time would tell.

Estherka was taken to Warsaw, where she was given over to Mother's competent hands. After introductions had been made, Mother asked a question that typified her straightforward, yet respectful approach. "Where would you like to go— to a religious or a non-religious institution?"

"Religious," answered Estherka, who could not remember the traditions of her home, yet vividly recalled her feelings in church. She was warmly accepted into the orphanage in Bytom, and quickly adapted—testimony to the sense of well-being and safety which the institution engendered.

Naturally, Estherka's individual experiences had left their mark. After months of tutoring, the young girl was unwilling to forgo further education. Thirsty for the many years of schooling denied her, she insisted on attending public school, even though most of the other children in the orphanage did not. Mother allowed this as the best course of action for this particular child. Estherka often stayed up to the wee hours of the night reading her textbooks until Mother would chase her off to bed, firmly insisting that she get a good night's sleep.

At Bytom, Estherka received instruction in reading Yiddish and Hebrew along with the other girls. She discovered that she could recall several Yiddish words she had learned from her parents. The lessons about Judaism were a different matter. "You people are all wrong!" she insisted. She would loudly denounce what she felt was the Jewish "heresy" being taught in class. "I know all about Jesus and Christianity! You have to believe in them!" After a while, however, she became tired of the severely disapproving looks she received: "If I'm going to be a Jew anyway," she told herself, "why should I bother defending Christian beliefs?"

When she gradually began to lose interest in Christianity, her teachers expressed their pleasure and approval. It wasn't long before Estherka became a proud Jew once again. In fact, she herself was once conscripted into the campaign to locate Jewish children and bring them back to their people. A girl in Russia had written to a friend of hers in Bytom, "If you're leaving for Israel, go to the Communist orphanage in the city and take out my little sister." Mother gave her consent to the mission, and soon Estherka was on her way with her friend.

Estherka entered the Communist institution and approached the eight-year-old girl. In a short while, the child agreed to go along with her. The three disappeared and resurfaced in the Bytom orphanage. Unfortunately, a doctor who was visiting there discovered the child's presence and summoned the police, who promptly raided the orphanage and took the child away.

From the time Estherka accepted her Jewishness, she became an integral member of the group of girls who blossomed under Mother's devoted care.

Estherka came to the orphanage at the beginning of 1947,

at the age of thirteen and a half. Although a group was organized to leave for France, Estherka had her eyes set on Palestine. By the time the orphanage relocated to Solice Zdroj in 1948, Estherka was growing impatient. One day, she and a friend sneaked out of class to join some activists doing target practice with real ammunition. These older Holocaust refugees were preparing to join the Israeli Haganah defense forces and didn't enjoy having teenagers hanging around. When Mother went searching for Estherka in the afternoon, she came upon the group.

"Here are your two girls," they told Mother in exasperation. "Do us a favor and take them back—and make sure they don't come here again!" The young girls tossed their heads defiantly and left with Mother.

By the time they got home, it was dark. Once inside, Mother, never one to mince words, gave them a piece of her mind: "Didn't you go through enough with one war? Do you need another?!"

She told the two that they should wait until the fighting in Palestine ceased, and then immigrate. Estherka eventually went to Cracow with a group of girls from the orphanage. Like the other children, they crossed the Czechoslovakian border using false passports with the help of bribed border guards. Following the crossing in late December, the group traveled in covered trucks to Austria, whence it made its way to Italy. On January 14, 1949, after a week of seasick travel, Estherka arrived in Haifa port on the freighter *Casserta*. Overjoyed, the girl threw her coat into the sea as the boat neared the port, gleefully announcing, "I won't need you in Israel!"

At the Kiryat Shmuel reception center, she was asked where she wanted to go. Studious as ever, she declared that she wanted to further her education. After attending several high schools, she went on to study in the nursing school of Shaarei Zedek Hospital in Jerusalem. There, she met her future husband, who was doing his residency in the hospital.

At present they live in Haifa, where her husband is a well-known gynecologist.

SNATCHED FROM THE VILNO GHETTO

As noted briefly above, the Bytom orphanage began with a brother and sister rescued by Rabbi Winkelstein. The children's parents, the Minikes, were a well-to-do Jewish couple living in Vilno. The father dealt in leather while the mother ran a grocery store. In May, 1935, their first child was born; they named her Chaviva. Occupied with her business, the mother hired thirty-five year-old Helena (Hela) Szemet, a Russian gentile, as a live-in nursemaid for the infant. Some two years later, Gershon was born. The children grew up happily under Hela's warm, expert care. With their parents away most of the day, the children became more attached to her than to their parents.

Chaviva Minikes.

Gershon was only four when the German attack began in June, 1941. The two young children would hide under their blankets in terror every time they heard the ear-splitting sound of bombs being dropped on their city. Soon the city was taken and Mr. Minikes' store was closed down. He tried to scrape out a living selling cigarettes. Harsh decrees followed the German occupation: All Jews were to wear yellow stars on their clothes; they were allowed to walk only on certain back streets; curfews were strictly enforced. After a few months, many of the men, Mr. Minikes among them, were rounded up by the Germans, temporarily held in the Lukishki prison, and then marched to the Ponary forest from which they never returned. The ghetto was rife with rumor. Some said the men had been taken to a labor camp; others that they had been killed. It was feared that the women and children would be next in turn.

Worried about her charges, Hela persuaded some non-Jewish friends, Nuta and Pavel, who lived on the outskirts of Vilno, to take in Chaviva. She herself remained with Mrs. Minikes and Gershon in their home. One day, Lithuanians working for the Germans knocked on the Minikes' door. Gershon's mother panicked. She begged Hela to hide Gershon so that nothing would happen to him. Gershon was thrust into the closet and commanded to remain silent. Instinctively, he knew that his life depended on it. His mother went outside to the Lithuanians. They put her under arrest, and then entered the house to search for others. They saw Hela and asked her to identify herself. She explained that she was the Russian help, and showed them her documents. Ignoring her claim that she was alone in the house, they began a search. They emptied the closet, but found no one, for Hela had, at the last moment, thrust Gershon under the bed. Gershon's mother was taken to the Ponary forest where she met the fate of her husband and the other Jews.

Hela registered the children as her own, even though she had never married. In spite of all her precautions, she still didn't feel safe, and would sometimes hide the children in closets and other such places. At one point, Hela took Gershon to his aunt who lived in a different district. Chaviva had been crying continually at the home of Hela's friends, who finally grew exasperated and insisted that Hela take her back. Hela returned with Chaviva to the empty Minikes house. The non-Jewish superintendent advised Hela to take Chaviva to the aunt as well: "There is no one from the family left." The two children reunited at their aunt's house. A week later, they joined the long procession of Jews forced to resettle in the old ghetto, whose inhabitants had already been killed.

The ghetto was extremely crowded, and it was obvious that it was only a matter of time before these Jews would share the fate of the others. Hela decided to act. She had taken over an empty apartment intending to bring the two children to live with her. When she went to the aunt's house to get them, she was shocked to discover that they had been taken to the ghetto three days previously.

Not willing to give up her precious charges, she ran to the gates of the ghetto and pleaded with the German guard. "My sister's children were playing with the neighbor's children three days ago, and we haven't been able to find them since! I'm sure they were taken by mistake and sent to the ghetto with the Jews!"

The German soldier looked at her suspiciously. "Do you have proof that they're your sister's children?"

"Of course I can prove that they're my sister's children! What do you think—that I would want some Jewish children?! I can bring you proof right away."

The soldier was convinced and allowed her to enter the ghetto to retrieve the brother and sister. Once inside, Hela located the Minikes' grandparents and asked them to permit her to try to save the children. The grandparents, fully aware of the fate which otherwise awaited them, agreed. They entrusted Chaviva and Gershon to Hela's hands, and watched from afar as she passed through the ghetto gate with the two children in tow. The children had distinctly Jewish features, but fortunately this didn't stop Hela from getting them out successfully.

Hela immediately took them to her friends Nuta and Pavel, who agreed to watch the two Jewish children until identity papers could be arranged for them. This was accomplished within several days, but Hela still feared to let them be seen outside, even to play with other children. Only at night were Gershon and Chaviva allowed to go outside and get some fresh air. Still, the children cooperated, aware of the danger which threatened them. When Hela's friends came to visit, the children had to hide in a closet in absolute silence. Now that Hela had no work, hunger set in. Finally Hela decided to go and sell sunflower seeds in the street. For hours every day she hawked her simple wares. The little profit she received was far from adequate for the three of them, but it kept them alive.

A year after taking the children in, Hela confessed to her priest that she was harboring two Jewish children. The priest advised her to convert them to Christianity. Gershon and Chaviva were thus baptized as Gzheshek and Lucia. Hela had them registered as her niece and nephew, children of her brother. From then on, the children dutifully attended church with their foster mother and were educated in all its rituals. Crucifixes, miniatures of saints and other religious symbols decorated the house. Hela was actually more concerned with survival than she was with religious salvation. Events proved her right. Once, for instance, while she was out shopping, a drunk accused her publicly of hiding Jews. Although she hastened to leave the store, the suspicious shopkeeper called a policeman, and the entire group paid a visit to Hela's house.

The policeman searched the house and asked about the children's whereabouts. "They are with friends," Hela answered simply. Glancing around the room, the policeman saw the hanging crucifixes, the devotional prayer books, and the statues. "How dare you accuse this pious woman!" he fumed. He turned on the drunk, and gave him a beating.

Hela always slept fully dressed with her shoes on. That way, if anyone suddenly knocked on their door at night in search of her Jewish charges, she would call out that she was getting dressed, but would instead use the precious seconds gained by the ruse to hide the two children.

Despite the love she showered upon them, they led a life of fear, never knowing what the next day would bring. Chaviva and Gershon had to fend for themselves much of the day since Hela was on the street trying to earn money for food. One year dragged into another. Finally, in the summer of 1944, the Russians re-occupied Lithuania. With the first taste of freedom, Hela placed the children in school. Chaviva entered first grade, and Gershon kindergarten. For practical purposes, they were Christian children, but Hela was not opposed to their returning to their Jewish heritage.

With the war over, a cousin of the children's parents stumbled upon the two orphans and mistook them for his own children. When apprised of his mistake, he immediately contacted the children's uncle and aunt in South America, who asked that Gershon and Chaviva be sent to them. The children refused. To them, their family housekeeper was the only mother they knew. They wouldn't hear of leaving her.

It turned out that an aunt, their father's sister, had escaped to Moscow and also survived the war. When she heard that her brother's children were alive, she came to Vilno to claim them. Hela nobly understood that she would have to give the children up, yet she begged their aunt, "I don't mind you taking the children anywhere—only please, not to the Bolsheviks!"

The aunt, however, saw how attached the children were to Hela and decided to leave them with her after all.

Upon hearing the story of these two children, Rabbi Winkelstein set out to bring them back to their people. But once again, the orphans themselves refused to part with their devoted foster mother. Taking account of the situation, Rabbi Winkelstein suggested that she convert to Judaism. Hela did so willingly. She took the name Sarah Rubinstein, chosen for her by Rabbi Winkelstein to symbolize the ruby-like luster of her devotion and courage.

Rabbi Winkelstein wanted the trio to come to Poland with a view to eventually getting them out to America or Palestine, something which could not be done from Soviet-controlled Lithuania. To facilitate their moving to Poland legally, he came up with another creative solution: a staged marriage for Sarah with a Polish citizen. She and the children could thus enter the country, where Rabbi Winkelstein planned to return Gershon and Chaviva to a healthy Jewish environment. Once in Poland the pair were "divorced," and Sarah Rubinstein (who never married) was free to stay.

Sarah and the children were taken first to Lodz. Chaviva proudly wore the crucifix she had become accustomed to during the past few years, completely unprepared for the rebuke which this display elicited. For many months afterwards she recited the only prayers she knew, Christian prayers, under her blanket.

Shortly thereafter, Rabbi Winkelstein brought the trio to Bytom, where Sarah was given the job of cook for the new orphanage. Chaviva and Gershon lived in a private room with her; later Gershon was moved to the boys' dormitory.

Mother took the two children under her wing. They were gradually reintroduced to the traditional Jewish life they had almost forgotten. It was a difficult adjustment, but soon the warm, positive atmosphere, together with the good food and pleasant religious instruction, had its effect. Mother paid special attention to the skinny little boy, making sure he was served double portions, and insisting that he take his daily spoonful of castor oil to invigorate his scrawny body.

After living in the Bytom home, Chaviva, Gershon, and their devoted foster mother—now Sarah Rubinstein—joined a group of orphans traveling to Israel by way of Czechoslovakia and Austria. While staying in the Bindelucher camp in Lunz run by the American Joint, Sarah became sick. The rest of the group continued on to their next stop, but Chaviva and Gershon remained behind until Sarah recovered. They then made their way through Italy on to Haifa.

Chaviva and Gershon found their place in a kibbutz. Naturally, they were joined by Sarah, an exceptional woman who spent the rest of her life in the pleasant company of the charges entrusted to her so many years earlier. Sarah had the satisfaction of seeing both children marry, raising children of their own, and marrying them off, before passing away at the age of eighty-six.

TWO BROTHERS, TWO SISTERS

Ruzia Halzband lived in Warsaw on Grzybowa Street together with her younger brother and parents. Her parents scratched out a living from an egg distributorship on Ogrodowa Street, on the side of Zelazna Street away from us. They lived in a tiny apartment on the top floor of a four-story building. The apartments in their building had no amenities; these were available only in a yard three houses away from them. For them, as for all the citizens of the capital, the War started with bombing raids. One such raid caught Ruzia emerging from the toilet. The blast wave knocked her onto the yard's stone pavement, causing her a permanent hearing loss in one ear.

Ruzia's father, like many others, utilized the chaos brought about by the war to steal his way from Warsaw to Russia to explore the possible benefits of fleeing east. They assumed that if conditions were bearable, they would be better off in the Soviet Union than under German occupation. Mr. Halzband was away for a few weeks without anyone hearing any word from him.

One day, Ruzia heard a familiar voice calling out from the street. It was her father, back from his reconnaissance mission. In her excitement, she threw open the window, knocking over a flowerpot which nearly hit her father. She ran to tell the others that Father was home, and after being warmly welcomed, Mr. Halzband announced his unequivocal conclusion to the family: life in Russia was indeed bearable, and they should get moving. The only thing left to decide was the timing.

The decision to leave as soon as possible became even easier to make when one day, within days of the father's return, Ruzia stuck her head out of the window and saw German soldiers entering one house after the other. Her heart went to her throat. It was common knowledge that they were rounding up Jews for work filling in the trenches that had been dug by the Poles. As rumor had it, some or all of the people so caught, never made it back. *"Tatte!"* she whispered, "the Germans are coming!" By a stroke of Providence, the front door of their apartment lacked an in-door lock and was locked from the outside with a padlock. Mr. Halzband told Ruzia to hang the lock on the door—giving the dwelling the appearance of being empty—and then go off with her brother on a little walk. (At that time, only men were being forced into the work brigades.) The ruse worked. The Germans came, saw the lock on the door, and left. Mr. Halzband emerged from the closet where he had concealed himself fearing that the German soldiers might break down the door.

Nothing remained for the Halzbands to do except flee to the Russian-occupied part of Poland. At that time travel by Jews was not yet restricted. The family's meager belongings barely filled a valise, so without drawing too much attention to themselves, they boarded a train for Brest-Litovsk, one of the towns along the newly designated border.

Once there, they joined a woman and her daughter in hiring a guide to take them across the border. The night of the crossing was pitch dark, and the small group followed the guide in utter silence. Suddenly, they found themselves at the edge of a deep ravine, which apparently served as a part of the newly drawn border between German- and Russian-occupied Poland. The guide instructed them to descend to the bottom and then climb up the other side. As they started their precarious descent, they lost contact with the guide.

In a few seconds they went from great hope to utter despair. They descended to the bottom and stopped to think. They were completely lost, and had no idea what to do. The children, sensing the gravity of the situation, started crying. Apparently they were heard by the Russian border guards, because almost immediately a rocket fired from the Russian side illuminated the lost and frightened group. The border guards descended into the ravine and took the six of them to the guardhouse. First they searched them for hidden valuables, but didn't find a thing. Then, knowing from which direction they had come, they told the frightened refugees: *"Davay obratno*—go back." When Ruzia's mother heard this, she whispered to her two little children to start crying again. They had no trouble executing this order, for it was only the appearance of the border guards that had shocked them into silence. Now their tears, sobs, and cries flowed freely. The fervent pleas of the parents and the tearful entreaties of the children (again as instructed by their parents in Yiddish) who kept on saying that the Russians were good and the Germans were bad, softened the hearts of the Russian border guards. They let the group leave the guardhouse.

Once free, they hired a horse and wagon for the several-hours ride to Bialystok. When they got off in front of the huge central synagogue, they found that hundreds of other refugees had preceded them. Fortunately, there was some semblance of order in the place. The community provided the refugees with meals and even opened classes in the women's gallery for the children.

This lasted for some time until one memorable Friday night when they were awakened and told to march down to the railroad station. Freight cars were waiting to take them to the vast forests of the Komi Republic, just as they took us.[*]

After two weeks of rail travel and one more aboard ship, they were deposited at some location along the Vychegda River and marched to a settlement which didn't differ much from the one that welcomed us. There were, actually, a few differences: they lived in a single, long barracks building, each family assigned only one, albeit a rather large, bed. Here,

---

[*] Whereas we were taken to the train station by truck, they were marched to it. The Communist authorities were apparently well aware of the difference in the amount of baggage carried by rich versus poor refugees.

though, there was no dearth of wood to stock the *pechka* (furnace).

This settlement, unlike ours, boasted a school, which the refugee children attended. But the adults had to engage in the same "gainful occupation" as in our place: felling trees and transporting them to the frozen river to await the spring thaw. Ruzia's father was given the particularly difficult job of uprooting tree stumps. Her mother was charged with keeping the last section of the "snow railroad" tracks free of freshly fallen snow. This was imperative because at the end of the line the ground sloped steeply toward the river. As in our settlement, at the edge of the incline the horses were unhitched from the log carrier, which was then pushed over the edge and allowed to slide down metal rails onto the frozen river.

One drab year followed another, until sometime late in the autumn of 1942, when the settlement's inhabitants were told that a ship would soon be coming to transport them from their settlement to a point where they could board a train to the south, toward Tashkent. The refugees waited hopefully. The ship arrived, but it proved to be too small for everyone. The strongest boarded first—which meant that the Halzband family was left behind. Another vessel was promised for the remaining refugees. Again, they waited. The ship finally did arrive, but by then the river had frozen at the banks. Unable to dock, the ship turned back.

Then tragedy struck. Ruzia's father, intent on not missing the opportunity to board the second ship, had stayed at the landing an entire night, wishing to be among the first. The disappointment of seeing the first ship leave, most likely coupled with the extreme cold he had to endure during the long night's wait for the second ship, took a heavy toll. He suffered a heart attack and died. The Halzbands lived for three days in the presence of the dead father's body until volunteers, twin brothers, dug a grave in the rock-solid, frozen ground of Komi. It was a traumatic experience which Ruzia remembers vividly to this very day.

But life continued, with the children going to school and getting a full day of excellent education. As opposed to the situation in Kortkeros, the language of instruction here was Komi, with only one period a day devoted to Russian as a second language. With nothing to do but attend school, the children spent long hours in the classroom and studied a wide variety of subjects (even French!). Ruzia's mother continued working at keeping the tracks clear of snow. Then, one day, tragedy struck the family again. Apparently deep in thought over her unfortunate situation, Mrs. Halzband failed to notice a fully loaded log carrier fly down the slope on the last leg of its journey to the river. She was gravely injured and taken to a hospital, where she died.

The children became wards of the state and were placed in an orphanage together with other Komi orphans. In typical Soviet fashion, they were never officially notified of their mother's death, and clung to the hope that she had recovered and would one day join them. It was only after Ruzia was in Israel for several years that she ran into the twin brothers who had buried her father. They told her that upon hearing that a Jewish patient in the Syktyvkar hospital had died of her injuries, they had gone to bury the woman, whom they identified as Ruzia's mother.

In the orphanage, Ruzia met Fela (Feige) Safian, a veteran resident of that institution. Before the war, Fela had lived in Chelm, Poland, not far from the old Polish-Soviet border. As soon as the war started, her father had taken her older siblings and crossed illegally into the Soviet Union. He planned on returning to pick up his wife and the two younger children, Fela and her brother. As Fela later learned, her father had left the older children with someone in Russia and set out on his way back to Poland, as promised. But he was never heard from again, although Chelm soon came under Soviet domination and he would no longer have had to cross a border to return to his family. Mrs. Safian was killed in an air raid, and the two orphans were left to their own devices.

Food became scarce and the two were continually on the verge of starvation. With no adult to take care of them, they were reduced to scavenging forÃoÅod. A favorite spot for this was next to the railroad tracks, since occasionally refugees passing through took pity on Fela and her brother and tossed them food through the train windows.

One day as Fela and her brother were sitting at the station near the tracks, a train full of Red Army soldiers on their way home made a brief stop at the station. A tall officer, most likely a Jew, jumped off the train and eyed them with curiosity.

"Where are your parents?" he asked the little girl.

"I have no parents anymore," she said, staring back at him.

"You are going on this train," the officer told them in a commanding voice. Resigned to their fate, the children allowed him to lift them onto the train; he hoisted himself into the car just as the train started to move. The officer fed the children and made sure they had water to drink. He was the only soul the children knew. Fela no longer remembers how or where they parted from him, only that she was somehow placed in an orphanage for older children. Her brother, as she later discovered, was placed in an orphanage for younger children, also in the Komi Republic.

The conditions in Fela's orphanage were not worse than other such institutions in Komi, but depressing nonetheless: little food, no heat, outdoor toilets, and so forth. Still, the arrival of Ruzia, a girl of her own age and about the same background, made her feel just a little bit better.

All this time Fela had no idea what had happened to her brother. At some time, most likely in 1944, Polish orphans in Komi were moved to several orphanages reserved for Polish citizens only, apparently in anticipation of their repatriation. At the first stage of their journey all these children, numbering about 500, were transported to Kotlas, which served as a staging area for the next leg of the trip. When Fela saw these children, many of whom were Jewish, she started going from one to another simply asking: "Are you Shlomo Safian?" Systematically, she asked every boy, until one answered "Yes!" —and it rang in her ears like the sweetest symphony.

Within a short time a part of the group that included Ruzia, Fela, and their brothers, were moved to the new "all Polish" orphanage in Oblovka, a town situated halfway between Moscow and Stalingrad.

The population of that orphanage numbered 127 children, 27 Jewish and 100 gentile. Changes were felt immediately. The language of instruction became Polish, of course. And inevitably, the deeply rooted Polish anti-Semitism quickly surfaced. Jewish children were routinely beaten up. Then the question arose of selecting the foreign language to be taught in the school. The Jewish children preferred German because of its similarity to Yiddish, whereas the Polish Christians wanted French, long regarded in Poland as the language of the educated elite. A vote yielded the expected result: 100 for French and 27 for German.

The Polish anti-Semitism came to the fore in a particularly ugly way one year before Passover. A group of Jews had appeared as if out of nowhere to bring their young co-religionists matzos and other kosher food for the holiday. All these were stolen by members of the majority population.

The orphanage was run by a certain Piotr Wojciechowski, who somehow managed to combine virulent anti-Semitism with a most benevolent educational approach to all the children, including his Jewish charges.

The children stayed in the orphanage until the end of the War, when Polish citizens started leaving the Soviet Union for their homeland. The train carrying Ruzia, Fela, and their brothers was met at its Polish destination by a priest who welcomed the children and directed them to Catholic-supervised educational institutions, among them, monasteries. Ruzia's and Fela's brothers were sent to a monastery in the vicinity of Katowice, Ruzia was sent to a Catholic orphanage in Skarb Romanov, not far from Lodz. So confident were the Church authorities that the children would never be able to meet one another, that they provided the sisters with their brothers' addresses. This allowed them, at least, to write to each other continually.

Not only the orphanage, but also the school the children attended, were under Catholic auspices. Ruzia sat in the first row because of her hearing disability, but when a priest came to teach them Catholic prayers, including genuflection, Ruzia moved to the back of the class, where she could more easily disregard him. This didn't solve all her problems, though, because on Sunday the children were issued special clothing in which to attend church. Ruzia didn't want to attend services, so she dreamt up all kinds of excuses until her true motivation became obvious. The school's principal called her over and told her that since she was in the school, she must follow the rules. To this Ruzia replied that she still expected to be reunited with her mother, who would never forgive her if she gave up the Jewish faith.

From that moment, the principal exempted her from attending church services, but she went out of her way to announce the reason for this exemption to the children. After hearing that, no one wanted to be her friend. Ruzia suffered painful isolation, with all the children regarding her as if she were abnormal. To his credit, the principal issued a strict order that she should not be harassed. The order was observed, but Ruzia noticed that a small boy began following her around. At that time she couldn't figure out why, but it later occurred to her that the boy was probably Jewish as well.

Some distance from Ruzia, in her orphanage in Gosciniec, Fela had begun to think about her future. She knew she was Jewish, and she didn't want to stay in a Catholic orphanage.

In a brave demonstration of strength of character, thirteen-year-old Fela did the unthinkable: she ran away. One night she stole out of the orphanage and walked the ten kilometers to Lodz to search for Jews.

She tried to remember how to distinguish a Jew from a Pole. She knew that Jewish men had beards, but so did some non-Jews. The same applied to hats. Still, Fela decided to ask anyone with a beard and hat if he was Jewish.

She found a place to sit, and waited in anticipation for someone fitting her mental description. The first candidate cursed her and turned away. The second stranger proved to be Jewish, and took her to the religious orphanage at 66 Zachodnia Street, which had previously hosted Mother and Lea. As soon as she had been welcomed there, she was asked if she knew of any other Jewish children sharing her fate. Fela told them about her brother and a second boy trapped in the monastery. She also informed them of her friend Ruzia who was in a Catholic-run school, and promised to ask Ruzia's brother for the girl's address.

As soon as the address was obtained, a lady was dispatched to Ruzia's orphanage, claiming to be an aunt. Ruzia recalls that she took an instant liking to the lady and was eager to accept her offer of taking her away. Fortunately, the priest who witnessed their encounter left them alone, giving the lady a chance to speak to Ruzia at length. She gave Ruzia full instructions concerning the "family details" that she was to pass on to the administration. Several return visits were required before the administration finally allowed Ruzia to move to the Jewish orphanage at Zachodnia Street, where she joined Fela.

Mother herself traveled to Lodz to bring the two girls to Bytom. Once they met Mother, they felt secure with her. It wasn't only the presents and the good food, or even the baths and outings. It went deeper than that. They suddenly felt that they had a mother. As Ruzia put it in later years, with tears in her eyes, "I had a mother. Her name was Sarah Lederman."

Mother taught the two friends, like all the other girls before and after them, everything they needed to know at that stage of their lives. Besides teaching them the basics of Jewish thought and practice, Mother filled them in on proper etiquette, the proper way to eat with fork and knife, good grooming, and everything else needed to help them to return to normal girlhood. These lessons were accompanied by loving pats on the cheeks, warm embraces, and plenty of kisses.

* * *

As related at the beginning of this part, Mother managed to remove Ruzia's and Fela's brothers from the monastery and bring them to Bytom. Extracting the boys from the monastery, however, was only one half of the task. The other half was to get them out of Poland, and quickly enough so that they could join their sisters immediately, without risk of a second separation. There was no normal way of achieving this. There was no way the brothers could leave Poland legally, and none of the usual illegal arrangements could be made at such short notice.

In desperation, Mother took the two boys to the Bytom railroad station in the hope that something could somehow be worked out. She started by inquiring about the train schedule to Czechoslovakia, and was immediately told that a freight train, carrying coal, was just about to depart. In a flash she told the boys to jump onto the back of the last car. She ordered them to hold on tight and to jump off when the train slowed down as it passed the first station in Czechoslovakia. She would arrange for them to be picked up there.

The plan worked. Mother established contact with the right people on the Czechoslovak side, and asked them to meet the boys. This information had to be transmitted in code form, by phone, with the assistance of an international phone operator, across a not-too-friendly border, via the rickety post-war phone lines. Or it could be sent by coded telegram, and one could then hope it would be delivered and received in time for someone to meet the children. This was by no means a sure thing.

In actual fact, the boys were met by the proper person as soon as they jumped off the train. From the border station the boys traveled, together with their chaperon, to Prague on a regular train.

As soon as the sisters learned of their brothers' imminent arrival, they organized a welcome party at the Prague train station, in which Lea participated. The train stopped, the doors opened, and, to the cheers of the sisters and their friends, out walked two black boys—covered with coal dust from head to foot.

It was fortunate that they arrived in Czechoslovakia while we were still in Diablice, because their sisters again insisted that they would not move without their brothers, and would not accept another promise that everything was being done to get the boys out "as soon as possible."

The boys joined us for the remainder of our stay in Diablice and then, with our entire group, traveled to Aix-les-Bains. And from Aix-les-Bains they and their brothers traveled to Jerusalem.

THE POLISH CAPTAIN'S ORPHAN

Although Mother was primarily responsible for the girls, her sweeping command took in the boys as well. Victor Ratner was one of those to benefit. Victor was born to highly assimilated parents living in Lvov (Lemberg) in 1933. His father, an attorney, and his mother, also a college graduate, conducted themselves as patriotic Polish citizens and raised their son to do likewise. Indeed, Victor didn't even look Jewish. With his blond hair and light blue eyes he looked the perfect prototype of a non-Jewish Polish child.

Life for the Ratners was as smooth as could be until the war broke out. When Lvov eventually reverted to the Russians as a result of the infamous Molotov-Ribbentrop Pact, Victor's father managed to escape being carted off to Siberia along with many other wealthy Jews by offering his legal services—accompanied by a sizable bribe—to the Russians. However, his success in evading the Russian round-up ultimately sealed his doom.

The fateful day in June, 1941, when the Germans betrayed their Russian allies, broke the Molotov-Ribbentrop Pact, and entered Lvov as part of their invasion of the Soviet Union, remained forever etched in Victor's memory. All Jews, without exception, were ordered into the ghetto. The Ratners, assimilated or not, had to join their brethren. Conditions worsened. Throughout 1942 most of the inhabitants of the Lvov ghetto were transported to destinations from which no one returned.

In December, when Victor was almost ten, his parents managed to buy false papers, which allowed them to leave the ghetto. A close friend of Mr. Ratner's had owned the building confiscated by the Gestapo for their headquarters. This man had been retained as superintendent, and now bravely decided to use the premises as a secret refuge for close friends. Above the Gestapo chief's fourth floor apartment was a secret attic room where four families, including the Ratners, went into hiding.

The attic was tiny. After three extremely tense weeks spent there, Victor's parents smuggled him out of the building and sent him to live with the family's former maid; for themselves, they found other quarters. Victor understood that the maid, Sophia Rabi, had agreed to take him in exchange for some kind of compensation.

When anyone came to visit her, she would hide the boy in another room. Victor did not leave the house except to attend church once a week. Never having experienced any religious services, he found that he liked the singing and dramatic atmosphere of the church. His perfect Polish helped foster his new identity as Sophia's nephew. He relieved his boredom by reading whatever books Sophia could get for him.

Twice a week he was taken to see his parents at their hiding place. They often expressed their regret at having circumcised him. They had done it because of pressure from their parents, who had threatened to cut them off from a large inheritance, but they had never imagined that it would later place his life in danger.

In those troubled days, Victor's mother discovered her Jewishness through Zionism. "If only we had our own country," she lamented, "such persecutions and atrocities would never have happened!" Circumstances eventually forced her to join Victor at Sophia's home. By April, 1943, Victor's father had been caught and sent to the Yanovska labor camp. Once, as a part of team sent to clean the sewers of Lvov, Victor's father managed to make a clandestine visit to Sophia's apartment to meet his wife and son. Victor was astounded when his father suddenly appeared and gave him a fervent hug and kiss.

"I don't know if I'll still be alive after this war, but I'm doing all I can so that you'll stay alive. You're the head of the family now. Hide your Jewish identity. Soon you're going to be sent far away."

Victor was very close to his father, but he took those earth-shaking words stoically. A minute later, his father had gone. Victor never saw him again.

Victor was sent to Sophia's sister, Zosia, who lived in Premishlan. Zosia introduced Victor to her family as Victor Kreshitzki, the son of a Polish captain killed by the Germans. Victor certainly looked the part, and since his intelligence bespoke high class, Zosia's husband and two children readily believed the story.

Victor took great precautions at all times to hide his Jewishness. He attended school in Premishlan with the local children, but he was especially careful not to uncover himself when he went swimming. Since school toilets in towns such as Premishlan did not provide sufficient privacy, Victor had to use the facilities when no one was around, for which reason he regularly suffered from stomach problems during his years in hiding. In spite of all these efforts to hide his true identity, he was still was unable to keep from blushing whenever he heard anyone discussing Jews.

One summer's day, Zosia's husband noticed Victor taking some papers out of a suitcase under his bed. He waited for the first opportunity when Victor wasn't home, opened up the suitcase, and discovered the letters that Sophia regularly brought Victor from his mother.

Although Victor did not know what had transpired, he immediately sensed a change in attitude towards him. The husband had been proud to host a Polish captain's son. But who wanted a Jew?

Events took a turn for the worse. Usually Sophia came to visit him and bring him news from his mother every two weeks. She was always friendly and usually brought him gifts. This time, however, she walked in and glared at him stonily. She stated briefly that his mother had been killed and that the Germans had tortured her into revealing Victor's whereabouts.

She would have to speak with her sister Zosia about finding a new hiding place for him.

The two sisters hurried into a side room and left him standing there. Without further delay, Victor ran out of the house and stood quietly under the window to eavesdrop on their conversation. He overheard Sophia tell Zosia that they had to get rid of him. Victor raced back into the house so they wouldn't suspect him of listening in.

A few minutes later they came out and took Victor with them to a field at the edge of town. Zosia watched him while Sophia went off. Victor sat on the ground, listless, not caring whether he lived or died. His father was probably dead, and now his mother, too. His friendly protectors had turned out to be enemies. From now on he would be a hunted animal. Who wanted life under such circumstances?

Sophia came back with a list of people. The threesome trooped from one address to another. Most of the people were members of the criminal underground. They looked frightening to Victor. Zosia kept watch on the boy while Sophia bargained. The first few times, sinister-looking men stared at Victor and then shook their heads. Finally one man, a *Volksdeutsch* named Bronislaw, gave Victor a look and then nodded his head. Sophia announced to Victor that Bronislaw would take care of him from now on, and Victor was unceremoniously handed over to this new "protector."

Bronislaw took Victor directly to an old aunt of his who lived in a village on the outskirts of Premishlan. This widowed aunt had no children of her own, and she, too, felt privileged at being asked to raise the orphaned son of a Polish captain who had been killed in action. Victor was enrolled in the village school, which had twenty pupils aged seven to fourteen. The children were duly impressed with his intelligence, and twice a week would make a small collection of butter to give to the Polish captain's orphan. The "orphan" dutifully handed this to the old aunt. He did everything she asked him to do and more, so she wouldn't regret taking him in. The old lady enjoyed the presence of the helpful Polish boy. She shared many interesting conversations with him, including her opinion of Jews.

"Jews stink," she once declared. "They're thieves, and they killed Jesus... I hate them." She often let him know in full detail why the Jews were getting everything they had coming to them.

Once he joked back, "What would you do if I told you I was a Jew?"

"Eh?" she cackled. "I would crack the ice on the pond and toss you in!" she said with enthusiasm.

Victor decided not to press his luck, and never brought up the issue again. Bronislaw knew that Victor was Jewish, but Victor realized the secret was safe with him. In fact, Bronislaw became almost a father figure to the boy. He let Victor play with his gun, shared news and "macho" conversations with him, and even spoke about father-son topics. Bronislaw also brought in the wide world with his weekly visits, since the old lady wouldn't let Victor out of the house, except to attend school, lest the Germans get wind of the fact that he was the son of a Polish captain. Bronislaw brought the boy clothes, gave him haircuts, and shared his sugar and jam rations with him.

Victor was thirteen years old when the war ended. One day Bronislaw sat him down for a blunt talk. "Look, Victor, you know what the Germans did to the Jews. There are almost no Jews left in Poland. But you were lucky. You're still alive, and you can make it here. You'll get some land, you'll grow up, and eventually you'll get married to a Polish girl." Bronislaw's eyes narrowed and he looked Victor straight in the eye. "But there's one thing you have to know, Victor, and it's the truth: Even if you throw in your lot with the Polish people, till the end of your days you'll still be told '*Zydy do Pales-*

tyny—Jews, go to Palestine!'"[*]

Victor felt a chill run down his spine. A bitter struggle churned within him. On the one hand, he hated being a Jew. He wanted to run away from the whole business. He still remembered the terrible year and a half spent in the ghetto. He remembered his beloved parents, and the anguish they had been through only because they had been born Jews. If they hadn't been Jews, he reasoned, none of this would have happened to them. Anyway, he couldn't even speak Yiddish, the language of his people. Why not just reject Judaism once and for all? He had been going to church for the past several years, even enjoying it, and he'd been successful as a Christian child. He knew by heart the Christian dogma—including the part that the Jews were guilty and deserved all that had befallen them.

But then he recalled his mother's words. She had often said sadly that their tragic fate resulted from the Jews' not having a country of their own. If only Jews had their own land, she used to opine, they could fight back and not have to suffer such atrocities. Victor thought and thought. Finally he told Bronislaw, "I want to go with the Jews."

In June, 1946, Bronislaw took Victor to a nearby city and handed him over to a religious Jew named Zalman Serebriansky, who took him to live with his family. Zalman was warm and caring, understanding of Victor's suffering and inner conflicts. He took care not to be too restrictive, and even let Victor enjoy the grown-up experience of smoking. Zalman slowly began to teach Victor Yiddish, how to read Hebrew,

---

[*] Bronislaw had good reason for returning Victor to his people. During the War he had taken advantage of his privileged *Volksdeutsche* status at the expense of the Poles. As long as the Germans were in power, he knew no one would touch him; but once they left his life would be in danger. By taking in a Jewish child, he hoped to establish a reputation that would help him later. Indeed, Bronislaw's name was cleared in a court case that took place shortly after the war. As he had calculated, saving Victor was a significant mitigating factor. His enemies, though, decided to take things into their own hands: in 1947 he was deliberately run over by a jeep.

and passages from Scripture. Zalman was actively involved in rescue missions of Jewish children from non-Jewish environments, which kept him away from home for extended periods. So, after taking care of Victor for several months, Zalman decided that the boy would be better off in the Bytom orphanage, where he would receive structured study and preparation for leaving Poland.

Upon entering the orphanage, Victor, like all the children before him, was told that he could have any one special thing he wanted. The rich lawyer's son had only one thing on his mind: a sturdy pair of shoes. During the four years he had lived in the village, he had not possessed shoes of any kind, and thus hadn't been able to leave the house during the winter. Although he now had a pair of shoes, he still dreamed of possessing the expensive kind his father and mother would have bought him.

Once the dream was a reality and the new shoes were in his possession, Victor guarded them with his life. He even took them with him to bed, placing them next to the cache of bread he hid under his pillow in case the severe rationing he had experienced during the War should return. During the night, he kept one hand on the shoes. He was not even willing to wear them until he was promised a new pair when these wore out.

Life in the orphanage was an unpleasant trial for Victor. He was unused to the separation between boys and girls. More significantly, he missed a mother's touch, someone to pat him on the head and ask how his day went or slip a piece of chocolate in his pocket. The orphanage staff, which consisted of men only, was not capable of providing such an atmosphere. Although Mother lived, of course, in the girls' orphanage, Victor had a special relationship with her, and he respected her greatly. Both Mother and Victor had been raised with a code of etiquette that eschewed eating with fingers, and similar breaches of good manners. Mother would, for instance, insist on the proper use of a handkerchief, which Victor admired. Theirs was an understanding that needed few words. Victor knew that anything he requested, be it a new article of clothing or food, would be promptly given to him by this strict, yet friendly, woman who beamed care and concern.

His other consolation was the presence in the orphanage of another boy, Moshe Sokolsky. Moshe was born in Warsaw and had been adopted by a priest at the beginning of the War. He eventually wound up in the care of a non-Jewish dentist. At the end of the War, he was returned to the Jewish people and sent to the Bytom home. Due to his upbringing, however, Moshe was not only a practicing Christian, but a zealous one at that. He suffered from severely divided loyalties: on the one hand, he knew he was Jewish and wanted to live among Jews; on the other, he remained strongly attached to Christianity. Moshe would attend synagogue with all the men and children in the orphanage, put on his *tefillin,* and pray fervently in Hebrew. Then, at the conclusion of services, he would sneak up to the roof, hold a crucifix, and repeat his Christian prayers. He found a sympathetic friend in Victor, the only other child in the orphanage who spoke Polish fluently.

In December 1948, Victor crossed the border illegally into Czechoslovakia. From there he traveled through Austria and Italy until he reached the port of Naples. Finally, at the beginning of 1949, Victor arrived in Haifa, filled with happiness at knowing that he had fulfilled his mother's lifelong dream. It was the first time, too, that he felt steady ground beneath his feet. Presently he is married and lives in Tel Aviv.

THE WORK CONTINUES

Mother perceived that Jewish children cared for by State-run Jewish orphanages were as much at risk of losing their heritage as those in non-Jewish institutions. She therefore spared no effort in trying to get them out of such institutions —and succeeded more often than not. Once, for instance, she heard of an eleven year-old girl in such a Communist-Jewish orphanage in Bilsk. Mother traveled to the city and located the girl, who readily agreed to go with her. Mother knew, of course, that if discovered, her act would be regarded as outright kidnapping. She therefore took the girl to a reliable family in nearby Katowice, instead of back to Bytom.

It didn't take long for the local authorities to find out who had removed the girl from the institution. They proceeded to conduct a search of Mother's orphanage in Bytom, but found neither the girl nor Mother. As soon as Mother was informed that the search was over, she returned to Bytom—only to be arrested.

She was detained overnight at the police station, all the while staunchly denying that she had anything to do with the girl's disappearance. Mother knew quite well, though, that her denials would get her nowhere, and she therefore offered them a deal: She would "help" the police look for the girl. Since Mother knew all the orphanages in Bytom, this seemed reasonable to the police, and they fell for the trap. Mother went from place to place, followed by a plainclothesman, making a show of searching for the girl. After finishing her rounds, she returned to the police station claiming that she simply had not been able to find the girl anywhere. Incredibly, the police accepted her story and let her go.

Information about Jewish children cared for in monastery-run and non-religious Jewish institutions at times came to

Mother in roundabout ways. This was the case of the Green-berg siblings. Like many of the children, Ruth Greenberg and her brother Shimon were orphaned in Komi. Ruth was placed in an orphanage for older children, whereas Shimon (then about three years old) was assigned to an institution for the very young. Upon her return to Poland, Ruth was placed in a convent in the town of Bytów (not to be confused with Bytom) close to the Baltic Sea. One day a sister of two other Jewish children who were there appeared at the convent and took them away.

When these children were questioned as to whether there were other Jewish children with them, they relayed the infor-mation about Ruth. For some reason, perhaps because of the extreme distance, Mother did not travel to Bytów, but sent one of the older boys, Samuel Payonk, mature for his age and highly reliable. Mother would not normally have entrusted him with such a mission. Most likely the decision to send him was made after the sister of the two children reported that she had had a very easy time getting her siblings out.

Samuel traveled to Bytów, presented himself as the girl's cousin and brought Ruth over to Mother's place. Like all new arrivals, she was asked whether she had any siblings. Ruth revealed that, indeed, she had a brother named Shimon, but had been separated from him while still in Komi and at pres-ent had no idea of his whereabouts.

This lead was enough for Mother. Someone was dispatched to the Central Jewish Committee in Warsaw and brought back the information that Ruth's brother had also returned from Komi and was currently in Warsaw at a non-religious Jewish orphanage conducted by the AJDC. Although the children in this institution attended a Jewish school, the study of Hebrew was their only exposure to anything connected to Judaism.

Mother felt that it would be only proper to get the boy out and provide him with a real Jewish education, especially since his sister was already in Bytom. But she feared that if she were to ask for the boy on the strength of having his sister in her institution, the AJDC orphanage administration might counter that the sister should join her brother at their place. She therefore decided on a quasi-"kidnapping."

Together with Ruth, Mother traveled to Warsaw and arrived at the school that Shimon attended. The normal procedure would have been to wait outside the school and then speak to Shimon as he left the building. However, Mother had a problem: since a number of years had elapsed since the children had parted, she feared that Ruth might not be able to spot her brother among the crowd of jostling children running out of school after the last bell.

Instead, knowing which class was Shimon's, she instructed Ruth to walk into her brother's classroom and ask for him by name. It is a tribute to Mother's sway over the children that Ruth, who was not yet twelve, mustered the courage to perform such a mission. She walked into the room, disregarded the teacher's verbal attempt to stop her, got her brother to identify himself and told him that she would be waiting for him after school. Mother then took Ruth for a walk. The pair returned in time for the bell, picked up Shimon and made their way to Bytom, where Shimon was assigned to the boy's orphanage.

The Greenberg girl presented a unique challenge. Mother was used to dealing both with children who had lived with non-Jews for an extended period, and those who had been in Catholic institutions for a relatively short time. But she was simply unprepared for the strength of Catholic conviction that Ruth, who had stayed in a convent longer than the other children, displayed. Still, the atmosphere, the warmth, the understanding smiles, and the hugs seemed to be having the desired effect, and Ruth appeared to be moving towards acceptance of Jewish religious life just like the children before and after her. Even so, it was very difficult for her to leave behind her Catholic upbringing and entrenched beliefs. She also missed the high-vaulted church with its stained-glass windows, organ, and other appurtenances of Catholic worship. She was also unhappy with the fact that now, after having found her brother, she had very little opportunity to see him, since he studied with the boys in a different part of town.

At about that time Mother heard of a Jewish woman who had given birth to a baby girl out of wedlock and was contemplating giving her away to a convent. Mother ran to the hospital, persuaded the woman to sign the proper papers, and hired a wet nurse. Some time later, the baby came down with whooping cough. The prescribed treatment at that time was a stay in Zakopane, a resort high up in the Tatry Mountains, the "Polish Alps." The elevation, with its air rich in healing-promoting minerals, was the best and possibly the only cure that could be offered to an infant at that time.

Mother, however, did not trust the wet nurse with the baby. She needed someone to keep on eye on her. Mother decided that she could solve both problems by sending Ruth to Zakopane. Mother hoped that the serene mountain atmosphere and the beauty of the fir-covered slopes, along with the feeling of responsibility for a young life, would "cure" Ruth of her Catholic longings.

However, this was not to be. Just as the baby was returning to good health, Ruth decided to run away, back to the Bytów convent. The wet nurse returned alone to Bytom and Samuel Payonk was again dispatched to the monastery to retrieve Ruth. Unlike his initial mission, this trip was unsuccessful. He was received at the convent with an overt show of suspicion and told that Ruth was in the hospital. There being only one hospital in Bytów, Samuel had no problem finding her. Ruth however, was not responsive to his entreaties that she come back to Bytom when she got well. He returned empty-handed. Mother felt that, given the circumstances of Ruth's loyalty to Catholicism and what had become a suspicious atmosphere at the convent, there was no chance of success, and no additional attempt at removing her was made.

Having recovered from whatever ailed her, Ruth returned to the convent. For a while she reverted to her cherished Catholic past and felt that this was the better way of life. However, she could not erase her Bytom sojourn from her memory. She could not forget Mother's words of kindness, the hours Mother spent talking to her and explaining what being Jewish is all about. Hence she could not shake off the feeling that she was in the wrong place. Although she could not work up the courage to leave the convent, she felt increasingly restless and unhappy.

Her moods did not go unnoticed by her principal teacher. This woman, although she was a nun, called her over one day and said: "Look my girl, I know what your problem is. In spite of having received a Catholic education, you are still Jewish, and this feeling has never left you. The convent is not for you. Find yourself a place with your fellow Jews."

Ruth transferred to an orphanage conducted by a Zionist organization and, in due course, arrived in Israel. Widowed in recent years, she lives here with her three children.

Shimon did not last long in Bytom after his sister left, and transferred to another orphanage. He, too, found his way to Israel.

On another occasion, information concerning a Jewish boy held in a monastery reached Mother from Switzerland. Needless to say, she was quite surprised to learn that this boy was the brother of one of the girls in her care. It emerged that the girl had never told Mother about him because while she had escaped to Russia, her brother had been placed in the monastery by their mother. (Either the girl had never been informed of this development, or had forgotten it.) Now, when questioned, the sister told Mother that she remembered her brother having a birthmark on one finger.

Armed with this knowledge, Mother traveled to the monastery. She arrived there to find the children kneeling in prayer.

Mother asked for the boy, and he was pointed out to her. The priest in charge was willing to give him up, but the boy refused to be separated from the priest, who, he said, was like a father to him.

Mother commonly encountered such reluctance, and had come prepared. "Your sister is staying with me," she revealed to him. "She even told me that you have a birthmark on one finger." The boy still found it hard to leave, but hearing of the existence of a sister exercised a tremendous pull on him, and so he let his "aunt" take him away. With that same opportunity Mother rescued another girl, also a sister of one of the girls in her care.

Mother at a Warsaw railroad station during one of her missions to locate still another Jewish child.

Mother never refused a request to rescue a child. She was not deterred in her mission by the need to travel large distances, or by the danger in rescuing children to whom she had no legal claim.

Mr. and Mrs. Eidelman were among the Jews confined to the Kovno ghetto in the spring of 1944. That was when the Germans, anticipating retreat under pressure from the Russian advance, decided to liquidate the ghetto. The Eidelmans saw no way to escape their fate, but, like many Jews in their situation, tried to save the life of their only son, four-year-old Yehudah.

Working through intermediaries (Lithuanian gentiles who could enter and leave the ghetto on business), the Eidelmans contacted a gentile family and made arrangements with them to take Yehudah in. Hidden in a sack of potatoes, Yehudah was shipped from Kovno to the town where the gentile family resided.

Yehudah lived with this family for nearly a year and a half, until six months after the Russians liberated Lithuania. His parents did not survive, but a aunt who was still alive knew the name of the family he had been sent to, and located him at the end of 1945.

At first the gentile family—who had become attached to Yehudah—refused to give him up. Fortunately, the Soviets, who took control of Lithuania, had passed a law requiring all abandoned children to be returned to their blood relatives. When the aunt threatened to report them to the authorities, the family agreed to part with Yehudah.

Retrieving Yehudah from his foster family solved only half the problem. For Yehudah to grow up as a proper Jew he had to leave the country, or else he would become a ward of the atheist educational system of the Soviet Union. Although the aunt was a Lithuanian citizen and could obtain a passport to travel to Poland, she had no way to take Yehudah out of there. No one was concerned about an elderly lady leaving the Soviet Garden of Eden for its Communist neighbor, Poland. However, a minor orphan was considered important: a future proud citizen of the great republic of Lithuania. A ward of the state was not to be relinquished to any other country, even to a Communist one.

So Yehudah's aunt had to find some other solution. In the end, she managed to locate a couple who were Polish citizens and therefore were permitted to emigrate from Lithuania to their homeland. Most probably in exchange for a fee, they agreed to take Yehudah along with them. Yehudah's aunt sewed a label into his coat containing his name and the name of Rebbetzin Shoshanah Soloveichik, her sister-in-law in the United States. She requested that Yehudah be delivered to the Rebbetzin in the event that he was lost.

The terror of the Soviet occupation which pervaded Lithuania at that time was so great that it can be only described by those who experienced it. Nevertheless, this did not prevent the aunt from accompanying Yehudah to the train station. She exposed herself to enormous risk in order to ensure that Yehudah indeed got on the train with the couple.

A gentile neighbor noticed them at the train station and asked Yehudah, "Where are you going to?" "Out of the country," Yehudah innocently replied to his incredulous neighbor. Had the man reported them to the police, the aunt would have been arrested and the whole plan aborted. But fortunately he did not say anything, and Yehudah was able to board the train without incident.

Since, at that time, minors were merely listed on their parents' passports and no photograph was required, all that one had to do to forge a child's passport was to add the child's first name to one's own passport and hope that the entry would not be detected.

With their "amended" passport the couple managed to pass the border police inspection when crossing into Poland. However, once the train was moving through Poland, the couple began worrying that their forgery had been detected. It might only be a matter of time, they thought, until they would be apprehended by the Polish authorities. In a panic, they abandoned the child at the next train station.

Fortunately for the boy, a Jewish man happened to be at the station and took Yehudah to his home. The man realized, however, that he had no long-term solution; the authorities were bound to discover that he was harboring an illegal guest. Inquiries brought the information that Mother ran an orphanage in Bytom and would be willing to take in any child, even one who was without any documents.

The man contacted Mother, who immediately suggested that he bring Yehudah to Bytom. He balked at this suggestion, though, replying that he was afraid to travel together with an undocumented child.

Undeterred as always by such considerations, Mother dropped everything and traveled to the man's town. Since Bytom is located close to the southwest border of Poland, whereas the Lithuanian border is at the northeastern extremity of the country, the trip, with train changes and time spent waiting for the next train, took almost an entire day and night. Mother did not want to burden the man's family with her presence and hence left for Bytom with Yehudah on the first available train, again traveling almost an entire day and night.

Yehudah proved to be undernourished and afflicted with impetigo, but Mother soon nursed him back to health.

In the meantime, word had reached Rebbetzin Soloveichik in America that her nephew had survived the war and was in Jewish hands in some undetermined place in Poland. She took the first available plane to Paris, which was then the hub of a large number of Jewish organizations, in the hope that she would be able to locate Yehudah. As she waited in the lobby of a hotel to meet an official who might have information about her nephew, she was approached by a total stranger. He asked her why she was waiting, and she told him. By an inexplicable coincidence, the man knew where Yehudah was: with a group of children in Czechoslovakia, where Mother sent her children on their way out of Communist hands. Rebbetzin Soloveichik immediately took a plane to Prague, where she was able to locate Yehudah. After arranging immigration papers for him, she took him with her to the United States, where he ultimately grew up to be one of America's outstanding Torah scholars.

*　*　*

And then there was a boy named Waldek. When it became obvious that being a Jew was dangerous, Waldek's father, one of the very few Jewish officers in the Polish police force, entrusted him to a fellow officer. The father subsequently vanished and was never heard from again.

The gentile officer took care of young Waldek, a task made

easier by the fact that the boy was not circumcised—until fear got the better of him. He may have been wary of the neighbors, who knew that Waldek was not his own son. Whatever his reason, the officer one day deposited the little boy unceremoniously on a street in a Warsaw suburb. Young Waldek's cries were heard by a Polish woman, a war widow with a little daughter, who took him under her wing. Indeed, she registered him with the local priest, who was in charge of vital statistics, as a son born out of wedlock. After her own daughter died an untimely death, the woman moved to Warsaw in an effort to further protect herself and the boy. She subsequently remarried, without even telling her husband that the boy was Jewish. Naturally, Waldek's uncircumcised state made this easier. She was still afraid, however, that his Jewish appearance would eventually give him away. For this reason,

Rz.-Katol. Parafia
SUB: STANISŁAWA B. M.
Warszawa-Wola. ul. Bema 73

Zastrzega się opłatę stemplową

Do spraw Kościelnych

Nr aktu 205

Rok 1942

Świadectwo urodzenia i chrztu św.

Wydane na zasadzie ksiąg metrycznych

Zaświadcza się, że Waldemar-Aleksander Hęciński

urodził... się   dnia   szóstego lipca

w Warszawie   tysiąc dziewięćset trzydziestego piątego   roku

z ojca

z matki Zofia Hęcińska

Ochrzczony... w tut. parafii trzydziestego października   19 42 r.

Uwagi Na marginesie aktu nie ma adnotacji o zawarciu związku małżeńskie-go.

Zgodność powyższego świadectwa z oryginałem stwierdzam

Warszawa   dnia 10 m-ca kwietnia 19

Proboszcz

A birth certificate issued by the parish priest, "attesting" to the (out-of-wedlock) birth of Waldemar (Waldek) Hecinski. Ms. Hecinski needed this document to protect the boy from suspicion that he was Jewish.

she kept him at home, not even sending him to school. Waldek was about eight at the time, young enough for his surrogate mother to postpone his schooling for another year without her new husband suspecting anything amiss. With the war over, Waldek entered school.

Mother was informed of Waldek's existence and attempted to negotiate with his foster parents for transfer of custody. After a great deal of bickering, they agreed to go to a lawyer and sign the pertinent document, but kept on pushing off having it validated in court. Unsure of the final outcome, Mother decided on a direct kidnap.

One day, as the boy was walking to school, a black limousine containing Mother and a uniformed Jewish chaplain serving in the Polish army pulled up along his path. Mother got out of the limousine, walked over to the boy and pointed out the chaplain to impress the boy with the officer's epaulets. The boy was duly fascinated, and as he stood there staring Mother took his hand and walked him to the limousine, which then drove off. For some reason, the child was not taken directly to Bytom, but to the office of a Jewish organization in Warsaw.

But matters became complicated before they could set off on the second leg of their journey. The boy made a ruckus, and someone called the police. Now Mother had no way out except to call Waldek's Polish "parents" to try to negotiate a deal. When that didn't work, the boy was returned to them.

Mother, never one to give up on a Jewish child, then took the courageous step of going to court with the non-validated custody-transfer agreement. Not surprisingly, she lost the case. Still undeterred, she reopened negotiations with the couple, and for a good price, finally succeeded in gaining custody of the boy. Waldek joined the orphanage and, like most of the children, eventually found his way to Israel.

* * *

MINISTERSTWO SPRAW ZAGRANICZNYCH

Nr p.

Zal.

Warszawa, dnia 23 września 1963 r.

O ś w i a d c z e n i e

Ja, niżej podpisany, Pszkit Stanisław ur.8.5.1905 roku
w Warszawie, z ojca Aleksandra i matki Rozalii z domu
Szczeblewska, zamieszkały obecnie w Warszawie, przy ul.
Chmielnej 126 m.28 stwierdzam co następuje:

W roku 1943 żona moja Zofia Chęcińska obecnie Zofia Pszkit
znalazła w lesie w Miedzeszynie dziecko pochodzenia izraelskie-
go - Waldemara Torn ur.6.7.1935 r. w Warszawie z ojca Jana.
Wyżej wymieniony przebywał u nas od roku 1943 do 1946.
Jesienią 1946 roku Gmina Żydowska zabrała go do Żydowskiego
Domu Dziecka w Bytomiu. Ojciec Waldemara Torna został zabity
przez Niemców na jego i mojej żony oczach. Waldemar Torn
był wówczas ukryty w wyżej wspomnianym lesie w krzakach.
Matka Waldemara Torna była więźniarką obozu koncentracyjnego
w Majdanku, z którego nie powróciła.
Nadmieniam, że Waldemar Torn w czasie okupacji nie uczęszczał
do szkoły z wiadomych przyczyn, natomiast po Wyzwoleniu
wyżej wymieniony uczęszczał do szkoły polskiej.

/Pszkit Stanisław/

Repertorium Nr A-III- /63
PAŃSTWOWE BIURO NOTARIALNE w WARSZAWIE
Al. Gen. Świerczewskiego Nr 58
Dnia dwudziestego piątego września
roku tysiąc dziewięćset sześćdziesiątego trzeciego
Poświadczam,że podpis powyższy uznał w mojej obecności za własno-
ręcznie położony Stanisław Pszkit,zamieszkały w Warszawie przy ulicy Chmielnej nr 126 m 28a,tożsamość którego ustaliłam na podstawie
dowodu osobistego WCA 105712.Pobrano opłaty skarbowej zł.10 /§ 1(
rozp. o opł.skarb./ i za dokonanie czynności notarialnej zł.10
/§ 21 rozp. o opł.not./.

Hanna Gibas
NOTARIUSZ

Sworn statement by Ms. Hecinski's subsequent husband, in which he
describes the course of events that brought Waldemar to his wife's house
and declares that his actual family name is Torn and that he is being
transferred to the Bytom Jewish Orphanage.

Difficulties abounded in running the Bytom orphanage. These included the special problems inherent in caring for children from orphanages run by non-religious Jewish Communists. These children couldn't understand why they were now forbidden to turn on lights or engage in certain other activities on the Sabbath. Children taken from non-Jewish environments also had a hard time adjusting, but they could more readily accept the explanation that in a Jewish institution certain actions and activities are not appropriate on the Sabbath. Mother solved the problem by dispensing large doses of love and attention to keep the children happy enough to forget their past.

One of Mother's most complicated and heartbreaking cases was that of Ihrka (Miriam), a Jewish girl living with a Polish family. The girl's paternal uncle lived in the United States, and with the War's end, he was eager for his niece to join him. Ihrka's whereabouts were known to a number of Jewish organizations, yet all their attempts to retrieve her had met with failure. But Mother was undaunted. She went to Ihrka's caretaker and said: "Look, Madam, I know that you have a Jewish girl for whom you did everything. I just came from America, from her uncle, who told me that he wants to take both of you there. You will live in a palace where your every whim will be catered to." The lady was interested. After all, palaces are not offered every day.

Mother continued: "At the same time, I cannot in all honesty tell those people in America that I have the girl if she is still staying with you! Here is my suggestion: You give me the girl and your personal data as well. I will apply for passports for both of you. Within two months, I will call for you. Here is my address. You can visit me and the girl anytime you wish. But first of all, I want to compensate you for all the expenses you incurred in taking care of her."

The lady agreed and mentioned an amount in zlotys— which Mother promptly paid. She then left with Ihrka.

Shortly thereafter, a representative of the local Communist-run Jewish orphanage, previously unsuccessful in taking Ihrka under his wing, visited the woman and asked for the girl again. At first, the woman refused to tell him where Ihrka was, but after several persistent visits, she told the man that a lady had come and promised to take both of them to America. The man was furious. He told her that it was nothing but an out-an-out lie, and that the girl would wind up with the "reactionary Zionists" in Palestine.

This frightened the woman and she came running to Mother's place. Perhaps afraid that Mother would be able to put her off in a direct confrontation, she chose a more devious route. She befriended a gentile household employee of the orphanage and learned from her what time the children went out for a walk. She then waited outside, and when the children passed by, she grabbed Ihrka and ran.

As soon as Mother heard of this, she declared an "all-stations alert," and the populations of both the boys' and girls' orphanages fanned out over the city in search of the pair. Ihrka and her caretaker were discovered just as they were about to board a bus. Mother had the custody transfer document, signed by the woman, in her possession. With this ammunition, Mother marched the two to the police station. There, Mother signed a document indicating that she took full responsibility for the girl. The Polish woman was detained for acting illegally, but Mother, out of pity, persuaded the authorities to drop the charges.

It was now imperative to get the girl out of Poland as soon as possible. Mother knew of several people who had valid passports with Czechoslovakian visas, one of them a man whose passport included his two small children, who were already in France. Since only the parent's picture appeared on the passport, this person could claim that Ihrka was one of his children. Mother herself would not have entrusted this particular individual with such a dangerous task. But, as was often the case, she was busy traveling in quest of more children, and so was not in Bytom to make the decision.

Unfortunately, there was a search at the border and the "enormous" sum of twenty American dollars was found on the man, thus making him answerable to charges of illegal possession of foreign currency. He was so terrified when the police led him away that he forgot all about the girl. Poor Ihrka, finding herself suddenly all alone in a strange place, started crying. She tearfully told one of the border policemen that she was the daughter of a Polish woman, gave him the address, and was promptly returned to her. The man who had posed as her father was subsequently released, and he returned to Poland. He eventually made his way to Israel, but the trauma of that event left him mentally unbalanced for quite some time, a state from which he never fully recovered.

Mother, however, would not give up on Ihrka. After consulting with a lawyer, she went to court. But despite the legally obtained custody transfer in her possession, she lost the case. The judge returned Ihrka to the Polish woman's custody, claiming that, legalities notwithstanding, Poland could not afford to lose its young citizens; it was obvious to the court that under Mrs. Lederman's wing the girl would leave the country sooner or later. The judge did rule, however, that upon attaining the age of eighteen the girl could choose to do as she pleased.

Mother wanted to appeal the verdict. But before doing so, she consulted her childhood friend, Fishel Finkelstein, who by now held a high position in the prosecutor general's office. He talked her out of it, claiming that it would entail too much exposure and might endanger Mother personally as well as her orphanage-rescue project. Mother took his advice. But this was not the end of the story.

The girl's uncle turned to Rabbi Chaim Kreiswirth in Antwerp for assistance. The Rabbi played a round of Mother's game, offering the girl the life of an American princess, this time dangling Hollywood stardom for Ihrka in front of the Polish woman. This was just in time, because Ihrka was already engaged to marry her Polish "brother." The Rabbi persuaded the woman to come to Belgium together with Ihrka, and somehow convinced her to leave the girl with him. Ihrka was later taken to the United States by her real uncle.

     * * *

After marrying in Israel, my wife and I lived in Brooklyn for five years, where my wife worked as a teacher. One day a fellow teacher, Mrs. Bruriah David, phoned us to ask a favor: There was a Polish girl staying with her uncle who would like very much to spend the weekend with a family whose background was closer to her own. The woman felt that since I spoke Polish, it would be appropriate for us to host her. My wife and I were quite happy to invite the girl, and I drove over to the uncle's house to pick up our guest.

As we sat down to one of the first meals, the girl suddenly said: "Lederman... Lederman... It sounds familiar. Did your mother run an orphanage in Poland? The minute Rebbetzin David told me that a Mr. Lederman was inviting me, a bell rang, but it took me a while to put two and two together."

Only then did I remember that one day Mother had shown me a picture of this very girl. "The trouble this Miriam [Ihrka] gave me," she had commented, "was more than I suffered from any other child."

But from the bitter came forth the sweet. Ihrka, now called by her Jewish name, Miriam, eventually became engaged to a Jewish boy who also hailed from Poland. Rabbi Chaim Kreiswirth, the man who had ultimately rescued her after the Holocaust, saw fit to fly to New York specially to officiate at the wedding. My wife and I also attended, as did the family from Antwerp with whom Miriam had stayed during her sojourn there.

     * * *

Mother rescued another Ihrka as well. The girl's mother, who came from one of the most famous rabbinical families, had married the Pole whose family sheltered her during the War. Shortly after giving birth to a baby girl, she died in an accident. The baby remained with her father, who had the obvious difficulty of both working and taking care of the child. For this reason, he was amenable to Mother's offer of a handsome payment for the child in exchange for custody transfer papers, and the infant Ihrka joined the other girls at the Bytom home.

Some time later, the father's parental instincts awakened and he showed up at the orphanage. He walked in, grabbed the girl's hand, and walked out. Hearing the hastily closing door, Mother ran after them and grabbed the girl by her other hand. Thus the trio walked down the stairs and into the street. Anticipating resistance, Ihrka's father had come accompanied by a large group of his Polish friends. These now tailed the threesome as they walked, in total and strained silence, down the street. As this procession was taking place, some girls from the orphanage met them on their way home from a walk. Mother shooed them aside, not wanting them to be involved in such unpleasantness, and continued walking with the girl and her father. Being more familiar with the city's layout than was the father, Mother managed to steer the pair straight to the police station. There, with a flourish, she produced the custody transfer papers, thus ending the attempted kidnapping.

Ihrka, like most of the children, wound up in Israel, where she was accepted as a member of a religious settlement. Unfortunately, she later suffered third-degree burns from a kerosene stove and failed to recover.

PART IV

JAIL AND FREEDOM

FOURTEEN MONTHS IN JAIL

Although Mother sometimes succeeded in retrieving children from orphanages run by the Communist state, she could not risk it too often. At the same time, she refused to give up on these children. So it was that she hit upon a new plan which, as it turned out, had momentous repercussions on her life.

She would prepare passports for the children, planning that if and when some legal way was found to get them out of Poland, she would collect the children in one fell swoop and immediately send them out of the country. Although passports were normally issued without much ado, an exit permit was also necessary for leaving the country. Such permits were not easily obtained. Mother had hopes that either the general situation would change, or that some other arrangement would be worked out by Jewish leaders abroad. In either case, she wanted to be prepared to act immediately.

It will forever remain a mystery how Mother found out what schools these children were attending, and how she identified them in person. The fact remains, though, that she contacted over forty such children.

The story she gave was usually the same: She had been contacted by the child's wealthy relative in America who wanted to adopt the orphan in question. Mother asked only that the child bring to school the following day a photograph of himself along with relevant personal information so that she could file a passport application. Then, she promised, when the time came, she would contact the child and take him to the "Golden Country."

The children were more than willing to comply, and in due time Mother filed over forty passport applications. The applications, however, had to be signed. Since it was too dangerous to go back to the school for the child's signature, Mother signed them all, making an effort to change her signature each time.

Mother did not depend on her skill in signature forgery; to be on the safe side, she paid off the official who processed these papers. All the applications were handled by the one and only passport office, which was part of the Foreign Ministry in Warsaw. Mother did not remove the passports from the office, since she was afraid the orphanage might be searched, in which case more documents than children would be found, implicating her. She depended on her bribed official to hold these documents for the children until needed.

Meanwhile, a new difficulty arose back at her orphanage: the girls became more and more insistent about wanting formal schooling. Mother resisted as long as she could, but eventually had to give in. The children were duly enrolled in local schools. But as Mother had foreseen, this led to undesirable developments. Happy at last to be like everyone else, the girls neglected their Hebrew studies, which continued to be given after school, in the late afternoon and evening. Even more worrisome was the fact that the children were now officially registered, making them highly visible to the authorities.

But this was not the only problem. The municipal authorities, who were never too happy with the presence of a religious Jewish orphanage, finally found an excuse to shut this one down. Here were children, enrolled in the city schools, who were living in an unlicensed dormitory institution—a clear violation of the law! Nor could a license be legally issued to this institution: an orphanage was not allowed to have its premises in a rented apartment. Also the required amenities to which the poor orphans were entitled, such as a gymnasium and a spacious dining hall, were all lacking. Therefore an order was issued to close the place down.

Mother had no chance of finding suitable premises in

Bytom, either because there were none or because of the price. Consequently, some time in the late summer of 1948 she decided to move all the girls in the orphanage from Bytom to the resort town of Solice Zdroj. She managed to rent a building there at an affordable price, and for a while things returned to normal—or appeared to, but this was only an illusion.

A short time after the orphanage had settled in Solice Zdroj, the head of the local health department paid a visit. She started with a "sanitary inspection," looking under every bed and every other piece of furniture in the hopes of finding dirt or dust. Her search was fruitless, though: as in Bytom, and in any previous place run by Mother, the building was spotless. Not a speck of dust was to be found.

Defeated on this front, the official was still determined. "Nice," she commented, "but you don't have a license." Mother immediately agreed to do everything necessary to obtain one. "Yes," the woman said, "but you don't have a degree." Mother countered by offering to take all the courses needed for a degree. But the official would not relent, and told Mother that an order to close the orphanage down would be forthcoming immediately.

Mother realized that this signalled the end of the orphanage, and of a chapter in her life. The hostile attitude of Polish officialdom towards her and the children in her charge was breaking all bounds. Her children would have to be moved out of Poland.

With the order to close down expected every day, arrangements had to be made right away to smuggle the children out of Poland. Not only that, but also they would have to be housed somewhere temporarily, until they could be taken across the border. Mother found a large apartment for rent in Cracow, moved the girls there, and immediately started preparations to get the children across into Czechoslovakia.

The border crossing took place on a bridge which spanned

the Oder River. Arrangements for the crossing were made by Rabbi Winkelstein. He knew that the border patrol guarding the bridge between Poland and Czechoslovakia did a ten-day tour of duty. This meant that once the soldiers were bribed, he had a full ten days to get the children across. At the rate of four children per day, the nearly forty girls then residing in the orphanage could be moved in one ten-day period.

At the beginning things went smoothly. A group of four children left each day, two younger and two older children, the latter acting as chaperones. The children travelled by train to a certain border town, with a guide (an older boy, specially selected for this job) to assure their safe arrival. They were told that after getting off the train they should look for a woman who would be wearing yellow shoes, and should follow this woman without saying a word. She would walk to a spot where the children would wait until nightfall, at which time either she or someone else would take them across the border, straight past the supposedly vigilant (and pre-bribed) border patrol. On the other side people would be waiting to pick them up and convey them to a transit point in Czechoslovakia.

The girls were now supervised primarily by the senior teacher, Miss F. It would have been dangerous for Mother to stay with them, because she could easily be identified as being in charge, but she visited them daily. It was hoped that within ten days everybody, including Mother and Miss F., would be in Czechoslovakia.

The plan was foiled, though. One day several policemen, apparently tipped off by the authorities in Solice Zdroj, showed up at the Cracow apartment, looking for the person in charge. It happened that Mother was there at that moment. The children immediately sensed that she was in danger, and before she realized what was happening, one of them had pushed her into the kitchen. Like our kitchen in Warsaw, this one had its own servants' staircase. The police were either unaware or overly confident, because they neglected to block off the rear exit.

Mother escaped and went into hiding; friends of hers extracted the children from the building and scattered them all over the city, among the large number of Torah-observant families concentrated there. The groups of four continued leaving, undetected. It seems that the police were primarily interested in laying their hands on the management, whom they had not yet identified. They soon did, however, with help from a most unlikely quarter.

One of the girls refused to continue staying with the family to which she was assigned. She kept on pestering Miss F. to allow her to move to a hotel. No longer able to resist, Miss F. gave in. By that time the last children were about to leave, and Miss F. hoped that the hotel stay would be short and pass undetected.

This was not to be. Hotels were under surveillance by the secret police, and it wasn't long before the girl was called in for questioning by the police. She told them all she knew, implicating everyone—not only Mother and Miss F., but also the border patrol team. That team, an officer and two privates, was arrested immediately. Mother and her children were in great danger too, but fortunately, by this time almost all the children had managed to leave. There remained only the girl taken by the police, Miss F., Mother, and the baby born out of wedlock, now recovered from the whooping cough. All the same, Mother would not trust it to anyone.

Now, the food in the hotel mentioned above was, of course, not kosher, so it had been arranged that the girl staying there would meet a messenger in a pre-arranged spot to get some food. When she failed to show up, the messenger called Rabbi Winkelstein on the phone and told him "that this girl had nothing to eat." People's senses were finely tuned in those days to catch hidden messages, so the rabbi understood at once that the girl had been arrested.

He sent an urgent message to Miss F. to meet her brother in Cracow—he was to warn to her not to try to cross the border, something which could not be mentioned on the phone. For some reason, her brother failed to arrive at the meeting point. Not knowing what to do, Miss F. returned to Bytom, where she was promptly arrested and put in solitary confinement in the special jail reserved for secret-police detainees, in the district city of Katowice.

Mother was in hiding at this time, and was obliged to make frequent changes in location, which prevented any contact with her. Unaware of the danger caused by the sudden turn of events, she went to the border and walked up to the bridge with the out-of-wedlock baby in her arms. She was apprehended by the new patrol team and was thrown into solitary confinement in the same prison as Miss F. The fate of the baby is unknown. Most likely she was placed in a Polish orphanage and grew up without ever becoming aware of her Jewish origins.

Conditions were harsh. Instead of a bed, the cell contained a narrow wooden sleeping platform with no mattress. For food, prisoners were given a quarter of a pound of bread daily, some soup, and water. Mother would not touch the soup. Choosing the traditional Jewish response to difficulty, she decided to fast, eating the bread and drinking the water only after sunset. She persevered for forty days, much like Moses on Mount Sinai. Unlike Moses, however, she grew so weak that she was unable to move from her sleeping platform. The prison doctor pronounced her dead, and she was removed to the prison morgue.

Mother stayed there immobile and unattended for about a day, until a passing inmate noticed that her hand was moving. Mother was then taken to the prison hospital, treated for her condition and returned to the cell. Now she realized that her life was in danger, she forced herself to eat the non-kosher soup. Even so, she developed jaundice, most likely because her

A letter written in code by one of Mother's friends in Poland to me in the US. In it she describes Mother (who was then in prison) as seriously ill, attended by the best of doctors, but nonetheless in poor condition. She writes that prayer is the best way to help Mother.

immune system was weakened by the fast, and for a while was very ill.

This period of solitary confinement lasted about three months, during which Mother and Miss F. were continuously interrogated. After this ordeal, the women were transferred to an ordinary prison, also in Katowice. Here, Mother's conditions of imprisonment underwent a fortuitous and dramatic change.

The prison doctor turned out to be none other than the very same doctor used by the Bytom orphanage. He immediately made good use of the poor condition Mother's fasting had brought her to and assigned her to the hospital ward. As a sick prisoner, she was entitled to receive extra food from the outside, in particular eggs, cereal, and butter, in relatively large quantities. While she used some of it for herself, Mother transmitted, almost daily, a pot of eggs and cereal cooked in butter to Miss F. This was accomplished through the services of a friendly warden and continued almost up to the trial, when the warden was replaced by a much less friendly woman.

Now Mother had no *kashruth* problems. None, that is, until Passover arrived. Even without a calendar, she made sure to find out the precise date of this festival. Eating forbidden *chametz* (leavened food) on Passover was more than Mother could bring herself to do, even after her previous life-threatening experience. But because she was allowed no visitors, nor any correspondence, she had no way of asking someone to send matzos—the only kosher-for-Passover food imaginable under the circumstances.

Mother always used to pray for help, but now she prayed for a miracle. Her prayers earned her the respect of her cell-mates, nuns imprisoned as part of the general persecution of the Polish clergy. They considerately conversed only in whispers and refrained from using the in-cell toilet until she finished her prayers. As Passover approached, her prayers and supplications became even more fervent. Then, on the night before Passover, Mother had a dream. Her father, whom she adored, came to her and told her not to worry, that she would not have to eat *chametz*. Mother woke up, not knowing what to make of her dream. On the one hand, she retained her childhood image of her father, a person whose word had the strength of the Rock of Gibraltar. On the other hand, she had to face reality: she was an observant Jewish woman in a place where she was granted no right to ask for anything—even if only for the pleasure of being refused. Not even her doctor friend could ask for something as outrageous as kosher-for-Passover food.

The hours piled up, with Mother torn between the vision of the promise and the reality of a Polish jail. Suddenly, she was called to the office and informed that she had received a parcel. It was opened in her presence to make sure it contained only what it purported to contain, and a package of matzos was thrust into her hands. Apparently the Jewish Communal Council, aware of Mother's internment, had managed to negotiate the supply of matzos. The same was done for Miss F., the teacher.

Mother had another interesting dream. She dreamt that she was with her father and her brother, Moshe Aharon, and that the latter was holding a heavy stick, about to strike her. Her father intervened, yelling: "Don't you dare hit my daughter!" Mother woke up visibly shaken. Her reaction was noticed immediately by her cellmates. To Mother's great surprise, the nuns volunteered an optimistic interpretation: "Your brother represents the many Jewish Communists who serve as prosecutors and judges. Your father represents the Father in Heaven, who is your Guardian and will protect you from your 'brothers.'"

When the trial date became known, a lawyer was hired. At Mother's suggestion, they decided on a line of defense. This was not easily accomplished since all messages had to be shouted over a seven-foot wall in the presence of the secret police! Still, Mother and her lawyer managed, primarily because Mother prepared the defense on her own. She claimed that she was illiterate and hence could not possibly have forged any papers. The lawyer did not, and under the circumstances could not, give any legal advice. She was reduced to listening to Mother.

In pre-war Poland few uneducated Jews—such as Mother was now claiming to be—spoke any Polish. This made it imperative to come up with an explanation for her ability to speak even the broken Polish she chose to use in keeping with her assertion of illiteracy. Mother claimed that although she had never gone to school, she had learned the language from a Polish housekeeper who had worked for her parents.

The defense, however, had the seemingly impossible task

of denying hard evidence, the most telling of which were the dozens of passport applications, signed in Mother's own handwriting, which had been discovered by the police. In addition to forgery, Mother was also charged with engineering illegal border crossings and running an unlicensed institution. These charges seemed very well supported, given the arrest of the bribed border guards (tried together with her), the evidence of the passport applications, and the readiness of the orphanage's Polish maintenance workers to testify against her.

The only hope lay in the fact that the trial was to be conducted by the Katowice Prosecutor General's office, where Fishel Finkelstein, whom Mother had saved from certain death by freezing in Komi, served as a high official. Only some kind of intervention by a person of his standing provided any chance that Mother's rather flimsy defense would be accepted by the court.

Fishel was approached by Mother's lawyer. In vivid testimony to the fear that gripped even the most highly connected, Fishel almost threw the lawyer out, informing her heatedly that the best he could do for her was not to report her to the authorities. Mother had no inkling of this response, which was probably fortunate, since she might have found it more difficult to play the simpleton if she had known how little chance there was that this line of defense would work.

The day of the trial arrived. Mother was asked to testify. As planned, she denied everything. Yes, she worked in the orphanage, but she was just a cook. She didn't even know how to read or write, so how could she possibly manage an orphanage and forge passport applications?! One of the maintenance workers couldn't contain himself and shouted out to the judge that Mother was the manager—and an actress to boot who shouldn't be believed.

Mother was charged with three offences: organizing illegal border crossings, administering an unlicensed orphanage, and forging passport applications. The last of these was considered by far the worst crime, so it was dealt with first. The prosecution called in a handwriting expert to examine the documents under oath. There being no readily available sample of Mother's handwriting for comparison, she was asked to write something on the spot. In keeping with her claim of illiteracy, she scribbled some unintelligible nonsense. The prosecution then triumphantly pulled out a sheaf of passport applications and asked the expert whether or not they had been signed by the accused.

It will remain forever unknown whether the prosecutor flinched when he discovered that the bulk of the applications were missing. Fishel Finkelstein's outburst at Mother's lawyer had been a sham. The debt he owed Mother was too great not to be paid back in kind. Disregarding the consequences, he had removed most of the incriminating evidence from the prosecution's file, leaving only the best forgeries. These were presented to the handwriting expert, who had also been approached by Finkelstein. She noted that Mother spoke only poor Polish, then testified that there was no similarity between the signatures and the sample of scribbling. The expert concluded her testimony by stating that since Mother did not know how to write she couldn't possibly have signed the applications.

The prosecution was furious. To its even greater chagrin, as it was preparing to press the lesser charges, the judge banged his gavel on the desk and declared, "All charges dismissed." Unknown to Mother, Fishel Finkelstein had paid a pre-trial visit to the judge as well. In a chivalrous nation like Poland* a debt of honor is not to be disregarded, not only by

---

* In addition to explaining the judge's acquittal of Mother, this national trait also explains the doomed Polish cavalry attack against German tanks mentioned above, as well as the rise of the Solidarity movement in the threatening shadow of the Soviet Union in recent history.

(In the course of my search for photographs for this book I discovered that some historians dispute the veracity of the cavalry-attack story. According to them, the brigade either was surprised by German armor or attacked German

the person who owes it, but also by that person's friend—even if he happens to be a judge.

* * *

The impossible had happened. Not only was Mother freed from the decade of imprisonment which would have resulted from a conviction on the charge of forging passports, but even the lesser charges were completely dropped. After fourteen months in jail she was now a free woman.

Her freedom, however, solved only one part of her problem. The other part was getting out of Poland. It was one thing to be released from jail for lack of evidence and quite another to be granted a passport and exit permit. It seemed obvious to Mother that the passport office, the scene of her "crimes against the homeland," would not be impressed with the court's verdict, so she did not even bother to apply for a passport. For the time being, all she could do was recover physically from her ordeal in prison and to wait for another miracle.

Neither recovering nor waiting were going to be so simple, either. Mother was released from prison in the middle of the winter with only the summer dress and open-toed summer shoes in which she had been arrested. In addition, she was penniless. This not only prevented her from buying some badly needed clothing, but also made it impossible for her to rent a place to live.

As a last resort, she turned to some of her pre-war circle of friends still in Poland and asked for their hospitality. Even this solution was not without problems. The women, although eager to help Mother, were afraid of being reported to the

---

tank teams who were taking a rest, and who managed to jump back into their tanks and annihilate the cavalry. The story that the Poles attacked was made up by the Germans, who told it to Italian war correspondents who in turn spread it through the world. The fact that, nevertheless, the Poles' version has been accepted implicitly and is printed in history books to this day testifies to the chivalry of typical Polish character.)

police by their non-Jewish neighbors. Knowing that Mother was a former political prisoner, they feared that the authorities would find some way of charging them with criminal activity for harboring her. As a result, she was forced to stay with each acquaintance for a day or two at most, and then move on.

During one of such stays, Mother reminisced with her hostess about their pre-war times. Mother happened to mention our former governess, Rachelka Silbiger. "Rachelka Silbiger!" the lady exclaimed, "do you know what happened to her?"

"No," Mother said.

"Has she worked her way up the social ladder!" came the answer. "She is now Mrs. Edward Ochab."

Mother couldn't believe her ears! She had the lady repeat the statement several times before she was convinced that she had heard correctly. Ochab had been Rachelka's Communist boyfriend from that era when the Communist Party was an underground movement, when he was jailed for his party activity, and Mother had helped Rachelka send him food and books to the prison. Now he was among the highest officials in the Polish political hierarchy, holding half a dozen important posts.* Mother didn't pay attention to the rest of the conversation. One thought possessed her. Perhaps Rachelka would be able to help her!

The lady gave Mother the Ochabs' address. It was in an elegant apartment house on Marszalkowska Street, Warsaw's main thoroughfare.

The security guards posted there not only turned down her request to convey the message to Rachelka that "Bolek's mother" had come to see her, but also ordered her to go away

---

* As listed in *Who's Who in the Socialist Countries of Europe*, vol. 2, p. 861, Ochab held the following positions when our story transpired: Deputy Minister of National Defense and head of Political Administration in the Polish Army, Chairman of the Main Board of Polish-Soviet Friendship Society, member of the Central Committee of Polish Workers Party, Deputy Member of Politburo, Secretary of Polish Workers Party Central Committee, Member of Parliament.

Pre-war photograph of Marszalkow-ska Street, Warsaw's Fifth Avenue and Broadway combined. Courtesy of Ginzach Kidush Hashem, Bnei Brak.

immediately. When she persisted, one of the guards angrily threatened to beat her with his rifle butt. Mother started begging for mercy. In the end the guard had pity on her. He conveyed the message, and, to his great surprise, was instructed to admit the visitor.

Rachelka welcomed Mother warmly, murmuring apologies for living in posh surroundings which did not exactly bespeak the "equality of men on earth" which she had preached with all the idealistic heat of her youth. The two women reminisced about the days when Rachelka had been my governess, including the time when the Polish police had sought to arrest her for her Communist activity, and Mother warned her to flee.*

---

* Thinking back, it is quite possible that the story I was told about my parents' renting a winter vacation place and then being unable to go was told to me just as a cover-up. What quite probably happened was that this was done intentionally, to remove Rachelka from under the eyes of the Polish secret police.

Eventually Rachelka asked Mother, with evident emotion, "Is there anything that I can do for you?" Mother answered that she had only one request: "I want to join my husband and children. I want you to arrange for me to leave the country!"

Rachelka immediately went in to her husband's study and soon came back with an officially stamped paper bearing his signature, which she told Mother to take to the passport office. Unfortunately, the document was not enough. The official in charge took one look at it before shoving it back at Mother and declaring: "Your request is hereby denied."

Mother was devastated, but, as usual, not defeated. She returned to the Ochab residence the very next day. The guards recognized her and granted her admittance immediately.

When Mother related the events of the previous day, Rachelka went in to her husband once again, but this time came out of his study saying that he could do no more than he had already done. "After all," Rachelka said, "you are a former political prisoner. It would be dangerous even for someone in our position to do more than we have already done."

Mother was not to be put off. "My two children are my entire life. If I cannot join them, go ahead and put me in front of a firing squad."

Rachelka was shaken. She took Mother's hand into hers and said, "I promise you I will do everything that is my power to get you of here. Come back tomorrow."

On the next day, when Mother came, Rachelka entered her husband's study, where she remained for quite some time. When she finally reappeared, it was with a piece of paper which now bore *two* official stamps. "I told him I wouldn't budge until this matter was taken care of," she said.

This time Rachelka gave Mother some clothes to make her look more presentable, and accompanied her personally to the passport office. They arrived in style, driven there in the Ochabs' official limousine. Rachelka went with Mother to the official in charge, and the necessary documents were issued.

Mother was free to leave Poland at last.

עסקנית-הצלה חרדית מפולין
עלתה ארצה

בשבוע שעבר עלתה ארצה הגב' לדרמן,
שהצטיינה בשעתה בפעולות נועזות ומסר־
רות למען הצלת ילדים בפולין והעלאתם
ארצה.

הגב' לדרמן נאסרה לפני למעלה משנה
ע"י המשטרה החשאית בפולין והואשמה
באשמת ריגול נגד המדינה.

הועד הפועל של פועלי אגודת ישראל
עשה רבות, דרך צינורות שונים, למען
שחרורה ועליתה של עסקנית חרדית זו,
ובשבועות האחרונים הוכתרו מאמציו ב־
הצלחה מלאה.

A news item in the She'arim newspaper reporting Mother's release from jail and subsequent arrival in Israel.

RETURN TO NORMALITY

Lea, the reader will recall, had joined Father in Israel already. After the initial excitement of the reunion had subsided, Lea had started looking for a school with a dormitory where she could continue her education. The dormitory was necessary because she could not stay in Father's cramped "apartment," actually a small room (ten by ten feet, about three by three meters) with a sink, small refrigerator, no bath or shower, and conveniences in the yard. Lea made inquiries and was advised to attend the girls' boarding school Beit Asher, located in Nachlat Yehudah, a suburb of Rishon LeTzion. With Father's blessings, carrying a tiny valise with whatever clothing she had, and clutching carfare money, Lea took the Number 4 bus to the Central Bus station in Tel Aviv.

The bus station, as Lea recalls it, was a veritable beehive, with barely a place to stand. She first waited in line to buy a ticket for what seemed an eternity, and then spent another such eternity standing in line to board the bus. The buses were infrequent and overcrowded and it was only in the evening that Lea climbed up the steps of the bus to Rishon LeTzion. It was pitch dark when the bus stopped along the Tel Aviv-Rishon LeTzion road at a spot totally deserted except for a signpost that read "Nachalat Yehudah." The driver told Lea to get off and to walk "straight ahead, straight ahead" perpendicularly away from the main road till she reached the dormitory.

Surrounded by darkness and accompanied by the howling of coyotes, Lea walked for an hour along a dirt path beaten through what is still known as the "sands of Rishon" until she reached the locked gate of the dormitory building, which stood in splendid isolation in the midst of sand dunes. She was welcomed by the barking of a dog and the braying of a donkey until finally the gate opened and the supervisor welcomed

The Beth Asher dormitory in Rishon Lezion where Lea stayed during her elementary school days.

Lea. To her joy, she met there several of her friends from Aix-les-Bains who had arrived in Israel before her. The next morning Lea began school and joined her friends in what was to be an hour-long trudge to and from school through citrus orchards. Life had returned to normal.

Upon graduating from elementary school, Lea entered the Beth Jacob Seminary in Jerusalem. The Jerusalem Seminary also had a dormitory for out-of-town students and for those without parents. However, they were now at least one year behind in their studies, based on their age. To remedy this situation, they took summer courses in mathematics, algebra and chemistry. This made it possible for them to enter the Seminary at the second-year high-school level.

Mother's release from prison and journey to Israel coincided with the end of Lea's first year of high school in the Jerusalem Seminary. Father informed Lea about Mother's impending arrival and told her that if she did not manage to get to Haifa on time to meet Mother at the port, she should proceed to the Haifa home of her cousin, David Gromb, one of Moshe Aharon's sons. The transportation situation being what it was, Lea indeed arrived in Haifa long after Mother had disembarked. Knowing she had missed the arrival of Mother's ship, Lea went directly to the Grombs.

When Lea entered, Mother was in the middle of reciting the Silent Prayer.* She heard the door open and most probably heard her nephew greet Lea, but nevertheless continued to pray. Lea stood in the room not knowing what to do—she did

---

* The Silent Prayer is recited while standing. Interrupting it is prohibited except in an emergency situation.

not want to interfere with Mother's prayer, but she desperately wanted to give her an enormous hug to make up for all the years of suffering and separation! Lea couldn't bear it another moment. She approached Mother from behind, embraced her warmly, and started crying. Mother too burst out in tears, but nonetheless continued the Silent Prayer until the end. For hours, tears of joy flowed, as did the stories which each told the other describing all that had transpired during their separation.

Both Mother and Lea were greatly surprised at Father's absence, but since Father did not have a phone, he could not be reached. The two spent the Sabbath with the Grombs.

Father appeared late Sunday morning just as Mother and Lea were getting ready to go to Tel Aviv on their own. It turned out that Father had had some urgent work to complete on Friday in the government office in which he worked at that time, and his boss would not allow him to take off. They all bid good-bye to the Grombs and traveled to Tel Aviv.

Mother's arrival, coupled with Lea's upcoming school vacation, precipitated an acute housing problem. The three of them could not possibly stay very long in Father's tiny room. Now Mother's fourteen months in prison and her activities in saving Jewish children stood her in good stead with the government, and she was soon assigned housing in one of Jaffa's abandoned apartments.

Now, with the family housed in a three-room apartment, Lea could live in Jaffa and attend a high school in Ramat Gan, near Tel Aviv, for her junior year. This entailed a long bus ride, for which Mother gave Lea the fare, but every day, unbeknownst to Mother, Lea would hitchhike any part of the way that she could and then walk the rest of the long way home. Then she would secretly return half of the money to the family "bank"—the kitchen drawer.

Mother wasted no time in returning to ordinary life. Not one to sit idle, and also concerned with increasing the income

המשרד הפרטי של הרב הראשי לישראל
Office of the Chief Rabbi of the Holy Land

JERUSALEM ירושלים
P.O.B. 1102 ת.ד.

כ׳ מנ״א תש״י .

לכבוד
הסוכנות היהודית,
מחלקת הקליטה,

שלום וברכה!

העסקנית שרה לדרמן ס-1946 היתה חברת
ועד ההצלה בפולניה והמנהלת של בית היתומות בביטום.
היא הצילה מאות ילדים מהנוצרים וסהמנזרים, ושלחה
אותם דרך הגבולות ארצה. העבודה היתה קשורה בסכנת
נפשות, והיא ידועה מהפעולות הנועזות שלה. בנובמבר
1948 היא נאסרה ע״י השלטונות בפולין, וישבה בבית הסוהר
14 חדשים. אחרי מאמצים גדולים מצד ראש הממשלה, משרד
החוץ וה״ב׳וינט״, שוחרה בינואר ש,ז. בבית הסוהר

Letter from Chief Rabbi Hertzog describing Mother's work in Poland.

of a family with two children of marriageable age, Mother started looking for employment. While Father managed to pursue his career as an accountant until 1976, he earned only a modest income.

Earning a decent income was not the only problem facing the family. Every aspect of life in Israel was fraught with difficulties during this period. These were the days of *tsena* (loosely translated, "frugality"), when everything was rationed and food was available only on presentation of government-issued coupons. With certain commodities, even if one had a coupon for them he would be lucky to get them. Sometimes one had to get up at two or three in the morning, only to stand on line till eight o'clock, by which time the commodity was often sold out. Sugar, eggs (meaning powdered eggs), flour, and potatoes were all scarce, and for that matter, everything else was scarce too. Still, Mother always managed to get everything that she was entitled to.

Once, Lea recalls, it was close to the end of the month and Mother ran out of money. As usual, Lea was sent off to school with a sandwich, which was supposed to keep her from being hungry until she arrived home at two or three in the afternoon. When Lea came home, Mother asked her to go right away and get a loaf of bread at the grocery store. She had no money, so she told Lea to buy the bread on credit. It was the 28th of the month, and Mother hoped to be paid in two days, when she would be able to repay the grocer.

Lea refused to do this. With the few potatoes still in the house, she claimed, they would manage somehow for two days without resorting to borrowing. They did not need to buy bread on credit.

Mother's eyes teared. She seized Lea, hugged and kissed her, and told her how proud she was of her. It was clear that independence and keeping free of obligations to others meant very much to her.

Citing a metaphor her father had taught her, Mother told Lea that borrowing money is like sitting in a cold room in the winter while holding a baby with a leaking diaper in one's lap. At first when the diaper leaks, there is a feeling of pleasant warmth. But after a few minutes the only sensation is that of being increasingly cold and uncomfortable.

* * *

After a while, Mother entered into a partnership in a small enterprise which produced cream-filled wafers. The wafer bakery was located in Jerusalem, but this was hardly an insuperable obstacle for Mother. She simply spent the week in Jerusalem and traveled home to Jaffa for the Sabbath. For sleeping, she just put two benches together in the back of the bakery next to the wafer machine. Lea was delighted to have Mother nearby and would come to the bakery after school to spend every possible moment together with her.

The business was highly successful and Mother was happy with the much needed income. However, this bliss did not last long. One day she noticed her partner behaving suspiciously. Close inspection showed that he had put a non-kosher ingredient into the wafer mix. Mother terminated the partnership immediately.

Mother once again started looking for a profitable pursuit, this time closer to home. She reached the conclusion that she should open her own bakery. As was the case with getting an apartment, Mother was at an advantage. She was able to obtain one of the hard-to-get government permits to set up a bakery. Since items such as flour and sugar were still in short supply and hence rationed, a governmental permit (in addition to a municipal one) was needed to operate a bakery.

Mother realized that her baking skills, while good enough for home baking, were inadequate for producing the variety of baked goods that a commercial bakery must offer. After several false starts, Mother met Mr. Meir Eisikowitz, a highly skilled pastry baker. Mother's most rigorous standards of *kashruth* and reliability, combined with the unequaled mastery of her baker partner, made her store *the* kosher bakery of the town. Indeed, when the Grand Rabbi of the Gerrer Chassidic movement would come to an affair in the Tel Aviv area, he would not touch any pastry except that supplied by Mother's bakery.

Mother tried her best to keep tabs on the children she had shepherded through the difficult transition from wartime to normal life—as normal as their lives could ever be. They would often stop by the bakery for a chat. These visits afforded both parties great happiness and satisfaction. To them, Mother was family, and over the ensuing decades she was the honored participant at many happy occasions celebrated by her former charges.

* * *

During all this time I was in New York, feeling very lonely. I wrote quite a number of letters home asking my parents to let me join them. Mother, however, constantly refused my requests. She was afraid of the security situation in Israel and that I might be drafted into the army with all its attendant dangers. (Yeshivah students were exempt from army duty, but Mother feared that this arrangement might be rescinded any time.)

Disappointed, I then asked that Lea be sent to the States to alleviate my loneliness. After many ardent pleas, Mother finally relented and agreed.

I arranged for a student visa from the Beth Jacob Seminary in Williamsburg, which Lea was to attend until graduation. The school had no dormitory, however, and we had no relatives with whom she could stay. Desperate, after shuffling her around every week or so among the families of my few friends, I suggested that she post a notice on the Seminary's phone booth asking for a place to live. The very same day a girl by the name of Shoshanah

Lea teaching in Rabbi Shimshon Brodski's school in the Bronx.

Lichtenstein offered Lea a place in her home. Shoshanah's parents were the owners of the Clinton Plaza wedding hall on the East Side, one of the former hallmarks of New York Orthodoxy, and a family overflowing with lovingkindness.

Mother and the Lederman family at the wedding of one of our sons. This was the last wedding at which Mother was strong enough to stay for a group photograph at the end.

Lea lived with the Lichtensteins until her marriage. I was free to come for the Sabbath as I wished, and fully exploited this privilege.

Lea advanced quickly in her studies: even before graduating from Seminary, she taught Jewish studies in the Beth Jacob High School on the Lower East Side of Manhattan, and in the Zichron Moshe School in the Bronx. In the early evening she attended Brooklyn College.

In the early autumn of 1956 she became engaged to Rabbi Aharon Feldman, a promising young scholar, the son of a prominent rabbi in Baltimore. Since my parents could not afford two tickets to America, they decided that Mother alone should attend the wedding, which took place on Chanukkah Eve of that year. Five years later the young couple moved to Israel.

Father died of a heart attack in 1976. Mother continued running her Tel Aviv bakery until she sold it in 1985, when

Mother and the Feldman family at the wedding of Lea's youngest son.

she was eighty three. But to keep busy, she continued to work as a salesperson until age ninety. Now finally retired, Mother is in the later half of her nineties and is currently living with Lea and her husband in Jerusalem, surrounded by scores of loving grandchildren and great-grandchildren.

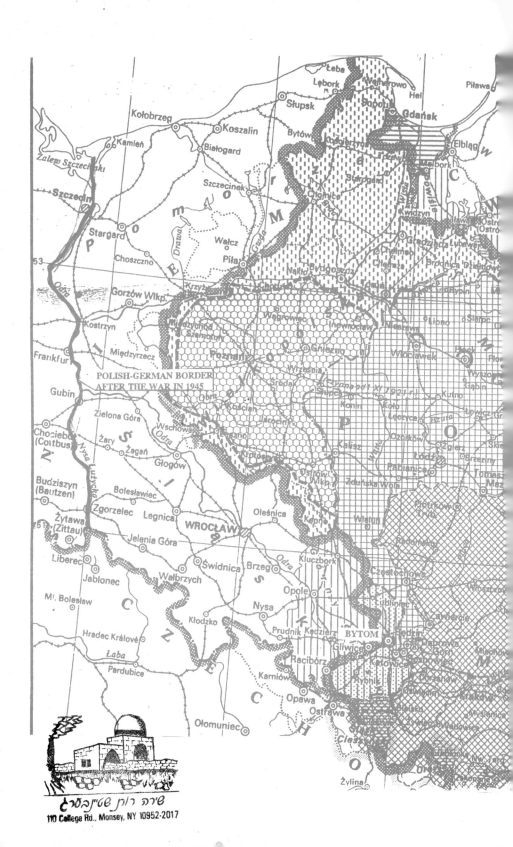

POLISH-GERMAN BORDER
AFTER THE WAR IN 1945